Indian and Nation
in Revolutionary Mexico

Indian and Nation in Revolutionary Mexico

Alexander S. Dawson

The University of Arizona Press Tucson

The University of Arizona Press
www.uapress.arizona.edu

 Published 2004
First paperback edition 2020

ISBN-13: 978-0-8165-2345-0 (cloth)
ISBN-13: 978-0-8165-4157-7 (paper)

Cover photo: Community members working on the internado at Ixtlán de Juárez.
(Courtesy of the Archivo General de la Nación)

Library of Congress Cataloging-in-Publication Data
Dawson, Alexander S. (Alexander Scott), 1967–
Indian and nation in revolutionary Mexico / Alexander S. Dawson.
p. cm.
Includes bibliographical references and index.
ISBN 0-8165-2345-2 (alk. paper)
1. Indians of Mexico—Government relations. 2. Mexico—Politics and government—
1910–1946. I. Title.
F1219.3.G6 D39 2004
323.1197'00972'09041—dc22
2003016948

Printed in the United States of America
♾ This paper meets the requirements of ANSI/NISO Z39.48-1992 (Permanence of Paper).

For Ian, who left just as this was beginning,

and Maia, who arrived just in time to see it end.

Contents

Figures

Acknowledgments

One of the delightful qualities of a finished book is that it offers the possibility of looking through its pages and seeing the debts one has accumulated over the long process of research and writing. For me, these debts begin with my undergraduate education, and the experiences I had as a student of Christon Archer. Other teachers also shaped this book profoundly, most importantly Paul Gootenberg, Barbara Weinstein, and Brooke Larson. I could not have asked for better advisors, and it is my hope that they see their probing questions, advice, and assistance throughout the pages of this text. As a graduate student at Stony Brook I also learned a great deal from other students, most notably José Gordillo, Sergio Serulnikov, Silvana Palermo, Catherine Stewart, Susan Gauss, and Derek Williams. Along with my other teachers, Herman Lebovics and Fred Weinstein, they shaped my interest in the Latin American past.

I enjoyed generous assistance from a number of individuals and institutions for the process of transforming my dissertation into a book. The funds to complete the research and writing were provided by the Social Sciences and Humanities Research Council of Canada, SUNY–Stony Brook, Montana State University, and the University of Florida. In Bozeman Billy Smith, Michelle Maskiell, Lynda Sexon, Jan Tarlin, Brett Walker, Michael Reidy, Robert Rydell, and David Large variously offered support, comments, and companionship through the long winters. In Mexico Jolie Olcott, Steve Lewis, Chris Boyer, and Rick López offered their friendship and helped me to find sources I would not otherwise have seen in the waning days of my research. Archivists at a series of institutions in Mexico were often helpful, but Angel Cabello Quiróz and Carlos Carrizales Barreto of the SEP archives were indispensable. In Gainesville, Charles Wood, Alejandra Osorio and Mark Thurner likewise offered important assistance, comments, and friendship as this project came to its completion. More generally, I have enjoyed advice and help from William Roseberry, Mary Kay Vaughan, Guillermo de la Peña, Claudio Lomnitz, Marjorie Becker, Ana Maria

Alonso, and Blancamar León Rosabal. Each of these scholars offered important aid, but Mary Kay went out of her way to help this book find a home at the University of Arizona Press, where I have had the very good fortune to work with Patti Hartmann. I would also like to thank the editors of *The Americas* for granting permission to include previously published material in chapter 1.

Other debts are not so easy to explain. To my family, Janet, Rick, Anne, and my late brother Ian, I owe a lifetime of thanks. This book may be on a subject of which they know little, but it is nonetheless a product of decades of long discussions around the dinner table, the inquisitiveness of my family life, and my parents' basic humanity. To Alejandra Bronfman I owe just as much. She marked these pages, shaping language and substance, and made this a much better book than it would have otherwise been. More than this, she has been a companion like no other, elevating not just my scholarship but my entire life.

Introduction

Remaking the Indian in Revolutionary Mexico

In the early afternoon hours of 25 September 1936, a motorcade of high government officials descended on the dusty town of Ixmiquilpan, Hidalgo, the ancient Otomí capital located in the heart of the Valle de Mezquital, for what promised to be an epic event. A crowd of onlookers had gathered expectantly, and as he exited his car, President Lázaro Cárdenas was greeted with loud cheers. He then slowly made his way into the Teatro Hidalgo, where the delegates to the Primer Congreso Regional Indígena awaited his arrival. Besides these 720 representatives of Otomí communities, another 8,000 congress attendees, including local, state, and federal officials, representatives of campesino and labor organizations, and several foreign dignitaries had assembled to find a solution to the "Indian question."

It was a quintessentially populist moment. Ensconced in the heart of a region known both for its pre-Columbian past and the horrific conditions of its present inhabitants, Cárdenas sat for several hours and listened as poor campesinos, many speaking Otomí, expressed themselves in what press reports indicated were "simple, but clear phrases." For the first time ever, they were gathered before the president to speak to him directly about their needs, inverting the traditional relationship between the all-knowing government functionary and ignorant peasant. At one point Modesto Esparza, of Tepenené, descended to one knee and tried to kiss the president's hand, as he asked for the materials needed to work a mine located near his village. Cárdenas recoiled, calling the act a sign of humiliation, and insisted that Esparza be seated at his side. Steeped in popular democratic symbolism and indicative of Cárdenas's profound respect for the dignity of the Indian, fleeting moments like this go a long way towards explaining the enduring affection for Tata Lázaro in the Mexican countryside.[1]

Press reports called the congress "a transcendental assembly," a sign that the Indians of the country were ready to "cast off their lethargy."[2] This was a particularly radical claim, given that throughout Mexico millions of Indians lived in misery, and were broadly perceived as a crippling burden to the nation. Just a few months before the congress, federal officials working in the Valle de Mezquital concluded that the extreme poverty of the region was a sure sign that the residents of the valley were "indisputably of an inferior race."[3] Many elite Mexicans would have been surprised, even horrified, to think that the Cardenista state would recognize Indians as a modern political constituency, similar to *agraristas* or workers. However, in this congress President Cárdenas challenged the world to see the Mexican Indian in a new light. At the same time, he challenged indigenous Mexicans to work with the federal government to end poverty, exploitation, and isolation.

For its public prominence and the ways that it rendered indigenous Mexicans as political actors, the congress at Ixmiquilpan was indeed a unique event. Yet because of its spectacular nature, critics might argue that the congress was just a show, an ephemeral moment where the state staged an illusion that would disappear with the reassertion of "real" politics.[4] While this view reminds us that we should not ignore the manipulative quality of state formation in Mexico, it falls far short of explaining the congress and the larger phenomena to which it was connected. Through the individuals who attended, the ideas expressed, and the ultimate outcomes, the congress was part of a much larger process whereby a generation of activists endeavored to remake the Indian and the nation in revolutionary Mexico. Inspired by the 1910 Revolution and hopeful for a more democratic future, they called for a nation based on economic and political equality, education, and cultural revival, and built with the tools provided by a growing body of scientific knowledge about the social, cultural, and racial characteristics of human civilization.

Their project was like any number of national projects undertaken in the industrialized West in the last century and a half, a simultaneous effort to define a national population and modernize it.[5] Over the course of two and a half decades these men and women, generally known as Indigenistas, were integral to efforts to create a new state and extend its authority across a national territory that remained largely outside the scope of federal control. Rejecting the Europhilic traditions of the past, they turned their attention to the Indian, both as the symbol of the national type and the object of reform. Though they shared no coherent ideology, revolutionary Indigenistas were united by their sympathy for the Indian and their desire to incorporate Indians into a reconstructed modern nation, in which living Indians were treated with respect and dignity, and their traditions accorded respect as the true national past. Through their efforts Indigenismo acted as a medium through which a series of actors, including social scientists, bureaucrats, intellectuals, teachers, and Indians themselves negotiated a new place for indigenous peoples in Mexico. And as was evident in Ixmiquilpan, these struggles would also contribute to the creation of new political subjects: Indians empowered to demand rights as citizens and act as agents in their own redemption. Although limited by a context in which the word "Indian" would remain for the most part a racial slur, these actors would nonetheless blur the boundaries that separated the Indian from the Mexican nation, and help create a new "pact of domination" between indigenous peoples and the state.[6]

Social Science and Revolution

The 1910 Revolution did not begin in Mexico City, but as the nation's capital it was both an intermittent battleground and a refuge for the young reformers who sought a role in national reconstruction in the aftermath of the war. At the National University, the National Museum, and in the bureaucracies of the revolutionary state, a generation of young men and women came together in the years after 1910 to create a blueprint for a more stable, prosperous, and equitable society. Yet how were they to create that new society? Most agreed that peasants had a right to land, and that the lower classes needed education. Even though they sympathized with the poor, most urban intellectuals did not support radically egalitarian social and economic projects, and were frightened by the agrarian communism and social inversions signaled by movements like the Zapatistas (the generic term for the agrarian and indigenous revolutionaries). Instead, they favored limited reform within a modernizing capitalist framework. Andrés Molina Enríquez, author of the influential prerevolutionary tract *Los grandes problemas nacionales* (1909), favored small-scale property holding as the solution to the agrarian problem. Similarly, presidents Venustiano Carranza and Alvaro Obregón considered the *ejido* a stopgap measure and widespread land distribution a poor solution to Mexico's problems. They likewise had little sympathy for the frontier culture and *serrano* values of the followers of Pancho Villa, as they favored a strong, centralized state. After ending the military threat from Zapatistas and Villistas, Carranza abandoned land reform in favor of increased production, anticlericalism, and education.[7]

Products of a northern bourgeois sensibility, both Carranza and Obregón believed that the solutions to Mexico's poverty and instability could be found in the same modernizing ethos that had enriched the nation's producers in the previous three decades. Scientific methods had improved livestock, produced better means of managing the treasury, revolutionized the nation's infrastructure, and could, they believed, also produce a better social order. By regulating what Michel Foucault called "bio-power" (Foucault 1978), administering a population and controlling its habits, the social sciences in particular could measure and define what that population lacked, and ultimately eradicate these deficiencies. Anthropology, ethnology, criminology, and a host of other human sciences found adherents among prerevolutionary elites, but Carranza and his successors would be the first Mexican leaders to make the social sciences a crucial tool in state-making. Mexico's first cohort of scientifically trained experts, uniquely qualified to solve the "Indian problem," emerged during these years, and combined advanced degrees from Mexican and North American universities, prestigious positions in the federal bureaucracy, and extensive experience in the countryside to speak with special authority about the Indian. Beginning with the Dirección de Antropología, founded as part of the Secretaría de Agricultura y Fomento in 1917, Indigenistas like Manuel Gamio, Carlos Basauri, Lucio Mendieta y Núñez, Moisés Sáenz, and Luis Chávez Orozco, used social science as never before to find new solutions for the Indian problem. They would populate a series of new bureaucracies, including the Secretaría de Educación Pública, the Departamento de Asuntos Indígenas, the Instituto Nacional de Antropología e Historia, and academic departments at the National University and Instituto Politécnico Nacional, giving social scientists unprecedented influence over public issues, and signaling a substantial commitment of resources towards using the social sciences to both define and improve the nation.[8]

Revolutionary elites found Indigenista social science appealing because it promised to extend federal authority throughout the national territory, a task that seemed particularly daunting in a country that had just experienced a massive civil war, and where the persistence of over eighty different ethnolinguistic groups suggested that Mexico was too backward and heterogeneous to ever constitute a modern nation.[9] In indigenous regions in particular, cultural and linguistic differences left federal officials completely at the mercy of local power brokers, who often impeded all efforts to extend the power of the central state. If it succeeded, the nationalist project undertaken by federal authorities would gradually extend their reach, undermining local autonomy throughout the country by instituting a new secular and modern set of cultural beliefs, a new property regime, new political institutions, and new infrastructures.[10]

Keenly concerned with remedying Mexico's backwardness, early Indigenistas believed that modernity and nationhood were essentially synonymous.[11] They celebrated an Indian past and folk traditions as the essence of Mexico's originality, but they believed that their nation needed to become a modern society. In this, Indigenistas adhered to the ideals that Néstor García Canclini argues constitute the four basic features of modernity. They wished to liberate people from their traditional values, to expand knowledge of and possession of the nation (and consumption generally), to encourage perpetual improvement of society, and to promote democratization (García Canclini 1995). Each of these projects called for the creation of a single, homogenous national community, which could only be created by assimilating all "inferior" groups into a modern, secular society. Indigenistas, together with other urban elites, made themselves the arbiters of the values that defined that society.

As members of intellectual communities that stretched from Mexico City to New York, Chicago, Berkeley, London, and Paris, Indigenistas were responsible for disseminating ideals that equated European and North American practices with modernity, and have often been accused of being agents of imperialism.[12] Indigenista social scientists, Arturo Warman and Guillermo Bonfil charge, relegated Indians to museums, denied them rights, and furthered exploitation even as they claimed to be lifting indigenous peoples to the level of all Mexicans. More seriously, they charge that Indigenistas idealized the mestizo (a mixture of Indian aesthetics and European rationality) as the essence of the national folk, calling for the complete incorporation of the Indian into the national mainstream. They also claim that since the only product of indigenous cultures that Indigenistas celebrated was folk art,

Indigenismo actually reinforced the idea that the Indian was an emotional primitive, while the European was the source of all modern life (Warman 1970; Bonfil 1970). Rooted in part in growing sympathy for ethnic self-determination and pluralism, at their most severe these critics argue that the same fundamental notion of the Indian prevailed from the nineteenth century through the late twentieth century, informing a range of apparently different policies built on the same basic ethnocidal urge.[13]

This, one might argue, is the point from which all studies of social science and state-making in Mexico should begin. We must take as axiomatic that Indigenistas created the Indian as an inaccessible primitive even as they claimed to be objective, sympathetic observers. Yet while this critique of orientalism is indeed a good story, like most good stories it relies on a vision of the past that distorts as much as it reveals. It reduces a range of highly contested efforts to a simple nationalizing project, and fails to adequately describe the complicated and deeply ambiguous experience of state-making and social reform. Scientific knowledge could justify an expanded federal bureaucracy that simply endeavored to dominate "primitives," but social science also served as a platform upon which a diverse group of activists developed innovative understandings of the national population, and even allowed some activists to question the very need for a unified Mexican nation.

Though privileged by their ability to claim a connection to modern science and intellectuals in the United States and Europe, these Mexicans did not merely reproduce first-world practices. Unlike in the United States and Europe, where multipolar social scientific establishments produced a diverse set of practices, in Mexico a small number of fairly powerful individuals designed and implemented scientific programs under the close tutelage of the state, with the single goal of transforming the lifestyles of indigenous Mexicans. The result was a social scientific establishment that was eclectic in its use of theory, often lacked disciplinary rigor, and proposed solutions before investigating problems. In Mexico social science would be judged more for how it served perceived national interests — providing immediate applications that could solve rural problems — than for how it stood up to academic scrutiny.[14]

This distinguished Mexican social science from metropolitan social science. More importantly, unlike foreign researchers, Indigenistas were not engaged in studying and preserving a disappearing other, but were instead trying to facilitate the disappearance of the other. Claudio Lomnitz notes that Indigenistas often chafed at the emphasis that foreign scholars placed on "traditional" Mexico, and sought to prove to the world that Mexico was as capable of being modern as any other nation. In this way Gamio and others were as closely linked to Mexican intellectual traditions as they were to their foreign mentors (Lomnitz 2001: 132–136). As Guillermo de la Peña suggests, Indigenistas like Gamio and Sáenz often served as "intellectual intermediaries" for their North American mentors (Franz Boas and John Dewey, respectively), acting as conduits through which some foreign ideas could be introduced in Mexico. They were however, selective interlocutors. Only some ideas would be translated (and often transformed), depending on their specific appeal to the modernizing project of the postrevolutionary state (de la Peña 1996).[15]

Indigenistas used a number of terms—Indian, Mexican, *campesino*, proletarian, and citizen—to express their desires to make indigenous Mexicans into modern political subjects, transforming them from nonpolitical primitives into modern political agents. Each of these terms already had a certain content, rooted in what most literate Mexicans considered to be "common sense," but they were not fixed, they were open to innovation.[16] To be sure, Indigenistas hoped to transform Indians into citizens by changing their lifestyles and value systems, but inasmuch as they could also change the content of these signifiers, Indigenistas hoped to transform the way all Mexicans understood their nation. For instance, they would constantly endeavor to empty the term "Indian" of its racial content. They celebrated Indians as the national soul and the potential equals of all Mexicans.

More than just remaking the Indian, Indigenistas were engaged in an effort to reimagine citizenship in Mexico. Indians had technically been citizens since the nineteenth century, but citizenship in Mexico had always been a freighted concept, rather than a concrete set of rights. It was a privilege conferred on those who proved modern enough to enjoy it, and was almost always reserved for males of European origin (or who aspired to a European origin). Indigenistas challenged this notion, if only in limited ways. Claudio Lomnitz's conceptualization of Mexican nationalism is especially instructive here. In contrast to Benedict Anderson's focus on fraternal citizenship, he argues that some forms of nationalism allow for dependent bonds within a hierarchy, in which women, children, the ignorant, and those viewed as lesser are included, but in a subordinate position. Indigenismo was part of this tradition, as Indigenistas generally envisioned an inclusive nation, but believed that not all Mexicans were ready for citizenship. Most were instead proto-citizens, incapable of rising to the level of citizen without state tutelage. In the short run democracy would be limited, but assimilation offered the promise of full citizenship in the distant future (Lomnitz 2001).

The Indigenista — and more broadly, revolutionary — concept of citizenship did not often confer the specific rights guaranteed through the judicial process usually seen in liberal democracies (effective suffrage, due process, etc.). Instead, Indigenistas used the title "citizen" more symbolically, indicating that the possessor of this privilege was a political subject with the right to represent themselves before the state, and the right to demand an education, land, and the fulfillment of the promises made in the 1917 Constitution. In this view, citizenship was not so much defined through individual rights as through the legitimation of corporate identities such as peasant and worker, and only respected inasmuch as those subjects proved themselves to be modern. This view of citizenship thus included the right to be a subject in the public sphere, but it also provided the basis for the state to exercise total control over those deemed not ready for citizenship. As such, citizenship was a claim, a will to an identity that would confer material and symbolic benefits on the possessor.[17] Like other signifiers, its meaning changed in different hands, as individuals with different interests — pedagogues, anthropologists, bureaucrats, and indigenous peoples — made strategic use of the term and linked it to other corporate, class, and ethnic identities, either making the Indian a political constituency or denying Indians rights altogether.

These efforts were particularly important in revolutionary Mexico, because the state was involved in a struggle over the language of revolution and nationalist ideology even as it struggled to extend its authority over the countryside. Federal officials spent a great deal of energy creating what Philip Abrams has described as a "mask," hiding the absence of a concrete state by disseminating illusions of control, coherence, and their legitimate monopoly on violence (Abrams 1988). Ultimately, their inability to impose a single set of practices or nationalist ideology would prove critical to the fate of Indigenista projects, in that while the ineffectiveness of the federal state could leave Indians and their advocates vulnerable to the capriciousness of local power brokers, it also created crucial opportunities for a variety of actors to shape revolutionary hegemony.

The story of Indigenismo was thus the story of an ideological project, but it was also the story of a struggle to extend the physical authority of the state throughout the country. This was a painfully slow process, punctuated by spectacular failures, which ultimately became critical to the evolution of Indigenismo between 1917 and 1946. While it is true that most early Indigenistas were guilty of revolutionary ethnocentrism, orientalizing the Indian and reinforcing neocolonialism, over time Indigenismo became increasingly complex as it was shaped by a series of popular and elite pressures. Initial attempts to solve the Indian problem, including Gamio's study of the Valley of Teotihuacán (1918–1921), and the creation of an Indian school known as the Casa del Estudiante Indígena in Mexico City (1926–1932), proved useful to nationalists who wanted to demonstrate the potential of the Indian, but also revealed that the nation Indigenistas imagined would be difficult to create. The indigenous Mexicans who benefited from these programs proved less compliant than their benefactors had imagined, and the wholesale incorporation of the Mexican Indian remained an elusive goal. Moreover, by the early 1930s their failure to assimilate the Indian mirrored the failure of the state as a whole to unite the nation under one dominant political regime. Key among these larger failures were the Callista efforts to extirpate Catholicism in the countryside, which ultimately precipitated the cristero revolt. By the end of the first decade of revolutionary reform many indigenous communities remained untouched by federal initiatives, and the power of the revolutionary state was mostly illusory.[18]

In the midst of this crisis, Indigenistas began to turn away from simplistic models of incorporation and ultimately came to question the very nationalist ethos they had originally used to secure a place of privilege within the revolutionary state. By 1932, ten years of failed revolutionary programs were casting increasing doubt on the project of simple assimilation. It was at this moment that the schools known as internados indígenas (Indian boarding schools), one of the first truly innovative programs of postrevolutionary Indigenismo, were created. Following a practice that Mary Kay Vaughan, Gilbert Joseph, and others have noted was crucial to securing federal authority throughout the national territory, these institutions forced the national state to accommodate to local conditions, varying its practices in accordance with the needs and demands of different groups (Joseph 1988; Knight 1994b; Joseph and Nugent 1994; Vaughan, 1997; Purnell 1999). Then, when Lázaro Cárdenas ascended to the presidency in 1934, Indigenistas were suddenly in a position to have a profound impact on the policies of the federal government.

A legend to this day for distributing eighteen million hectares of land, nationalizing the oil industry, mobilizing workers and peasants, and implementing a system of socialist education, Cárdenas promised to fulfill demands that had long remained ignored. On the campaign trail he promised that indigenous communities would be targeted for substantial land reforms, major developmental and educational projects, and scientific study and improvement. He also promised to create a new Departamento de Asuntos Indígenas, which would concentrate the energies of social scientists and the Mexican state on Indians in ways never before seen. Though this agency would undertake many efforts aimed at simple incorporation, its structure also afforded opportunities to a number of Indigenistas who, increasingly ambivalent about the assimilationist ethos of Mexican nationalism, designed innovative programs that recognized Mexico as a plural nation. The 1930s thus represented a turning point for Indigenismo, when a crisis over assimilation and the government's momentary turn to the left converged to generate projects that could reshape both the Indian and the state.

During the 1930s a new actor became increasingly important to these struggles, as the object of social reform (the Indian) used the forums created by revolutionary Indigenismo to talk back to the state. Using the very language created by Indigenistas, many of the participants in Indigenista programs made themselves into political subjects; they became Indians empowered by the state to demand rights as citizens and act as agents in their own redemption. That they succeeded to the extent that they did reveals a great deal about the importance of discursive practices in the creation of revolutionary hegemony, and in particular about the role of Indigenismo as a "language of contention" (Roseberry 1994). These actors were given a new name, *indígenas capacitados,* which they could claim as long as they acted within the scientifically defined parameters of the "modern." In the absence of a hegemonic project based upon mass participation, they were among the crucial metonymic signs upon which the Mexican state depended for its legitimacy.[19] Indígenas capacitados, like Indigenistas, were actors in the "war of position" that characterized state formation in Mexico. This was (and remains) an ongoing process; the hegemony of the Mexican state has never been complete. Rather, since the 1910s a plurality of forces have continually reshaped the limits of federal authority and the mechanisms of consent and dissent that govern Mexican society (Laclau and Mouffe 1985: 136). Indigenous actors played a role in this process by selecting the needs and demands that they placed before the state, and protecting and preserving knowledge of local cultures. Sometimes they simply refused federal officials access to local patrimonies, but more often they played a mediating role, allowing the state into local communities in exchange for certain concessions. It was this give-and-take that allowed subaltern groups to challenge the terms of their own domination, and that was critical to the relative stability of the postrevolutionary regime.

The Organization of the Book

As part of an overall structure that examines the process whereby Indigenismo was translated from a nationalist desire into a set of practices, chapter 1 examines Indigenista efforts to reshape the relationship between Indian and nation in the immediate aftermath of the 1910 Revolution. Revolutionary Indigenismo first gained national prominence through Manuel Gamio, whose Dirección de Antropología (1917–1925) acted as a key forum for both reimagining the Indian and promoting social reform. Assimilation served a number of ends during the eight-year life of the agency, allowing Indigenistas to create new images of the Indian and the nation, and project a simple process whereby all Indians could be made full members of the national community. Though based in a profoundly superficial understanding of the countryside, this program proved appealing to revolutionary officials because it was so straightforward.

By the early 1930s, the flaws in this program were increasingly evident, leading to a crisis in Indigenismo. As a result Indigenistas created a series of new programs, the most significant being the internados indígenas, the subject of chapter 2. Conceived in light of the failures of assimilation, the internados were the first program designed by the Secretaría de Educación Pública (SEP) that sought to approximate education to local conditions. The internados faced serious problems early on, but after Lázaro Cárdenas ascended to the presidency at the end of 1934, they were expanded significantly and became central to Cardenista efforts to serve indigenous communities. The internados were used to experiment with the use of local vernaculars, integrate local cultural practices into the educational process, and even to promote ethnic identities as a mechanism for empowering indigenous Mexicans.

Chapter 3 focuses on the struggles over Indian policy in the Departamento de Asuntos Indígenas (DAI), founded in 1936. Working through this agency, Cárdenas tried to establish official channels through which traditionally oppressed groups could both communicate their demands and receive the benefits of modernity. Ideally, in return they would offer their support to Cárdenas and defend the emergent state from attacks by conservative groups.[20] The DAI also had a role in the development of social scientific practices in Mexico; it was within this agency that social scientists, privileged as never before by the revolutionary state, came to question the underlying precepts of Mexican nationalism. Concluding from their work in indigenous communities that the incorporationist project was deeply flawed, many agency employees came to articulate a pluralistic vision of the nation, in which indigenous Mexicans would play a more important role in determining their own destinies. The nation they imagined would respect, rather than seek to eradicate, indigenous cultures, languages, and forms of social organization.

This development created conflicts between social scientists and political elites. Cardenistas understood Indigenismo as a means through which they could undermine exploitation and racism in the countryside by building connections between indigenous Mexicans and the central state. In revealing the incompatibility of nationalist agendas and scientific practice, social scientists undermined the Cardenista project. Increasingly vulnerable to attack, some Indigenista social scientists expressed overt support for the nationalist agenda even while they critiqued it in subtle ways. Others, including a growing number of linguists, cultural anthropologists, and teachers, openly challenged the need for a single national culture, calling for a radical reconstruction of the relationship between the state and indigenous communities. Their successes, along with their failures, reveal a great deal about the possibilities for and results of radical undertakings within the revolutionary state.

Chapter 4 examines the Congresos Regionales Indígenas that took place under the auspices of the DAI between 1936 and 1940. Two decades of Indigenista practice converged with Cardenista populism in these events, where for the first time, self-identified Indians from specific ethnic communities gathered in public forums and addressed national audiences. They spoke as "Mexicans," and made demands of the state based upon their rights as citizens. The *ponencias,* petitions, and complaints made by these rational political agents not only affirmed their place in the nation, but further justified intrusive and colonizing practices against those who refused to cooperate with the state.

However, these events were not simply forums in which a patron-client relationship between Indian and state was affirmed. The contrasting agendas promoted in these forums revealed deep fissures in revolutionary Indigenismo, indicating not only the extent to which the struggle over the "Indian problem" had changed since the 1910s, but also the ways in which indigenous peoples shaped that change. Conceived in moments of political and social crisis, when the Mexican state was struggling with powerful foreign and domestic enemies, the congresses offered popular groups a certain amount of leverage to make demands in return for supporting Cárdenas. As such they provided local power brokers the opportunity to contest and transform the nature of revolutionary reforms.[21]

In chapter 5, I assess the consequences of two decades of postrevolutionary Indigenismo. The chapter begins by examining the impact of Indigenista programs undertaken in the Valle de Mezquital after the congress at Ixmiquilpan, and then turns to a larger examination of the ways Indigenismo changed after 1940. Indigenistas' dependence on the federal state came into high relief after Lázaro Cárdenas left the presidency. Leftists were purged from the bureaucracy, projects were defunded or canceled altogether, and the ideological orientation of the remaining Indigenista projects was dramatically transformed to suit the interests of a state more concerned with control than elevation. Moreover, if their early successes showed the possibilities of destabilizing race as a discrete social category in revolutionary Mexico, events after 1940 showed that Indigenista ideas simply competed with, rather than supplanted, biologically determinist views of the Indian. Indigenistas may have shifted the ground in the debate over the Indian, but even at the height of their power they remained unable to convince many literate Mexicans that the Indian was not an immutable racial other.

The conclusion explores the legacies of revolutionary Indigenismo through an analysis of perhaps the most important outcome of revolutionary Indigenismo, the indígenas capacitados. Educated and empowered in Indigenista programs, the capacitados were uniquely situated to take advantage of the openings created by Indigenismo. Their story, however, is also very much that of the vagaries of revolutionary state formation. Their personal successes did not easily translate into larger transformations in indigenous communities, and their history as agents of emancipation is meager at best. As enforcers for the state, defenders of local cultures, and interlocutors between the two, the capacitados used the language created through Indigenismo to shape revolutionary hegemony.

Finally, a note on language: I use the term *Indian* in order to reflect the language used during this period to describe a variety of ethnic groups. Indigenistas used the words *indígena* and *indio* to convey meanings that English speakers at the time would have understood to mean "Indian." I also use the ethnic categories of the time to describe various groups, including Tarascan for those who are today called Purépecha, and Otomí for those who today call themselves Ñhañhu.

Indian and Nation in Revolutionary Mexico

1 The Indian and the Nation

We could classify the majority of the inhabitants of the Republic as Indians, because to some extent, we all carry the blood of our aborigines in our veins. — *Carlos Samper*[1]

Long before Independence, Mexican elites looked to the Indian as an important nationalist symbol. In an era when Europeans dismissed the Americas as degraded and inferior, creole Mexicans celebrated ancient Mexican artifacts as signs of Mexico's potential greatness. Missing from most of their musings, however, was any consideration of the place that living Indians would play in their nation. This practice expanded during the nineteenth century, so that by the time of Porfirio Díaz's dictatorship (1876–1911) living Indians had more or less disappeared from the public sphere. They were merely specks of paint on Velasco's great landscape paintings, and shunned in the great cities of Mexico. The term *Indian* was even stripped from the liberal universalizing language of the Constitution in 1857, and organizations based in racial or ethnic identities were made illegal. As a juridical category the Indian simply did not exist any longer. To be sure, Díaz built statues commemorating Cuauthémoc on the Paseo de la Reforma, but nineteenth-century nationalists saw the contemporary Indian as completely degenerate. Most hoped that the Indian would soon disappear, and few imagined that Indians, innately slothful as they were, could possibly be a factor in national politics.[2]

Events after 1911 showed these elites just how wrong they were, and their responses ranged from horror to hope. A decade of civil war left over a million dead and Porfirian dreams of economic progress in tatters. Conservatives understood the conflagration of revolution as a frightening descent into anarchy—an affirmation of just how barbarous rural Mexicans were—and called for an escalation of discipline and control to put an end to incivility. Some urban and educated Mexicans, however, tired of a generation of dictatorship and cognizant of the limits of nineteenth-century liberalism, used this moment to call for a radical reconstruction of Mexican state and society. They would "remake the ancient virility of the race . . . form citizens who are anxious to discharge their civic duties, aware of public authorities, and capable of sacrifice and discipline in the interest of the collective good."[3]

Inasmuch as they invoked the Indian as a nationalist symbol yet also saw living Indians as the subjects of their program of social reform, this new generation of Indigenistas represented a clear break from past practice. Moreover, the word they used to describe that subject—citizen—reveals a great deal about their project. They imagined a single Mexican community, defined by the political rights and obligations that they associated with citizenship in a modern nation. Yet while North American and European elites could describe a broad segment of their population as citizens (limited, of course, by notions of race, class, and gender), in Mexico the very concept of the citizen evoked a much more complex set of images. Mexico was deeply segmented into diverse cultural, linguistic, and ethnic communities, and if reformers hoped to ever create a citizenry, they would first need to create a national community.

The Race Question

Indigenistas in the early revolutionary period used a series of concepts to describe the process they wanted to promote. Most commonly they called for the assimilation of the Indian into the nation. But the idea of assimilation has a problematic history in Mexico, where beliefs about racial inferiority raised serious doubts about the prospects of assimilating indigenous peoples. Revolutionary Indigenistas inherited images of the Indian that were rooted in four centuries of colonial domination, and built on a series of polarities—the Christian versus the heathen, the *gente de razón* versus the savage, the masculine versus the feminine, and culture versus nature.[4]

Basing their notion of community in the perceived qualities of blood, many nineteenth-century nationalists used the work of Cornelius de Pauw, Comte de Buffon, Arthur de Gobineau, Jean Baptiste Chevalier Lamarck, Césare Lombroso, Paul Broca, Samuel Morton, and Francis Galton to prove the irredeemability of non-Europeans. Nineteenth-century science provided precisely the evidence they needed to see non-Europeans as "primitives," incapable of redemption. More than this, many European thinkers were particularly critical of miscegenation, arguing that racial mixing resulted in offspring who inherited the worst traits of both parents. The scientific methods they developed to prove these views, including phrenology, anthropometry, Spencerian sociology, criminal anthropology, and eugenics became essential to late nineteenth-century statecraft.[5]

Given their ability to entrench the boundaries that had long defined Mexican social hierarchies, practices such as the measurement of cephalic indices found many aficionados in Mexico, as did those racial ideologies that described contemporary Indians and mestizos as degenerated organisms.[6] These were powerful ideas, but even prior to the 1910 Revolution some nationalists were skeptical of scientific racism. These intellectuals reasoned that, if followed through to their logical conclusions, the precepts of scientific racism denied the possibility of a modern Mexican nation. In the decades after Independence many public figures (Benito Juárez, most notably) modified or rejected racial determinism and imagined a nation in which the majority of Mexicans could participate based on citizenship rather than race.

Some drew on the anthropological concept of social evolution to describe Mexico as an evolutionary hierarchy from the primitive to the modern, arguing that the stages of society were not racially determined. In the late nineteenth century, prominent intellectuals including Alfredo Chavero and Justo Sierra developed complex evolutionary schemes for pre-Columbian and contemporary Mexican races, making evolution integral to the Mexican past and present. Others, including Vicente Riva Palacio and Francisco Pimentel, were troubled by the heterogeneity of the nation, but called for the mixing of all groups into one culture and race, rather than the elimination of those that did not meet European standards. They envisioned a slow whitening of the population, which although based in notions of European racial superiority, rejected Gobineau's claim that racial mixing was tantamount to degeneration. Some even explicitly denied the racial inferiority of the Indian, and argued that with better hygiene, living conditions, and education, Indians could be the equals of whites.[7]

By the last decade of the nineteenth century a number of important intellectuals had committed their energies to exploding the myth of Indian racial inferiority. At the first National Pedagogical Congress in 1889, delegates signed an open declaration that Indians were not racially inferior, arguing that with the proper education they could aspire to accomplishments equal to that of any other group. Sierra similarly launched a series of attacks against those who saw mestizos as degenerate, arguing that such a view had no scientific merit. To him, the mestizo was the most dynamic element in the Mexican past. Andrés Molina Enríquez likewise argued that racial mixing could create a single national "soul." Turning race theory on its head, he argued that "the Indian races could be considered superior to whites because of their higher levels of resistance, which itself is the logical consequence of selective adaptation, and in accord with Darwin's theory of natural selection." His mestizo was the product of a coupling of the masculine European and feminine Indian, creating a nationalism that was simultaneously modernizing and nativist.[8]

These critics found a ready ally in Franz Boas, whose antiracist ideas became increasingly well known in Mexico through his involvement in the creation of the International School of Archeology and Ethnology, which opened in Mexico City in 1911. Arguing for the significance of culture and environment in human societies, and warning that anthropologists should not make normative judgments about other cultures, Boas was instrumental in challenging the racialist and hierarchical assumptions of anthropology. His presence in Mexico was particularly fortuitous for Manuel Gamio, who was able to secure a scholarship to study at Columbia University with Boas in 1909, becoming the first Mexican to earn a Ph.D. in anthropology at a foreign university.[9]

As a rising star in the government after he returned from New York, Gamio repeatedly promised that anthropology offered the means for "good government" in Mexico, principally because of its potential to unite all Mexicans into one culture. Anthropology, he argued, was uniquely suited to provide knowledge about the physical and mental capabilities of the population, and "deduce the appropriate methods to facilitate their normal evolution."[10] In this promise Gamio departed sharply from Boasian anthropology (Boas being a strong critic of both nationalism and evolutionism), but his claims were well suited to the needs of the revolutionary state and the native intellectual tradition of viewing the Mexican people in evolutionary terms. Mexico's cultures needed to be studied, understood, and improved. This could be done without turning to either genocide or racial mixing, and out of it a single nation could be created.[11]

Gamio expanded his vision for the role of anthropology in state formation in *Forjando patria* (1916), which called for effective and efficient cooperation between social scientists and the government towards "the achievement of an ideal social, economic, political and physical life." He emphatically asserted that Indians were not racially inferior, but lamented that the country was a series of *pequeña patrias,* linguistically and racially heterogeneous. He argued that Mexico needed a nationality based on ethnic, linguistic, and cultural unity. *Forjando patria* identified the 1910 Revolution as a popular mandate for the "fusion of the races," meaning in particular, linguistic, cultural, and social unification, so that Mexico would "constitute a powerful country . . . and a coherent nationality."[12]

Forjando patria caused an immediate stir in Mexico, so impressing Alvaro Obregón that he declared it required reading for all Mexicans.[13] Gamio's ideas were tailor-made to fit the needs of the revolutionary state, as he simultaneously advocated unifying the nation through the use of modern scientific methods, and to some extent avoided sticky questions like egalitarian social reform or land redistribution. His proposals also convinced Venustiano Carranza to provide Gamio with the resources to found the Dirección de Antropología (DA), in May 1917. Coinciding with the promulgation of the new Constitution, this decision represented a strong endorsement of Gamio's social scientific vision. Given the resources to hire a staff of forty, the DA represented a unique opportunity for a number of young intellectuals who would become national figures in the following decades. Many of them lacked more than a cursory knowledge of social scientific methods, and Gamio would have to resort to giving classes in anthropology to his colleagues, but in spite of these obstacles the DA was hailed as profoundly important to the creation of a modern nation.[14]

Its promise to use science to classify and transform an otherwise unknown national population made the DA an ideal forum for generating the "controlled fictions of difference and similitude" that are essential to most forms of nationalism. Furthermore, the DA and the social scientific federal bureaucracies that would succeed it over several decades were examples of the axiom that the "regulative strategies" of the state "produce the subjects they come to subjugate" by creating the very categories through which the population could be understood. The DA would collect scientific data on Mexico's heterogeneous "population," and "territory," both as a means of diagnosing national needs and facilitating progress. Racial data would be a part of these studies, but most of the work would focus on regional cultures, languages, economies, histories, climates, geography, flora, and fauna.[15]

The categories and territorial divisions promulgated by the DA laid the foundations for the "state simplifications" that would be central to the mandate of anthropology as an exercise in state making.[16] The nation was defined through a series of discrete characteristics, both human and geographic, that would be either preserved or improved in the interest of progress. Typical of this, population studies were to divide the "material" and "popular" components of culture into separate categories so as to improve the one and preserve the other as a nationalist treasure trove. The DA would also determine if the methods of production and capacities for development of each community were "normal" or "abnormal." This would in turn reveal the "evolutive state" and precise needs of every member of the "gran familia" that constituted the Mexican nation. Indian traits in particular would be evaluated as either positive or negative, thereby providing the means for deciding which characteristics should be preserved and which should be discarded as these communities were transformed into productive members of the national polity.[17]

References to Mexico's gran familia underscored the fact that, although the DA was principally involved in the study of a diverse population, its ultimate goal lay in incorporating Mexico's Indians into the national life and increasing their affinity for the nation. Gamio thus sought to understand differences principally in order to eliminate them. Its very mandate called for the DA to foment a process of "racial approximation, cultural fusion, and linguistic unification" that would unite all Mexicans in a coherent, modern, and secular nation, both through the knowledge it produced, and through efforts on the ground. Moreover, the agency was given the mandate of promoting economic improvements in the regions where it worked, a task that employees of the agency would undertake by petitioning for land redistribution, working to increase wages in the zones where they operated, building schools, creating workshops, implementing applied rural education programs, and introducing mechanized agricultural and industrial skills.[18] As a whole, these efforts indicated that the employees of the agency believed they understood the solutions to the "Indian problem" even before they studied rural problems. Assimilation would be the answer.

Denying Biological Inferiority

More important even than improving the lot of the Indian, the DA's most significant goal lay in proving the redeemability of the Indian, which Gamio chose to do through a study he began in the Valley of Teotihuacán immediately after the agency was created. Drawing on Boas's desire to integrate historical, social scientific, and scientific study, Gamio chose this site for a number of reasons. Though the population had been labeled white in the 1910 census (designated as such because the region was universally Spanish speaking and heavily Catholic), Gamio believed that the residents were racial Indians, and thus represented a good test of the comparative roles of culture and race in human society. It was also a region where 90 percent of the land was devoted to the production of commercial crops for consumption in Mexico City, and offered convenient access to the capital.[19] A study of the Tarahumara, Yaqui, or Lacandon might reinforce notions of essential Indian alterity, but in Teotihuacán Gamio believed he had an Indian population that could be used to disrupt traditional images of Indianness.

One of the first tasks that Gamio and his cohort undertook once they arrived in the valley seemed to affirm the racializing tendencies of Mexican scientific circles. Drawing from the best anthropometric traditions, they lined up as many residents as they could for skull measurements. Paul Siliceo Pauer measured 2,540 men and 1,637 women in Teotihuacán, mainly according to stature, cephalic index, nasal index, pigmentation, facial characteristics, and disease. Using these and other measurements he determined that there were 5,657 Indians, 2,137 mestizos, and 536 whites in the valley.[20] These classifications unquestionably had the effect of reinforcing racial stereotypes, especially since Gamio concluded that the "majority of the inhabitants still remain in the backward stage of indigenous civilization."[21] Although he would repudiate these measurements as having "no scientific significance whatever" within two years of publishing the study, at the time they had enormous power to fix the alterity of the Indian.[22]

His results however, were much more complex than a first glance suggests. The somatological measurements fixed racial alterity, but other aspects of the study in Teotihuacán exploded racial categories. Along with classifying the civilization of the valley in racial terms, Gamio also created a system of classifying the population according to whether they were of "indigenous" civilization or "modern." Several factors were indicative of indigenous civilization, including consumption habits (corn, chiles, pulque, tortillas, and frijoles), living conditions (traditional dwellings), and social and cultural practices. This last category included the use of traditional medicines under their indigenous names, the preservation of oral traditions, and the demonstration of what he called a "typically Indian spirit." Using these markers, Gamio determined that 5,464 valley dwellers belonged to indigenous civilization, while the remaining 2,866 were modern. This meant that while most of the local population had adopted certain features of modern civilization (such as metal implements, firearms, and modern clothing), only a small number of the residents in the valley were in fact modern. Nonetheless, at least 113 of those determined to be racially Indian did belong to a "modern" civilization, thus proving that simple biological categories were inadequate tools for describing the region. Substituting the terms "culture" and "civilization" for race, he determined that 67 percent of the population had Indian characteristics, that 65 percent still "cling to a markedly indigenous civilization," and 2,886 "have developed culturally and are fast attaining modern civilization." These numbers indicated that several hundred of those whom he described biologically as Indians would be described culturally as mestizos.[23]

Gamio was particularly impressed by the fact that Spanish had replaced indigenous languages throughout the region and that some Indians had successfully adopted "modern" traits. Moreover, the long history of "fusion, intermixture, substitution, and elimination"[24] made the valley a model of national unification.

> They have been in constant intercourse with one another for the past four centuries. . . . There does not exist a real racial problem in this district as is the case in other parts of the country. There is, in fact, no aversion against the Indian, except that, because he is invariably poor, he is disdained rather on account of his humble station in life than for his personality. . . . If the Indian amasses a fortune or in any

> other way distinguishes himself, he finds no difficulty in mixing with the other classes, or rather, with the white race, for with the mestizos he is in constant intercourse. If at present the mestizos make up one third of the population, there can be no doubt that as soon as the economic standards of the Indians improve—and they will, we hope, improve before long, for there is great need for it—the mestizo element will spread until it permeates the whole population, which would then have made an important step ahead in its evolution through the fact that it would become racially homogeneous.[25]

These somewhat ambiguous phrases reveal *mestizaje* as both a cultural and racial process. Indians were as capable of becoming modern as any other sector of the population, when not mired in poverty. Gamio was explicit in arguing that the "decadent" cultures of the valley were products of colonialism and Catholicism, not race.[26] In fact, the only racial differences that Gamio saw between Indians and whites in the valley were those that favored the indigenous population, which he believed was better adapted to the climate and physical conditions of the region.[27]

Like others who argued that it was rural life that determined the backwardness of the Indian, Gamio suggested that simple improvements in living conditions could easily unleash the potential of the Indians.[28] Drawing from Lamarckian eugenics, Gamio described these Indians as degenerated, but capable of regeneration if conditions were improved. He argued that when Indians moved to cities and became members of the Mexican proletariat, better wages resulted in improvements in "their food, dress, habitation, in their amusements and in their savings." Gamio attributed these changes to the fact that in the cities the indigenous laborer had access to some education, and "joins to a certain extent the social phases of the white race and the mestizos and becomes acquainted with modern civilization."[29] Critically important was the fact that urban living would also improve the diet of rural peoples, which Gamio found appalling. Believing that the vegetarian habits of the countryside could not possibly provide adequate nourishment, he and others suggested that Indians needed to eat meat. Later, after a 1929 visit to Japan during which he was awestruck by the powers of the soybean, he also suggested that the traditional tortilla be substituted with one made of at least one-third soybean paste and two-thirds maíz.[30]

These observations were informed by Gamio's belief that the country was divided into three principal groups, the indigenous, mixed, and modern cultures. These broad evolutionary categories were based mainly in material issues, including dress, food, literacy, and lifestyle (the extent to which it was informed by scientific knowledge), as well as Gamio's sense that a modern culture was an "efficient" culture, that mixed cultures were minimally efficient, and that indigenous cultures were deficient. Of the sixteen million inhabitants of Mexico, he claimed 18 percent of the population was modern and efficient, that 75 percent was intermediate and minimally efficient, and that 6 to 10 percent were deficient. He described Teotihuacán as medieval, placing its residents in the middle category. He gave them credit for having produced some of the nation's most important folk traditions, but denied them the right to full citizenship.[31]

Gamio's approach to the folk cultures of the region was typical of the much broader tendency in Indigenismo to appropriate local folk practices for the nation, while simultaneously calling for their improvement. As a mixed, or medieval culture, Teotihuacancos were repositories of the values, popular practices, and folk traditions that gave the nation its form. Regardless of whether they were Indian or mestizo, they possessed a series of talents and sensibilities that Indigenistas could celebrate as nationalist icons. In his writings on the region, as well as in journals like *Ethnos* (published by the DA, and dedicated to the popularization of anthropology, ending Indian poverty, and the development of a "true" national identity) and *Mexican Folkways,* Gamio and other Indigenistas made the Indian and indigenous folk cultures the core of the nation.[32]

The value that Indigenistas placed in these cultures should not be underestimated. Gamio and his cohort were emphatic that Indian and "popular" art forms represented one of the few original or unique sources for a specifically Mexican culture. Rooted in the splendor of pre-Columbian civilizations, these practices were intuitive, instinctive, and based in everyday popular activities. They formed the basis of the revolutionary nation and attested to the "formidable creative power that rests in our race."[33] Nonetheless, that popular culture needed improvement, much like the material culture that Gamio saw in Teotihuacán. For example, indigenous ceramics in the valley were beautiful, but technically inferior, produced inefficiently, and needed to be "remodeled to suit modern tastes." Gamio thus tried to introduce ceramic techniques from Puebla and suggest new motifs to the artisans of the region. Likewise, while he believed indigenous dances and music were beautiful, Gamio hired Manuel Ponce and Carlos Cháves to transform them to suit the needs of a national audience.

Following Gamio's lead, the SEP instructed teachers throughout the country to promote indigenous motifs by tapping into the "innate plastic intuition that lies hidden in the folk." In a practice that extended well beyond the revolutionary period, federal officials tried to eliminate the "profane" aspects of folk cultures, introduced models from the national archives in order to promote improvements in weaving and other art forms, and endeavored to standardize regional cultural and artisanal expressions to suit the demands of the market. Some would object, claiming that as the basis of the nation, popular arts could not be improved without putting the national culture in peril, but the perspective argued by Gamio—which called for improvements in the popular arts in order to produce economic benefits for local artisans—ultimately dominated. It also fit the larger Indigenista project perfectly. Improving popular arts was like improving the Indian generally. The Indian would be made more valuable as a citizen and Indian cultures would be made more perfectly representative of the uniqueness of the nation.[34]

Drawing influences from Sierra, Chavero, Riva Palacio and other nineteenth-century nationalists, Gamio mixed an evolutionary vision of the nation and a commitment to mestizaje with a limited reading of Boas's cultural relativism to argue that the Indian was not inherently inferior. It was limited, because Boas would have objected both to Gamio's image of the "foggy"-headed primitive, and to his use of a model that posited linear evolution from the primitive to the modern.[35] True cultural relativism would have actually made a homogenous nation impossible, so Gamio adopted the Boasian concept that behavior was culturally determined (allowing the primacy of biology to be discarded), but mixed it with a vision of cultural evolution that was closer to Tylor than Boas. Gamio also drew on a much simplified notion of cultural diffusion, based in part on the observable diffusion of cultural practices (folk culture) from European to Indian in the past, to argue for the state as an instrument of accelerated and directed diffusion. Gamio thus chose to define Indians as hybrids, people who were Mexican in their spiritual culture but primitive in their material culture, distorting cultural anthropology in the interests of nation building.

Though he would ultimately conclude that his cultural classifications of the population were too simplistic (arguing for a more complex combination of racial, linguistic, and cultural characteristics to define the Indian), decades later Gamio remained proud that at Teotihuacán "cultural data was introduced for the first time."[36] Because these concepts usually relied on permeable and not fixed categories, they did not produce a concrete image of Indian alterity. The culturally backward Indian was already a member of the folk, and just needed an education in modern living to enter the mainstream. Gamio was joined by dozens of other authors in promoting this image of the Indian, many of whom drew from work at the DA and SEP during the early 1920s to publicly claim the redeemability of the Indian as a potential citizen.[37]

Numerous Indigenistas drew from Gamio when they portrayed an Indian subject who had gone through many transformations since the conquest, and who had already assimilated other of the values of modern civilization. In some cases this practice was as simple as noting the growing tendency of many Indians to speak Spanish, use western forms of dress, or play western sports, but in many instances Indigenistas described cultures that actively demanded the "advantages of civilization."[38] Addressing this issue in a 1928 pamphlet designed to orient rural teachers in their task of educating the Indian, Carlos Basauri highlighted the Indian's intelligence (especially with regard to scientific knowledge), discipline, dedication to work, and innate loyalty as key qualities that made Indians likely to succeed in modern civilization. He did note that Indians had a unique "ancestral physio-psychological inheritance," but argued that "these racial differences may benefit them, because if the ethnic values they enjoy were adapted to modern civilization, they would be converted into a potent element of indisputable value to human society." As such, he claimed that Indians should never be judged on the basis of skin color, or "hierarchies based in the blood that runs through their veins." Instead he called for recognition of the "true value that we find latent in this race of bronze, and of the moral, social, and economic benefits of joining this valiant contingent to the rest of the Mexican population."[39]

Basauri did not eliminate the primacy of biological categories, but instead used these characteristics to celebrate the Indian and critique the notion of Indian inferiority. Similarly, Antonio Gutiérrez y Oliveros's *Valores epirituales de la raza indígena* (1929) identified twenty-eight positive features of the Mexican Indian. The physical features described a strong, robust, racial type, with no deficiencies from a physiological point of view. Gutiérrez also noted the Indians' aptitude for science and the arts, and "great talent for imitation . . . the Spaniards could do nothing in front of the Indians that was not immediately imitated."[40]

In the same vein, in 1924 Gamio suggested sending Indians to the Paris Olympics because of their "marvelous energies and physical resistance." He claimed the "organic resistance of the Indian" was superior to that of whites and mestizos, because the process of natural selection and the extreme difficulties that indigenous Mexicans had faced over the centuries (massacres, infirmities, alcoholism) had left only the most resilient alive. Turning traditional eugenics on its head (and contradicting his own writings), he added that Indians lived a more nutritionally frugal life, and that they exercised in "clean air, contributing directly to the preservation of healthy organisms." Since these habits produced Indians who could run up to eighty kilometers per day, Gamio advised the government to find Indians to compete in sports such as distance running and steeplechase, events he felt confident that "our Indians" could win.[41]

As Alan Knight notes, the deeper implications of these comments are unmistakable. Even when they were said in praise of the Indian, they indicated that the Indian was a race apart.[42] This tendency was even more pronounced in one of the seminal nationalist texts of the era, *La raza cosmica*. In the text José Vasconcelos wrote that the Indian "will have no other choice but to diffuse and perfect himself in each of the superior varieties of the species."[43] Vasconcelos despised indigenous cultures and felt ambivalent about mestizaje, only ambiguously suggesting that it represented an improvement on European racial stock, in part because "our Indians . . . are not as primitive as the Red Indian."[44] Similarly, many teachers, social scientists, and intellectuals persisted in using terms like "atavistic" (popularized to describe primitive races by the Italian criminal anthropologist, Césare Lombroso), "savage," and "indolent" to describe the Mexican Indian, and continued using scientific measures of race after they fell into disuse elsewhere.[45] Even when their usage of these terms differed from earlier writers, the persistence of racializing practices reflected the important legacies of racial thinking within the revolutionary state.

Yet if we simply dismiss Gamio, Basauri, Gutiérrez y Oliveros, and others for their racialist overtones, we risk interpreting them too narrowly. Postrevolutionary intellectuals inherited a series of nationalist sentiments that were impregnated with racial thinking, and even when they tried to discard the language of racial difference in favor of a more inclusive sense of the nation they could not always do so.[46] While the persistence of racial images in these texts sometimes indicated a given author's desire to fix Indian alterity, it could also signal that author's unreflexive use of inherited terminology. Sometimes their words implied that Indians were as capable as any other Mexican, a position they often established through reference to a series of racial qualities ("moral, physical, and intellectual, in the arts, sciences, and politics") that were often thought lacking in Indians.[47] Consciously seeking to counteract the influence of those who saw in the Indian "the cause of all of our national disasters," they created an Indian who was a racial ideal.[48]

A 1938 editorial in *El Universal* expressed this tension perfectly. The writer condemned racial prejudice because it masked the fact that inequality was truly rooted in cultural problems, and could be resolved through education. His evidence for this claim was that "a high percentage of the organized workers in the country and the city are of pure Indian race."[49] If these Indians were of pure race, then the Indian was an identifiable racial type, opening up the possibility of essential differences between whites and Indians. On the other hand, these Indians were also as modern as any other member of the national community.

In the early 1940s Gamio clarified his own views on this issue, arguing that he had been observing cultural problems all along. Two decades after Teotihuacán he decided that Siliceo Pauer's measurements were a waste of time because the race of most of the inhabitants of Teotihuacán was impossible to determine. More importantly, he concluded that decadence was entirely a product of poverty and poor nutrition, and that even if the biological development of Indians was generally deficient, it was the result of illnesses and cultural factors, not heredity. He would never waver in denying claims that Indians were racially inferior, and would remain emphatic in arguing that mestizaje was both a cultural and racial process.[50]

These assertions reflected Gamio's individual understanding of eugenics, which he relied upon to describe the deficiencies of Mexico's indigenous peoples (Gamio headed the Mexican delegation to the International Eugenics Congress in 1921). In part due to his efforts, eugenic language increasingly found its way into the reports of federal officials in explaining the problems of the countryside during the 1920s, a development that became even more pronounced after the founding of the Sociedad Eugénica Mexicana para el Mejoramiento de la Raza in 1931. Discussions of malnutrition, poor hygiene, degeneration, and repeated denunciations of the deleterious effects of "premature sexual unions" became commonplace in efforts to explain rural poverty.[51]

Adolfo Velasco, of the Escuela Central Agrícola, in Santa Lucio, Durango, provided a notable example of this practice in an essay he submitted to *El Maestro Rural* in 1933, titled "Some Considerations on Physical Anthropology as it applies to Education." In the article he concluded that the Indian's "stunted stature and deficient volumetric indices," were in part the result of Indian adolescents marrying too young (sixteen to eighteen for males and fourteen to fifteen for females). He argued that people at these ages were not sufficiently developed both physically and emotionally to rear children, and that the results were stunted growth, high rates of infant mortality, a melancholy spirit, and a general degeneration of the race. Velasco indicated that each generation had a potential to develop to its fullest, but was stunted by the decision to marry young, before their stature had reached its "normal development." As a result, he saw "a reversal through which they become impaired and degenerate . . . a decline in their physical, moral, and spiritual capacities." This observation suggested that the sins of the parents were visited on the children in ways that had multigenerational consequences.[52]

While he indicated that there were many living Indians who were beyond redemption, Velasco's words allowed for an interpretation of eugenics that did offer hope for the Indian. In an era when North American eugenics was heavily Mendelian (which saw genetic material as unchanging and racial mixing as invariably negative), most Indigenistas adopted positive neo-Lamarckian eugenics, which offered hope for regeneration. Neo-Lamarckian thought, which argued that acquired characteristics (both good and bad) could be inherited, appealed to Mexicans because it offered the possibility of improving the race. Indigenistas thus focused on alcoholism, venereal disease, unhealthy motherhood (the opposite of puericulture), delinquency, and tuberculosis as racial poisons that produced "organic hereditary degenerations."[53]

These views kept the possibility of national progress open, and as Nancy Stepan argues for Brazil, reflected a desire to "rescue their country from the charge of tropical decay and racial degeneration."[54] Furthermore, Indigenistas were generally much more definitive than their Brazilian counterparts in arguing that the Mexican Indian was in no way racially inferior, rejecting both immigration and a general process of whitening as the means to improve Mexico's racial stock. Though they believed that racial mestizaje was a natural ongoing process (it had, after all, been going on for four centuries), it was the cultural process of mestizaje that Indigenistas saw as essential. Even Velasco offered hope, suggesting in classic neo-Lamarckian fashion that an end to premature sexual unions would bring an end to degeneration.

That Indigenistas often used the terms "Indian race" and "Indian culture" interchangeably, leaving the meanings of both indeterminate, reveals a great deal about the ambiguous role that eugenics played in Mexico. Most found it impossible to even designate which Mexicans were truly Indians. Indigenistas used a variety of racial and cultural data, along with their own imaginations, to define both the Indian and the mestizo, and in turn described a variety of national types. According to wildly divergent accounts, Indians made up between 30 and 50 percent of the national population. Experts set their numbers at between two and ten million, with the indeterminacy rooted in questions of whether the category should include "a portion of the mestizos who live in the countryside subjugated, like the Indians."[55] This ambiguity was reflected in the practice of federal educational inspectors, who often relied on linguistic and cultural categories to describe the "race" of Indian communities, defining a community as Indian only so long as the majority of its inhabitants did not speak any Spanish. Sometimes the same inspector would change the racial designation of a given community as the work of the rural school progressed.[56] Likewise, many leading figures came to believe that a combination of cultural markers, and not biology, were the bases on which the national population should be classified. Making this an official policy, in 1930 race was eliminated from the national census in favor of linguistic classification.[57] In their words and deeds these representatives of the revolutionary state thus revealed the constructedness of race. If mestizaje was as much a cultural as a racial process, any Mexican could be a mestizo as long as they displayed certain sensibilities associated with modernity.

Gramsci introduced the concept of "contradictory consciousness" to describe contexts where two incompatible conceptions of the world seemingly exist in an individual's worldview (Gramsci, 1976: 325–326). This is particularly useful in understanding Indigenistas, whose projects and ideas were often fraught with the tension between race and culture. Typical of this tension was Pierre Morpeau's 1931 comment that "it is clear that the solution to the racial problem in Mexico lies in giving a better, a much better culture to the Indian, and not only the Indian, but the mestizo as well, and the population in general."[58] Morpeau may have been confused, or he may have been making a subtle point, but over time many Indigenistas came to see this tension as something that needed to be resolved. This task was usually accomplished by consciously replacing the concept of "race" with that of "culture."[59]

In spite of their power to challenge long-held assumptions about the Indian, these practices did not represent a simple departure from racial hierarchies. Even though race had assumed a heightened importance because of its capacity to exclude anyone defined as Indian from the nation during the late nineteenth century, systems of hierarchy and domination in Mexico were never wholly based in a scientifically clear concept of race. Race served as a catchall explanation for poverty and inequality during the prerevolutionary era, the basic point of reference for explaining the Indian. However, racial categories also utilized a series of long-standing hierarchies, based in class, gender, education, morals, customs, eating habits, language, and dress to describe the Indian. When Indigenistas challenged race, they did not also challenge these other hierarchies, but instead reinforced their importance as obstacles that had to be overcome in the interest of national development. Thus, even as Indigenistas aggressively denied the importance of race as a marker of the national population, they would leave unchallenged other key mechanisms for defining the Indian as an impoverished subject and incomplete citizen.

On the other hand, while cultural prejudice was often simply a form of "racism without race"—substituting a prejudice based on moral or cultural superiority for one based on biology—descriptions of the nation rooted in cultural differences offered certain important promises to indigenous peoples.[60] Unlike race, culture was not fixed, but open to innovation and improvement. Mexico could be divided into permeable categories based in the cultural distinctions between educated and illiterate, middle and working class, agrarista and fanatic, and (perhaps most importantly), urban and rural.[61] While most rural Mexicans would remain hopelessly primitive within these new categories, cultural, as opposed to racial differences, could be overcome. This would create important new possibilities for individual indigenous Mexicans, who during the 1920s and 1930s demanded rights based upon their own successful incorporation into modern civilization. Thus, even though the Indigenista effort to deny biological determinism was ethnocidal, it departed from the exclusionary past, endeavored to empower Indians as individuals, and reflected a willingness to grant rights to those who were willing to assimilate.

Redeeming the Indian Race

Indigenistas believed the Indian was perfectly capable of entering the modern world. It simply remained for the state to find the means of assimilation—a process that most believed would be accomplished principally through education. In the relatively conservative political climate of the 1920s, education promised to obviate the need for massive land reforms or the redistribution of wealth, because rural Mexicans would acquire the capacity to improve their lives without recourse to the state. With education, all campesinos would make their lives more efficient and productive, make better use of the resources that they had, and become a more stable and secular political constituency. Education would also impart to all Mexicans—Indian, mestizo, or white—a deeper sense of community, a desire to cooperate with one another for the improvement of all. Assimilation through education seemed a much better alternative to the Indian policies found in other countries, where isolationist practices like reservations "condemn [Indians] to a slow, agonizing death."[62]

Early directors of the SEP, including Vasconcelos and José Manuel Puig Casauranc, believed that a school that focused exclusively on introducing students into modern civilization would be the most effective means of incorporating and homogenizing Mexico's Indians.[63] Operating as a modern, secularized version of the sixteenth-century missionary project, the school would teach students to speak Spanish, salute the flag, celebrate national holidays, sing the national hymn, venerate national heroes, and learn the nation's history. At the same time, schools could teach Indians to make the soil more productive, and teachers, acting as both economists and sociologists, could create a new generation of more intelligent rural dwellers, with better homes, better methods of living, better cultivation, better health, better means of communication, and a "better spiritual atmosphere."[64] In this schema modernity was measured by a number of things. A modern community would have large numbers of Spanish speakers, and clean schools and homes. Its residents would use new agricultural techniques, engage in activities like beekeeping, and be willing to go to a doctor and use modern medicines.

Modernity would also include the diminution of those practices that José Puig called "the tragic triangle of fanaticism, alcoholism, and premature sexual unions, the factors of racial degeneration."[65] Degeneration in this instance was in part signaled by the cultural backwardness that many revolutionaries identified with devout Catholicism (and the resistance to the state that this often provoked). It was also a product of the lived effects of alcohol abuse, and the supposedly noneugenic impact that teenage pregnancy had on children and their parents. By eliminating these backward practices and imposing a new, secular and modern sensibility on the countryside, the school would be the core instrument in creating a true nation. Healthy motherhood would be central to these efforts. Programs like the Misiones Culturales promoted puericulture as one of their chief responsibilities.[66]

These programs thus envisioned a uniform set of practices through which all indigenous Mexicans would come to enjoy the benefits of modern civilization and abandon their barbarous tendencies. No provisions were made for differences in regional economies, cultures, and ecology.[67] The assimilationist ethos was so dominant that, when in 1927 the federal director of education in Puebla discovered teachers using Nahuatl to help their students learn, he ordered that they immediately cease using the language. He also forbade its use in the classroom or on the playground, even though most were only using it to explain lessons that the students did not understand. The director believed the use of Indian languages slowed incorporation, claiming further that it "retards the consolidation of our nationality."[68]

Early press reports suggested that SEP efforts yielded great success. Indian students, it was said, traveled many miles just for the privilege of learning to read, supported their schools enthusiastically, and eagerly demanded the fruits of modernity.[69] Yet the assimilationist project of the SEP fell into crisis very soon after it began.[70] Between 1921 and 1924 the SEP enrolled 65,000 students in 1,089 rural schools, with 1,146 teachers and 102 missionaries, but their efforts largely failed in monolingual Indian communities. In these communities teachers came into profound conflicts with residents and local authorities. These struggles in return often left schools empty. If left unchecked, these failures threatened to undermine both the SEP's assimilationist program and their claim that the Indian was the racial equal of whites and mestizos.[71]

Facing these challenges, in 1925 Puig announced a plan to open a special school designed to create incontrovertible proof of the Indian's capacity for assimilation. The school, called the Casa del Estudiante Indígena, would place racially pure Indians who were "without culture" in a boarding school in Mexico City, where they would take part in the variety of excellent educational opportunities in the city, and emerge as modern citizens. Though racially pure Indians, these students would become fully modernized (and for that matter, Mexicanized) in the Federal District.[72]

Students for the Casa were chosen based on a number of criteria. Puig and the school's director, Enrique Corona, sought out intelligent, healthy adolescent Indian males from every major indigenous ethnicity in the country. They also preferred students who had one or two years of rural education, required that students understand the Indian dialect of their region perfectly, and declared that they would "reject those Indians . . . who have already been incorporated."[73] Puig and Corona believed that this combination of qualities (racial purity, backwardness, but inherent aptitude) represented the ideal foundation for a program that could both prove Indian assimilability and make "social leaders"—

young men who would return to their communities after their education and successfully introduce modern beliefs and practices.

The Casa produced a mixed record concerning race and assimilation from its very inception. The first cohort of students included dozens of mestizos from regionally powerful families (drawn to the school due to its generous funding) who were ultimately rejected in favor of youths Corona described as "little savages," who "gave the impression of strange little animals, with bright, intelligent eyes."[74] In areas where young Indians did not come forward voluntarily as prospective students, local representatives of the SEP procured students by any means necessary. At times they even hunted them down, "trap(ping)" "completely savage" students after violent struggles. These students were closely supervised once they arrived at the school for fear of flight.[75]

Corona relied on a series of somatological measurements to examine these students for racial purity and root out the mestizos, repeatedly asserting that over 90 percent of the students in the school were pure Indians. To prove this, doctors and anthropologists regularly visited the school and generated physiological classifications of the different Indian "races" represented at the institution. Their reports showed a fixed biological sense of race, which included types and location of body hair, skin and eye color, and the shape and size of facial, skull, and body characteristics, all based on multiple minute examinations.[76]

Treating the school like a museum, anthropologists, archeologists, and artists also examined students to collect racial and cultural data. In one of the earliest investigations in the school, Carlos Basauri examined the "anthropological characteristics" of the students as part of an ethnological and anthropometric study of the various distinct Indian races. Basauri made students in the Casa an essential part of race-making in Mexico by fixing their difference, calculating "the cephalic indexes, nasal and biachromal measurements . . . to form comparative tables, and establish the differences that exist among the representatives of every Indian group and every race."[77] Following Basauri, representatives from the National Museum and Department of Fine Arts of the SEP conducted similar studies that used Casa students as specimens. They studied the racial makeup of students, along with cultural practices (regional dances, etc.) that they brought to the school, often justifying their projects in terms of the cost effectiveness and convenience of studying a diverse set of cultures and races in one location.[78] Lost on them was the Boasian imperative that cultures needed to be studied in their own context.

Undermining Race in the Casa

The significance of these race-fixing practices should not be minimized, as they clearly indicate the ways in which scientific racism and cultural prejudice were integral to the school's practices. However, they must be understood in the context of a larger set of practices at the Casa that in some ways undermined race as an essential category. The very pedagogy of the school mandated that teachers recognize ethnic diversity, but deny that the races were truly discrete categories. Students were taught that Indians were in no way inferior to whites or mestizos. Moreover, the tests performed on students in the school confirmed this very assertion. Mental examinations carried out at the Casa in 1926 and 1927 demonstrated that the aptitudes of indigenous students in the school were on a par with mestizo and white students at other schools in the city. The tests also suggested that those differences that could be seen between the Casa's students and those from other schools in the city were merely a result of their rudimentary Spanish or social conditions that the students faced prior to attending the Casa. These tests were particularly important given the larger failures of rural education, and the results were highly publicized as incontrovertible evidence of the capacity of the Indian. As time passed Corona and the Casa's advocates made almost no reference to the nearly 30 percent of students who ran away, dropped out, failed, or were expelled, but repeatedly provided examples of actual Indians who, hailing from the most primitive circumstances, had adapted to and prospered within the school.[79]

The success of the school depended on the ability of the students to fulfill three different demands. They had to succeed in their studies in order to prove their capacity for education. They also had to acquire a series of cultural and civic sensibilities that would reveal their potential as citizens. Lastly, they had to successfully translate the benefits they had gained within the school into practice in the countryside. In achieving the first of these goals, they could clearly rely on Corona's complicity. While internal documents suggest that some of the other teachers were not so impressed, in his reports he unfailingly boasted

A group of Huichol students arriving at the Casa del Estudiante Indígena in 1926. Photos like this measured the primitive state of the Indian through dress, perceptions of cleanliness, and the seeming "indifference" that photographers captured in the subject. For a comparison, see the photograph on page 26. (SEP, 1927, 60)

that the Indian students in the Casa were enthusiastic and able learners.[80] Corona argued that beyond simply being good students, they undertook and succeeded in difficult technical projects with little support from outsiders. These assertions were given public confirmation when industrial products manufactured by students from the Casa won a gold medal at the Hispanic Exposition in Sevilla in 1929.[81]

Corona also reported that between 80 and 100 percent of the students in the school passed their exams every year, and that "96 percent of the Indian students have been fully incorporated into the Mexican social community."[82] Disproving the belief that Indians had no capacity for living in the modern world, he argued that these results showed that the Indian had "an unlimited potential for progress."[83] Others agreed, as federal officials who visited the school, members of the press, and even President Calles marveled at how students in the school were transformed "from savage Indian[s] to Mexican gentlemen."[84] Their successes were also displayed through student participation in school organizations, community projects, civic ritual, and sports

Photos of the same Huichol students two years after they were admitted to the Casa del Estudiante Indígena. Photos measuring the progress of students at various SEP schools were very common during the revolutionary period, and invariably measured modernity through dress and European standards of personal hygiene. (*Muncher Illustrierte Press,* October 1931)

competitions in the city. In one of their most notable achievements, students constructed the Parque Anáhuac, a playground with basketball, tennis, and volleyball courts that they built and then ceded to the community. The products they made in their workshops (industrial, woodworking, furniture making, and otherwise) provided much of the money to pay for these public works.[85]

The students' public demonstrations affirmed both their modern sensibilities and their commitment to return to their homes and work for the Revolution. Typical of this, Mother's Day celebrations at the school featured a program called "Tribute from the Casa del Estudiante Indígena to the Mothers of the Colonia Anáhuac," with poems written by Indian students in their own vernaculars and read for the mothers of the neighborhood around the school. The iconography of the event was striking; the students maintained their indigenous identities by using Indian languages, but placed themselves within modern society through their participation in a secular civic holiday. As the symbolic children of these women, they were also loyal sons of the nation.[86]

Similar messages could also be found in the periodical students published, titled "El Indio." It contained poems and testimonials about the plight of the Indian, assertions of the talent of the Indian (through the very production of the text and in the content), and celebrations of the redemptive role of the school.[87] Along with the plays and musical performances put on by the students, these practices celebrated Indian students in the Casa as the source of *mexicanidad,* further undermining the idea that the Indian was a distinct racial other and blurring racial boundaries. In these forums Corona and other SEP officials took students they believed were richly talented and innately artistic, and set out to transform their sad and "profane" traditions into something useable for national pride. This was central to the mission of the Casa, where SEP officials sought to "shape the national soul," and articulate the national culture as a function of Indian, mestizo, and *criollo* traditions.[88]

This ethos clearly informed the first major cultural event at the school, which took place in December 1927. In what was described as a public demonstration of "Action Theater," students displayed a number of "Indian customs," and performed a student-written play titled "The Wedding." Mixing Indian and mestizo folk iconography, the performance included numerous folk ballads and ended with a rousing rendition of the national anthem. The performance not only reinforced the image of Indian artistic sensibilities in ways that pleased Casa administrators, it also delighted the numerous city luminaries who attended the event. It was described in *El Universal* as a "hit," in which it was "simply marvelous to witness the total transformation of the young Indians."[89] Students maintained the artistic and theatrical reputation of the school in later fiestas, sometimes gaining national and even international attention for their artistic productions. On one occasion in December 1929, students performed "Regional Mariachi Music," and staged a series of dramatic plays. These performances included "The Rural School Combats Alcoholism," written by Casa student Cupertino de la Cruz, along with "The Wise Rabbit: a Folk Legend from the Isthmus," written by Magdaleno Cruz, also a student from the school. Like other comedies and dramas performed in the school's theater, these later events celebrated the rural folk and the redeeming role that education could play in the countryside.[90]

In these events, indigenous artistic traditions were complemented with mestizo *corridos*, mariachi music, and creole *jarabes,* producing a subject who was the perfect synthesis of Indian past and mestizo present. This was a contradictory image, in that by demonstrating their artistic abilities, these students sometimes reinforced stereotypes about indigenous artistic sensibilities in ways that reinscribed their racial alterity. Producing fine objects of art reinforced notions of essential Indian artistry, while folksy renderings of the music of Tata Nacho (the popular musician and composer Ignacio Fernández Esperón) surrounded by sets decorated by Carlos González evoked compliments that focused on the charming "simplicity" of Indian students in the Casa.[91] However, these performances also created a number of other images that suggested much about the capabilities and modern sensibilities of the students within the school. As the purveyors of Indian folk traditions, students of the Casa were themselves important nationalist icons, but in their assimilation to a higher culture, they became the living symbols of a realizable revolutionary future.

Of course, these living symbols needed to do the work of the Revolution in order to fulfill their mandate, and it was in this task that the Casa saw its greatest trials. Corona regularly claimed that upwards of 99 percent of the students returned to the countryside as missionaries of progress, but others were unconvinced.[92] Perpetually questioned for the cost of producing his "civilized Indians," by the early 1930s Corona's tales of success were increasingly scrutinized.[93] Rafael Ramírez, Corona's superior within the SEP, attacked the school in internal communications for both its high costs and the insufficient numbers of rural teachers it produced. Ramírez weighed in publicly on the matter in late 1930, lauding the school for proving that Indians could incorporate into the mainstream, but lamenting that the process was very slow, and that students often did not return home "because they feel repugnance for rural living, and a repulsion for life amongst their brothers." In a period of declining budgets such as was at hand, Ramírez argued that the budget of the school could be used to establish as many as six boarding schools (internados), which would accomplish the same ends as the Casa.[94] His reservations were manifested in the budget for the school, which fell from an allotment of $190,410.00 in 1930 ($952.05 per student), to $109,932.48 in 1932 ($574.32 per student) [all values in pesos]. By mid-1932 he became so alarmed that he appointed a special investigator to look into the problems at the Casa. He chose the educational inspector Manuel Mesa, who visited the school in mid-May.[95]

Mesa's report was extraordinarily critical of the school. While conceding that the Casa showed that "Indians are capable of instruction and civilizing influences, and their aptitudes do not depend on the color of their skin, or on other ethnic characteristics," he lambasted the school on a variety of grounds. He complained that the costs of producing rural teachers at the school were far too high, that physical conditions were deplorable, and that there were numerous mestizos in the school. Most importantly, he argued that Corona's representation of the successes of the school in producing rural teachers could not be trusted, as the students in the school were ill-prepared to be rural teachers, and many of them had avoided this profession altogether. He noted that over one-third of the total students (314) had left the school without completing their studies, and that by 1932 the school had produced only seventy-nine rural teachers (23.5 percent of former students). Most of these, he believed, were not particularly good teachers. Based on these conclusions, the Casa was closed at the end of 1932, and its students dispersed to a variety of schools in the Federal District and around the country.[96]

The Crisis of Assimilation

The Casa's failures in promoting a larger process of assimilation left SEP administrators in a crisis. To be sure, some rural schools had prospered during the 1920s, but the lamentations of rural teachers about the vast problems of rural education far outweighed these successes. According to struggling pedagogues, the Indian was "atavistic," "indolent," and was either "glacially indifferent" or fought every federal program with a deeply ingrained "spirit of resistance."[97] These problems were probably most acute in the Misiones Culturales which traveled through the countryside during these years, and which produced some very stark images of Indian alterity. Often sent into regions where the rural school had yet to make any inroads, the Misiones Culturales mixed the modernist message of the SEP with a complete ignorance of local conditions in an often horrifying and ineffective blend. Shocked by what they saw, cultural missionaries described malnourished children with distended stomachs not only as hungry and ill, but as "degenerated" and "mentally abnormal," and mobilized racial imagery to explain communities that seemed to "lack any desire for improvement."

They were rendered as irrational, wild, inward-looking, and often incapable of civilization.[98]

Whether they attributed their problems to Indian degeneration or to the poor design of SEP programs, by the early 1930s most Indigenistas agreed that they had accomplished very little in ten years of work. Looking over their recent experiences, SEP administrators were conscious of the ways that Manuel Gamio's desire to develop scientific knowledge about the Indian had been ignored during much of the previous decade, as self-confident educators implemented programs designed to bestow a superior culture on a poorly understood Indian community. After a decline in Gamio's political influence led to the closure of the DA in 1925, the SEP had devoted few resources to studying rural education. Since that time all responsibility for producing scientific knowledge of the Indian had fallen upon poorly prepared teachers, who received a cursory introduction to physical anthropology, ethnography, ethnology, folklore, and linguistics through Carlos Basauri's Sección de Etnografía in the Departamento de Enseñanza Rural.[99]

In 1931 the SEP created the Comisión de Investigaciones Indias as the first step towards resolving this crisis. Although assimilation remained the principal goal of the Comisión, it would henceforth be undertaken through a program that considered local conditions more carefully. Charged with finding "the most appropriate method of education for incorporating this race into modern civilization," the Comisión undertook two major research projects during its relatively short life.[100] The first was directed by Basauri, and took place in a series of schools in the Valle de Mezquital, Hidalgo, in April 1931.[101] Basauri's project was short-lived however, because in 1932 most of the resources of the Comisión were reallocated to the Estación Experimental de Incorporación del Indio, in the Tarascan village of Carapan, Michoacán, under the direction of Moisés Sáenz.

Like Gamio had more than a decade earlier, Sáenz parlayed a graduate education from Columbia University (he studied education under John Dewey) into an appointment as Subsecretary of the SEP in 1924, where he was an important architect of the rural school and the Casa. Long a proponent of stimulating economic development and incorporating Indians into the mainstream, he offered a more optimistic vision of Indian redemption than did Basauri, who by 1931 was increasingly obsessed with endocrinal problems and hormonal imbalances (in part due to his interest in Italian criminology). By contrast, Sáenz endeavored to resolve the crisis in assimilation by assembling Mexico's most important experts on indigenous issues in one location and conducting an intensive study of the problems and possibilities of Indian education. Staffed by Sáenz, Basauri, Pablo González Casanova, Miguel Othón de Mendizabal, José Guadalupe Nájera, Catherine Vesta Sturges, and a host of other prominent Indigenistas, the project promised to find the most rapid means of incorporating the Indian into civilization.[102]

When they entered Carapan on 24 July 1932, Sáenz and his cohort were self-confident missionaries of the Mexican state, carrying with them the expertise needed to interpret the social conditions they found and design a program to save the Indian.[103] Sáenz had chosen Carapan for the experiment because he believed it was a typical Indian village, but also because he believed the large numbers of agraristas in the area would ensure his team ready support in the community. Though violent agrarista-cristero conflicts had engulfed the region for more than a decade, Sáenz was confident that the young cohort of agrarista males, advocates of modernization and civilization, would be allies in what he hoped would be a swift transformation of the community.

A few weeks later Sáenz and his colleagues were disillusioned, frightened, confused, and filled with doubt as to their own abilities to solve the problems they faced. Their problems had begun within days of arriving, when even as they established themselves in the old *curato,* they found themselves the subject of violent attacks from locals. In spite of initial promises from the local agrarista leader, Ernesto Prado, no one would help with even the most basic tasks, and it soon seemed that the project was in danger of total collapse. In the following weeks the Estación faced other, nearly violent conflicts with the villagers, who at one point even tried to prevent them from entering the school. Sáenz was flabbergasted by the shouts of residents in these confrontations. As they marched, the assembled crowd chanted "Viva Cristo Rey!" and "We don't want to change, we are ignorant and we want to remain ignorant!" "Get out of here!" "Who are you to advise us?"[104]

Sáenz would soon enough learn that many of these attacks had been orchestrated by his erstwhile ally, Ernesto Prado, as part of a larger strategy for monopolizing local power for his own clique. Prado went so far as to write to Sáenz's superiors in Mexico City, accusing members of the Estación of being in league with the cristeros. Yet Sáenz learned this too late to do any good. Crippled by conflicts, the Estación would last only eighteen months. Most of its participants would leave the region deeply aware that they left in defeat. As Sáenz later acknowledged, the combination of apostolic zeal, romantic desires, and the demand for practical scientific results from Carapan was fatal to the project. The program of studies had been designed in Mexico City by pedagogues with little knowledge of the *meseta tarasca,* and the professionals assigned to the school were mostly unfamiliar with the culture and politics of the area, resulting in a school that was simply a "mirage of idealism."[105]

Sáenz concluded that in spite of outward appearances, local conceptions of the world were fundamentally different from those of the investigators. Together with linguistic barriers, these differences led to moments of total incomprehension at Carapan. This was only made worse by a long history of exploitation by outsiders, which prompted a great deal of resistance to outside influences and refusals to proffer assistance to the Estación. In part this was a product of the "ill will of the Prados," caciques who could exploit both members of the Estación and the community simultaneously, but it was more directly a result of the profound cognitive gap between the Estación and the locals. Mexico was an unreal world for them, Spanish a foreign and largely useless language, and the print traditions of a larger Mexican society incomprehensible to people raised in an oral culture. Even though some came to have deep affection for Sáenz, the gulfs that separated residents from the Estación were too vast. Never before had so many important experts seen how little they actually understood about the complexities of education, incorporation, and progress.[106]

Sáenz's ultimate lament on his experiences in Carapan, that "the more we came to know them the more Indian they seemed to be,"[107] reflected one of the first moments in which a powerful activist, while eschewing racial stereotypes, acknowledged that the gulfs between indigenous Mexicans and their educators could not be overcome through a simple process of assimilation. He remained committed to the Mexicanization of the Indian, but in the aftermath of Carapan neither he nor most of his cohort at the Estación believed that this change could be imposed in a straightforward manner.[108] Even before the SEP closed the Estación, this lesson, like others drawn from a decade of assimilationist programs, was being considered. After Carapan SEP officials found it increasingly difficult to view the rural school as a simple instrument in transforming the countryside.

During the coming years, this lesson would inform a host of federal initiatives, from the internados indígenas, to the Departamento de Asuntos Indígenas, and ultimately the Congresos Regionales Indígenas. Driven by their desire to understand the failures of revolutionary programs and the consistent hostility with which many indigenous communities viewed their erstwhile benefactors, a growing number of Indigenistas would use these initiatives to question the very nationalist underpinnings of the programs of the revolutionary state. Taking Sáenz's concern about the penetrability of the Indian seriously, but also committed to rejecting racism, these institutions provided forums for articulating a host of new ideas about social reform, prompting the federal state's first halting steps towards recognizing Mexico as a plural nation.

2 The Problems and Promise of the Internados Indígenas

The Indian can only be redeemed and elevated by the Indian.
—Luis Monzón, 1933[1]

The summer of 1932 was a long one for Rafael Ramírez, the chief of rural education at the SEP. Budget cuts had been crippling his agency for nearly two years, the experiment in Indian education in Carapan fell into deep crisis within weeks of being founded in July, and the Casa del Estudiante Indígena, long the symbolic centerpiece of the government's program of Indian redemption, was rocked by a series of student protests that threatened to destroy the school. Yet while the first two issues may have caused Ramírez considerable concern, the third was likely a source of some relief, as Ramírez had long been looking for reasons to close the Casa, and had probably even caused some of the problems. Ramírez, it seems, was tired of the great expense of educating students in the Casa, displeased with the behavior of its director, and thought the school had failed miserably in its efforts to produce social leaders who would take the modernist ethos of the Casa and translate it to the vast Mexican countryside.

The failures of these social leaders were even more serious in light of the fact that the SEP had generally failed to find enough good teachers who would work in indigenous regions. Summarizing the miserable results of these programs in a report on the Misiones Culturales (the other key program of Indian education), Rufino Tamayo lamented that they had left little more than a series of unfinished buildings, empty theaters, and antipathy for the federal government in their wake. He lamented that the Misiones "are almost entirely staffed by individuals who lack, in the first place, the required skills in the respective specialties, and in the second place, a true spirit of responsibility." These problems, Tamayo observed, were made worse by the fact that Mision staffs knew very little about local conditions, and were inclined to "undertake subterfuges in order to avoid their work and remain in the cities."[2]

It was thus unlikely that the Casa, the Misiones Culturales, or Carapan would offer the solutions to the Indian question that Ramírez was looking for. In light of this, in October 1932 he announced that he was closing the Casa, and that in the future its mandate would be undertaken through a series of internados indígenas, to be established in Indian regions throughout the country. In a major departure from the policies of the previous decade in rural education, these schools were charged with harmonizing their practices with local cultures and conditions, and using local idioms as a means of communication and teaching. The internados would be specifically targeted for those areas where the problems faced by rural educators required special efforts. Located "in the heart of Indian regions," "whose backwardness could not be overcome with the rural school," the internados were meant to rehabilitate Indians without removing or alienating them from their home environment, so that they would in turn educate their communities. They would serve specific ethnic communities, defined as such through racial, linguistic, economic, and geographic criteria. If all went according to plan, each internado would design programs that were uniquely attuned to local conditions, drawing on local cultures, using local languages, and appropriate for the "cultural level" of the communities it served. They would also be charged with accepting, even encouraging the influence and participation of local leaders and parents.[3]

Admission was limited to Indian adolescents (fourteen to twenty years old for males, twelve to eighteen for females) who "lack any elemental culture" (meaning they could not speak or understand Spanish) and were in good health. Prospective students would also need to be "of pure Indian race and habitually use the language of their ethnic group as a means of expression and communication." In accordance with the civilizing ethos, education in the internados would first focus on teaching students to speak, read, and write in Spanish, after which the school would teach "satisfactory customs and habits, and . . . superior forms of personal, domestic and social life." Students would also study the "popular arts" of their regions, participate in sports, and receive technical and agricultural training. The latter was perhaps the most important aspect of their education, as students would learn to use modern technologies, organize and run cooperatives, and study a variety of academic subjects oriented towards elevating the living standards of their communities. In order to achieve these ends the schools were to have no less than twenty-five hectares of land for cultivation.

In theory, these practices would help students remain connected to their cultures so that they would emerge as leaders who carried with them both the positive qualities of Indian cultures and the progressive values of the school. They would become "social leaders," content to remain in their home communities as agents of progress. SEP officials downplayed the possibility that once they were transformed into leaders, students from the internados would no longer be ideal representatives of their communities, and might use their role as interlocutors to act as caciques because they believed the countryside needed leaders who could bring modern values to the masses. Facing a program of Indian education that had largely failed, this risk was worth taking.[4]

Its overall program made the internado indígena similar to other rural schools, particularly the rural agricultural normal school. Both focused on issues such as hygiene and health, regional economic development, agricultural skills, home economics, and a variety of academic subjects. And while they were not normal schools, students from the internados could go directly into rural teaching after their four- to six-year agricultural and technical education. On the other hand, internados were unlike other rural schools in that they were meant to be open to mutual influence from the community and the teacher, and "have a flexibility that makes them adapt and fit to the needs of the social topography."[5] SEP officials hoped that in harmonizing their pedagogy with local ethnic, social, cultural, and economic practices, the schools would have a beneficial impact in the larger community, "shaking the Indian races [out of their lethargy] and stimulating them to work for their own improvement."[6]

In privileging local cultures and vernaculars in the internados, SEP officials acknowledged for the first time that each educational environment represented a distinct culture, and that local cultures and languages had to play a role in the educational process. For some, this merely meant that education had to be made more rudimentary because Indians were too primitive and their "mental capacity" too limited for them to prosper in ordinary rural schools, or that the school should find a more effective means to supplant the retrograde cultures of indigenous Mexicans. However, in making a place for local cultures in the internados, the SEP created the possibility that local communities might have a role to play in setting the curriculum of the schools.[7] In fact, by placing the internados in Indian regions, calling for regionally specific practices, and encouraging an active relationship between the internados and local communities, the internados created an unprecedented opportunity for community influence on the direction of education.[8] At a time when many rural schools still refused entry to Indian children who wore traditional dress, the internado was a site in which indigenous youths could make a claim both to education and to a right to maintain their culture.[9]

A Shaky Start

The SEP opened eleven internados in 1933, locating several in some of the most impoverished regions of the country. These founding acts took place with a great deal of public fanfare, but the problems that experiments in Indian education faced outside of Mexico City became apparent almost immediately. Not only were internados often hastily organized, loosely overseen and poorly funded, they lacked materials, adequate lands and buildings, and properly trained teachers. Schools were often created in converted churches on the verge of collapse, endangering those children who could be enticed to enroll. Where church buildings were unavailable, some early schools operated in stone huts without roofs, windows, land, or even the most basic necessities, forcing teachers and students to make do with what they could siphon off from the desperately impoverished communities where they were located. Many schools lacked electricity, potable water, beds, clothes, and even food. Not unlike many types of schools during this era of rapid expansion and inadequate resources, students often lived in "absolute misery."[10]

In all but a few cases the individuals who staffed the first internados lacked any experience or expertise in Indian education. Ill-prepared to implement their specialized program, many treated the internado as a typical rural school.[11] SEP officials did prioritize the hiring of bilingual teachers, which meant that at least some former students from the Casa and other young indigenous males educated in rural normal schools found positions in the internados.[12] However, they too did little to make the program a success. Many teachers and directors quickly ran into serious trouble, and within six months several schools that had opened at or near capacity emptied. Internados in Caró (Mexico), Quitiyé (Querétero), and Zongozotla (Puebla) were typical of this trend. In

Caró, only four Indians remained of forty original students by July 1933. Inspections of Zongozotla around the same time found that the sixty-six students in the school were almost completely ignorant of Spanish, that the internado had no agricultural parcels, and that the shoe-making operation profited only its teacher. In Quitiyé, the school had half the number of students it was designed for, with twenty-six men and four women. Of these, eleven were too young and two were mestizos, lowering the number of acceptable students to seventeen. Of the director at Quitiyé, one inspector wrote that "he is an optimistic man, with great initiative and a real interest in seeing the school prosper, but he lacks a clear vision of the mission that should be undertaken in this type of school." This was a generous assessment, as the same inspector had recommended firing the entire staff at other internados.[13]

By mid-1934 many schools were either empty or filled with mestizo students, a situation that several directors justified by claiming that they could find no Indians willing to enroll.[14] The lack of cultivable lands at some schools only aggravated the problems, as students were unable to grow food or cultivate foodstuffs to raise money for provisions. Typical of these problems were the conditions found at the internado in El Carmen, Guerrero, located on a 125-hectare hacienda that had been abandoned for twenty-four years. The land was ill-suited to agriculture, the small number of animals (including only one horse) were the personal property of the director, and there were no small industries. Its forty students (thirty males and ten females) ate poorly, and had no interest in their work. These problems resulted in high rates of desertion, making one inspector lament that it would be impossible for the school to produce "social leaders . . . individuals capable of properly emancipating their racial brothers from the ignorance, misery, ignominy, and corruption in which they live." Describing the "deplorable conditions" in the school as absolutely ill suited to elevating students from their "trogloditic life," he concluded that the school should be closed.[15]

Some inspectors responded to these conditions with an increasingly despairing voice, but Luis Monzón, who in late 1933 was given a special commission to examine the problems of the internados, saw an opportunity in this crisis.[16] Having inspected several schools, Monzón concluded that the internados faced a daunting task, but argued that they could succeed if they were organized differently. Monzón believed the schools had an important role to play in introducing new technologies and ideas into indigenous communities, but suggested that the schools were even more essential as mechanisms for undoing the "oppression and misery that has imprisoned the Mexican Indian for centuries." This, he believed, was the underlying cause of the apathy that he saw in indigenous communities, and could only be overcome through the work of Indians themselves. It seemed to Monzón that the good intentions of teachers and directors, as well as federal assistance, would be misplaced if the schools were not reorganized to reflect the belief that "the Indian can only be redeemed and elevated by the Indian." This should be the core mandate of the schools, which should take only "pure Indians" and transform them into the redemptive force that indigenous Mexicans needed.[17]

Monzón harbored no illusions that these leaders could be easily produced. Even when they were at the school, the students in the internados faced incredible pressures to contribute to the economic, social, and religious needs of their communities. He believed that when they confronted these pressures, many students "being Indians, and for that matter, given to a well-known racial indolence, wind up deserting the school, and take to their communities of origin a poor impression of the internados." Having returned home they became ill, forgot the lessons they had learned in the school, and reverted to their old ways. This was a problem that could be overcome, but given the poor provisions, planning, and conflicts that crippled the schools, it was not a problem that could be overcome without major reforms.[18]

Monzón's reference to the "well known racial indolence" of Indians seems to suggest that he saw these subjects as profoundly inferior and incapable of self-determination, but it is one of the curious characteristics of this era that this was not his intention. Monzón was simply attempting to articulate his belief that, given the vast cultural differences that separated Indian communities from the national mainstream, the impetus to change indigenous communities had to come from within. Although his earlier reports had mentioned the importance of a "culture of action" and class-consciousness, he now turned his full energies to arguing that self-empowerment was the key to elevation. Concluding that "Indian" social leaders (ideally those educated in internados) were the sine qua non for the "transformation of our aboriginal races," he insisted that in the future "Indian teachers must come from the Indian race." He also suggested that administration, construction, maintenance, and provisioning be left to the Indian students, creating in them a spirit of redemption that they could bring to their communities. The mestizo or white teacher might remain the agent of civilization, but they should not play a central role in this process, lest the indigenous student remain alienated from power. Monzón thus suggested that all intermediaries—himself included—be marginalized.[19]

After he traveled to the Yucatán on a series of inspection visits during the following October, Monzón further refined this vision. Observing the Maya, he was struck by the "biological features, the language and primitive habits, unique to the race, and completely distinct from those that characterize the other Indian tribes of the country."[20] This in turn reminded him of a visit he had made to Japan several years earlier, during which he had been impressed by the ways that the Japanese had preserved their nation in the face of European and North American colonial empires. From the Japanese model Monzón concluded that Mexico's indigenous peoples could use the internado to follow a similar practice—namely, they could selectively adopt certain features of Western culture while preserving their autonomy from their traditional overlords. Monzón argued that the practices within Mayan internados should differ from others, as a reflection of the cultural distinctiveness of the Yucatán, just as Tarahumara, Huichol, and other internados should reflect distinct cultures and act as unique means for self-expression and development. Further, he argued that the goal of complete incorporation should be abandoned. As sites where local cultures could mediate their relationship with the Mexican state, he believed internados could reorganize power structures and allow indigenous Mexicans to preserve and promote their own cultures, traditions, and languages.[21]

His conclusion, that Indian cultures were distinct systems, which could and should not simply be transformed into a mestizo hybrid of Indian aesthete and rational European, stood in sharp contrast to the practice of using education to create a single national culture that obliterated local peculiarities. Nonetheless, Monzón remained the voice of paternalistic authority on indigenous issues, as was revealed in a proposal he submitted to the SEP after his visit to the Yucatán. Calling for a new Federal Department of Indian Affairs, Monzón proposed a series of radical reforms that would be imposed on Mexico's indigenous peoples, who he believed were imprisoned in a "state of complete misery, ignorance, and ignominy."[22] Beyond addressing the standard litany of issues (land reform, aid, education, sanitation, nutrition, hygiene, etc.), his proposal was anything but respectful of indigenous cultural autonomy. He proposed, for example, programs that would move Indians out of sterile areas (such as unhealthy and inclement mountainous regions), and settle nomadic groups in colonies.[23] Perhaps even more importantly, nowhere in his reports did he suggest that the department consider the "rights" of indigenous peoples to cultural self-determination, a key concept that would ultimately inform Mexican pluralism.[24]

These omissions must temper any tendency to see incipient pluralism in Monzón's remarks, yet they should not serve as the basis for assuming Monzón was cut from the same assimilationist cloth as his precursors. Rather, Monzón reflected a trend followed by a small but growing group of individuals (mostly educators, linguists, and ethnographers) who believed that the revolutionary state had to make Indians active agents in their own redemption, and who increasingly felt that the cultural differences found in indigenous communities needed to be more effectively accommodated by the schools. Although overseen by powerful interlocutors like Monzón, if implemented these programs would inevitably relocate some power from the Indigenista to the Indian.

Making Changes

Rafael Ramírez was initially reluctant to follow Monzón's advice. Ignoring Monzón's radical approach, he suggested that most of the problems would be resolved once Indian communities came to understand the mission of the internados.[25] His prediction was not fulfilled however, as problems continued in some schools and deepened in others. In Matlapa, for instance, changes in personnel in the wake of Monzón's inspections led to brief improvements, but the crises quickly resumed as community leaders fought with the school and student enrollment declined. Similar issues troubled other schools, as once cooperative relationships with local communities and students soured.[26] Finally, in early 1936 SEP officials decided to overhaul the program under the auspices of a new agency, the Departamento de Educación Indígena (DEI). Headed by Carlos Basauri and endowed with a total budget of

$1,646,470 for the 1936–37 school year, the DEI was to undertake much needed repairs at existing internados, ensure that provisions reached students, and expand the number of schools.[27]

More importantly, the DEI promised to implement programs that were more closely suited to the needs of specific communities. Conceding that many of the serious problems the internados had faced were due to the tendency of some directors to treat their schools as if they were simple rural schools, Basauri promised to reform the pedagogy of the schools to ensure that they conformed to local cultures and needs. They would undertake special efforts to avoid alienating students from their environment, implement a more aggressive program of ethnographic study, and pay more attention to "the individual idiosyncrasies of each of the Indian groups."[28] Parroting Monzón, Basauri was particularly critical of the type of "mestizo education" and hostile environments students had thus far experienced in the schools, claiming that these practices "could not possibly banish from the Indian conscience the belief that whites were their bitter enemies."[29]

Basauri also emphasized the role of social scientific methods in the future direction of the internados. In this, he echoed the concerns expressed by a variety of Indigenistas dating from Manuel Gamio in the 1910s to the recent declarations of Moisés Sáenz and Monzón, to declare that the "most complete understanding of the social and biological environment" was "indispensable" to the success of these schools. He promised to commission specialists to study the "physical-geographic environment, the human element, industries, agriculture, social, economic, and sanitary conditions; in a word, all of the economic and ethnographic characteristics" of each internado. These studies would create empirical bases for designing programs carefully suited to specific ethnic groups, and would "serve as a basis for precisely orienting the educational labors with the students, and the work of cultural diffusion in the nearby communities."[30]

In spite of the claim that this program would make education fit the needs of individual communities, the DEI maintained a strongly incorporationist tendency. Writing about the mandate of the agency, Basauri observed that:

> the general denomination "Indian" has been arbitrarily applied without a scientific basis since the colonial period, at which time it

> was meant as a racial classification, to establish the rights, obligations, and privileges of the different "castes" and social classes. Today this denomination has been converted into a vague term that describes a large part of the campesino population; but it carries with it an implicit meaning, independent of any ethnographic value, a cultural significance: Indian is synonymous with backwards.[31]

From this, Basauri concluded that the internados should serve individuals of *cultura indígena* (composed of Indians and mestizos), who were designated as culturally and psychologically deficient.[32] This Indian was a cultural (as opposed to racial) other, and while this meant that Indians could be made modern, they (like the rest of the rural folk) would need to shed their Indianness in the process.

First and foremost, these cultural Indians would need to shed two of the impediments that separated them from the modern world, illiteracy and ignorance of Spanish. As Sáenz had seen in Carapan, one of the most glaring problems facing Indian education was the linguistic barrier that separated teachers and students. In the Casa, where the vast linguistic diversity had made Spanish a necessary lingua franca, educators paid only limited attention to the need for instruction in indigenous languages. However, the internados presented an entirely different challenge, as students in the schools typically shared a common language that not only acted as a barrier between students and teacher, but which they would need to use if they were to communicate to their brethren after they left the school. If students deserted their schools en masse because they simply could not communicate with their teachers, the entire program of Indian education would be placed in jeopardy. These potential social leaders had to be enticed to remain in the internados, and what better way to do this than to create an environment where they were more at ease? It seemed only natural that the solution to this problem lay in using the new mandate of the DEI to promote the study and use of Indian vernaculars, if only in the interest of eventually assimilating the Indian.

This was just the course taken by the agency. Under the DEI the internados became critical to the first systematic efforts in revolutionary Mexico to use indigenous languages and train bilingual teachers. These efforts accelerated after Indian education was put under the jurisdiction of the Departamento de Asuntos Indígenas (DAI) in January

1938. At this time teachers who spoke local languages were given special priority in the Brigadas de Penetración Cultural Indígena, Misiones Culturales, and the internados.[33] By 1939 the DAI also founded several *Academias de Lenguas Indígenas,* which both trained teachers and created employment opportunities for educated Indians. To be sure, many of the Indigenistas who worked in these forums utilized Indian languages and developed programs for the Indian's "cultural plane" paternalistically, lowering the system of education to what they believed was the Indian's primitive state. Even so, by increasingly opening these programs to influence from the community, and prioritizing a multilingual environment, federal officials created a context in which indigenous communities were given an unprecedented role in their schools. They in turn used that opportunity to demand schools that conformed to their own perceived interests.[34]

Friends and Foes on the Ground

As of August 1936, the internados, now known as *Centros de Educación Indígena* (CEI), became the centerpiece of Cardenista efforts to educate the Indian, and during the following year their numbers would swell to thirty-three (see appendix A). Cárdenas promised that these new schools would have more than adequate levels of funding, lands, and an orientation that harmonized them to the needs of specific communities. The reforms were accompanied by an aggressive press campaign, in which Cárdenas promised that he would turn his personal attention to the problems faced by the internados.[35]

This promise prompted a flood of requests for internados during the following few years. Over one hundred communities requested new internados in the 1936–37 school year alone. Hundreds of residents attached their signatures or thumbprints to these requests, which often took advantage of the specific components of the program to demand internados. No longer were the schools justified simply because a community was poor and illiterate. Now many claimed the right to an internado for linguistic and cultural reasons, occasionally even including maps to indicate which villages spoke an indigenous language, which were truly Indian, and which were mestizo and should thus be excluded. These requests not only reinforced the impression that education was a popular demand, but SEP officials interpreted them as a sign that the internados had finally awakened "the desire for liberation" and cultural development within the Indian community. A simultaneous increase in scholarship requests was interpreted similarly.[36]

SEP officials may have mistaken a strategic choice to demand schools for an "awakening" in the countryside, but it nonetheless seems clear that the new prestige afforded the internados after 1936 and the possibilities they seemed to offer for a more locally sensitive system of education had a great deal of appeal in rural Mexico. More than this, though, internados offered local authorities access to federal largesse. With the improved funding after 1936, internados often came with a number of important benefits, including trucks, sewing machines, agricultural implements, carpentry and iron-working tools, medicine chests, beds, motors, ovens and motorized corn mills, as well as other icons of modernity like radios and movie projectors. The schools may not have created demands for these objects and services, but they did create new civic spaces in which the authorities in indigenous communities could expect that these and other demands would be fulfilled. As an added benefit, a new internado might offer the opportunity to settle some old scores, as the need for an agricultural parcel might also provide the justification for expropriating a local hacienda or attacking a neighboring community for its lands.[37]

In some cases, community leaders offered to make extraordinary concessions in order to have an internado founded in their community. In November 1936 residents of the pueblo of Coapilla, Chiapas, promised to donate twenty hectares of community land and give voluntary labor to construction and maintenance if an internado was founded to serve the three thousand Indians of school age in the municipio. They also promised to enroll their children and publicize the school so that it could fill its complement of students. More generally, writing in a tone that was both an offer of support and a warning, they promised to "watch over it to ensure its progress."[38]

In another case the residents of San Fernando de Matamoros, Zimatlán, Oaxaca, fearing that an internado to which they had already contributed material and labor was about to be moved, offered the school an extra twenty hectares and better community cooperation if it remained in place. Twenty-three signatories from the community complained that they had given the internado the church, and that eighty "citizens" from the community contributed thirty-five days of labor to

Residents and teachers from Amatenango del Valle, Chis., sent this photo to President Cárdenas in October 1935 as part of their efforts to have an internado founded in their community. The sign in the photo reads "Long Live Our Protector, Señor Presidente de la República, General Lázaro Cárdenas." (AGN)

the school. The contributions were made, they bemoaned, because they were told the school would remain there permanently. They finished with an apocalyptic tone, claiming "this race will be lost if the internado is moved to another place."[39]

The complaint by the residents of San Fernando de Matamoros was typical of the complicated ways that community residents viewed their schools. They wanted the material benefits of the school, and having tapped into *cofradía* networks for its construction and provision, they felt that they had a proprietary interest in the school whether their children filled its classrooms or not. They also expected that federal funds allocated to the school would not be cut, that the school would support the community, and that local customs and systems of land tenure would be respected.

Federal officials did not imagine that indigenous communities might mobilize the ethnic identities that they associated with backwardness in order to exclude non-Indians from these schools. This was, however, just what many indigenous Mexicans did. Balking at the SEP's notion of cultura indígena (an effort to avoid balkanization of the country and deracialize the Indian), community members repeatedly pushed to eliminate mestizo students from the schools, often to the chagrin of high-level officials, and in direct repudiation of the 1936 reforms to the schools.[40] In this they promoted their own notion of ethnicity and called for schools that served their specific ethnic, cultural, and linguistic communities.

Locals strove to control the schools in many other ways. They endeavored to oversee the personnel in these schools, supporting teachers with whom they sympathized and attacking (often viciously) those who did not meet local demands. Community leaders petitioned the SEP and DAI for special scholarships for their children and more aid to their schools, sometimes also requesting that levels of support be indexed to local costs of living. They sought to regulate the size of the agricultural parcel, offering more land when the school was under threat, but petitioning to have land taken away from the school when it was used poorly or prejudiced their interests. Representatives of Indian communities also repeatedly demanded that the state staff these schools with adequately trained teachers and teachers who spoke local dialects. These requests came to be one of the key ways in which indigenous authorities endeavored to take advantage of the program but dictate the ways in which it was implemented.[41]

Sometimes this perceived arrangement meant that locals would keep students out of the school during harvest cycles, or call on their children to help at home during periods of illness and community strife, but it also meant that community members responded to disrespectful teachers by withdrawing their children.[42] The promise to "watch over" the school was not limited to the buildings. It also indicated that community members would watch the teachers, ensuring that the school did not violate community standards. When teachers aggressively attacked local religious and cultural sensibilities, community members responded with various forms of hostility. This did not mean, however, that they did not support the school. Rather, these conflicts often simply indicated that community leaders wanted a change in practices or personnel. When federal officials closed an internado, it was not uncommon to see a flood of protests, the lot of which claimed that the school, even if troubled, was highly valued by the communities it served.[43]

These ambiguities were beyond the ken of many school directors, much to the detriment of everyone involved. Those who proved grossly paternalistic or heavy-handed found themselves confronting hostile communities, which in turn only reinforced their own sense of superiority. Some, like Professor Juan F. Campos G., director of the Huichol internado in Bolaños, Jalisco, responded to these problems by acting increasingly authoritarian. Lamenting that the adults in the Huichol community had unequivocally refused to send their children to the school, Campos went so far as to ask Cárdenas to order these communities to send their children to the school. Calling the Huichol race "perhaps the most refractory in accepting civilization," Campos believed that nothing short of a presidential order would fill the school.[44]

Local leaders had different explanations for why attendance was so low. Federico Antuna H., of Bolaños, complained that the school lacked windows, and asked that an inspector visit "so that he can see the poor treatment of the children."[45] He explained that the Huichol parents wanted to take their children out of the school not because they were refractory, but because a child had died, and the buildings were in terrible shape.[46] Local indigenous authorities complained similarly. In December 1937, Cenovio de la Cruz, gobernador del pueblo indígena de Tuxpan, Jalisco, asked Cárdenas's intervention because "the children in the internado complain that they are poorly cared for, and the building is in a horrific condition."[47]

Given the discretion they enjoyed in running their schools, a director's inability or unwillingness to build a cooperative relationship with community leaders could prove disastrous for the school. Conflicts between communities and directors were one of the most common sources of problems in the internados. Directors became lightning rods for the pecuniary problems in the schools. Dissent often arose because local communities had voluntarily contributed to the school, only to find their assistance abused and promises of remuneration unfulfilled. In one case, the residents of Chenalhó, Distrito de Las Casas, Chiapas, contributed food worth $2,395.75 to the local internado on the promise that they would be repaid by SEP officials. When school officials denied their requests for payment, they complained to Cárdenas that as poor campesinos, this "fraudulent" behavior represented "an irreparable prejudice" to their community.[48]

Similarly, residents of Techímal, Hidalgo made it very clear that although their internado "has been a source of great excitement and rejoicing, because our racial brothers have at last come to our defense," the demands made by the director were too much for them to bear.

> We are truly disconsolate about the situation we face; because from the start of June of last year, we have been forced to work without pay in the (construction) of school buildings, from ten to twelve hours of work [per day], without any kind of remuneration, despite the precarious situation in which we find ourselves. In spite of all that has been said about the minimum wage, about benefiting the proletariat, they make us do forced labor without any remuneration. . . . We ask that the Law of the Minimum Wage be enforced, and that each of us be paid fifty centavos in wages. That would be very satisfactory. We, the suffering and silent Indians have always earned 25 or 35 centavos daily as our wage; with this we can only eat chiles and tortillas, and are forced to dress in shabby clothing.[49]

Directors also faced severe criticism when they took animals from local campesinos on the pretext that they would be used to train students in animal husbandry, but then appropriated the herds for their personal needs without compensating already impoverished locals. Adding insult to injury, the herds were often poorly cared for, and disappeared while under the care of the internados, destroying the little capital that many campesinos possessed. Directors tended to treat those who complained about these impositions brusquely, insinuating that by demanding their animals returned they were undermining the work of the Revolution.[50]

If some of these directors were insensitive, others were simply interested in lining their own pockets. Directors committed a host of abuses, stealing from the schools, exploiting locals, violating local customs, providing rotten and inadequate food, hitting students, and demanding excessive work. Others gave preference to mestizo students, made fun of students when they spoke their maternal tongues, prohibited their traditional dress, or forced students to cut their hair. At various moments these conflicts left schools virtually empty, even as their directors continued to take the full allotment of funds. Federal officials acknowledged and tried to limit these abuses, yet they were difficult to prevent. A limited staff and meager resources made oversight extremely difficult, and the individual schools were generally left to the whims of their directors.[51]

On the other hand, the victims did not take these abuses lying down. Community members, teachers, and students formed organizations, protested, went on strike, and wrote countless letters to federal officials about these abuses, all the while insisting that these schools meet their own perceived needs. They also aggressively demanded the right to self-representation in these forums, refusing to allow traditional interlocutors to speak to the state on their behalf. At one point, students at the internado in Zongozotla, Puebla, complained of suffering under a "dictatorship." "The food they provide us is inadequate, and poor, owing to the fact that the meals consist of nothing more than frijoles and plantains." Going on, they complained that "instead of receiving instruction in our classes, we are forced to carry boulders every day, clean out canals, and perform other tasks that place our lives in danger."[52] In another instance, the director of the internado in Vícam, Sonora, came under fire for misrepresenting the demands and needs of local communities to federal authorities, leading to a broad community mobilization. He was accused of insulting the local population, public drunkenness, and absconding with the money sent to feed students.[53]

These conflicts did not only pit communities against the internado, they also saw students and teachers struggling against directors. This was the case in Zongozotla in 1938, but was most strikingly evident in a student strike that took place in Caró, Mexico, during July 1934. A large group of students, led by the school's professor of agriculture, created such a stir that they forced the school's director to flee the region, and he refused to return out of fear for his own safety. It took a special intervention by the state's Director of Federal Education, the expulsion of several students, and the banishment of the subversive teacher from the area to quell the movement.[54] The conflict resulted in severe sanctions for the protesters, but revealed a school in which at least one of the goals of Indian education had been met. Within the internado at Caró students and teachers had formed powerful bonds, even if they were using those relationships to cause trouble.

Sometimes it was not corruption, but agitation that caused these conflicts. Taking their role as agents for social change seriously, rural teachers in many regions used their status as intermediaries to make alliances with agraristas during the 1930s, often acting as scribes for petitions and advisors to agrarian committees. These teachers might put their skills into efforts to defend communities and denounce exploiters, becoming representatives of these communities before the state, but if not carefully handled their role as agitators could result in serious conflicts with municipal authorities, merchants, and Catholics, leaving teachers vulnerable to attack. In the worst cases, these conflicts became violent. Local authorities and landlords, sometimes infuriated at the anticlerical or coeducational programs in the internados, or merely angry at the threat they posed to the local balance of power, threatened students and teachers, causing panic in the schools.[55]

Factional conflicts in indigenous communities left internados extremely vulnerable, and meant that local support for the school could shift dramatically over time. Popular directors and teachers could descend from the most praised to the most despised member of the community in a matter of months.[56] Hostile non-Indians might attack the internado as well, if it seemed to threaten the local political order. Complaining of this in 1939, Professor Amado González Dávila of the internado in Nayarit lamented that because the school was located in a mestizo region, not an Indian region, local mestizos were able to subject the school to "constant political attacks."[57]

This was also the case when the internado in Chalcatongo, Oaxaca, became enmeshed in a series of factional struggles over the control of the municipio of Tlaxiaco between 1938 and 1940. The director, Mario M. Valdés, supported a group of agraristas in their bid to control the municipio, and ultimately became a lightning rod for those who resented his attempts to wield federal power in favor of the agraristas. Underestimating their own power, Valdés and five allies were arrested and imprisoned for several years for the murder of one of his political enemies. Ironically, the man he was imprisoned for killing, Juan Cortés, perished as he and a group of reactionaries assaulted the school in June 1938 in an effort to drive out the director. His death then became the pretext for dismantling the agrarian faction.[58]

Promises Fulfilled

Student revolts, corrupt directors, and angry communities provide stark images of the internados, and have indeed led several scholars to conclude both that they failed to accomplish their goals and that they were emblematic of the larger failings of revolutionary Indigenismo.[59] However, as Elsie Rockwell notes, the presence of conflicts over the schools does not prove the absence of support.[60] Dissent was a natural by-product of the relationships between schools and the communities where they were located. Local authorities from indigenous communities repeatedly tried to make the internados meet their expectations, and school administrators tried to make the communities conform to theirs. More importantly, an exclusive focus on the conflicts over these schools masks the fact that they produced many success stories, instances where in spite of their problems the internados made important gains in the communities they endeavored to serve.

Oddly enough, the eventual jailing of Mario M. Valdés, the director of the internado in Chalcatongo, Oaxaca, came about because after a slow start, a portion of the local population came to support the school, offering both their children and provisions. As remains a problem today in many indigenous communities, the successful incursion of competing powers was the catalyst for a conflict that would not have occurred had the school lacked any popular support. Religious, class, ethnic, gender, and generational conflicts were all played out in struggles over the internados, as shifting coalitions supported and then opposed the schools as part of their strategies of local domination. Over time students and teachers became embroiled in conflicts with local authorities over control of resources, pedagogy, and community leadership, leading to acrimonious attacks and counterattacks.[61]

As students became more comfortable in the schools and built relationships with their teachers, the conflicts with local communities sometimes became worse. In 1943 there were several instances of assaults on teachers and students in internados, including notorious ones against the internado for women in Galeana Morelos,[62] and another bloody assault on students from the internado in Comalco, Mexico. Evidently, the incident at Comalco occurred when a group of locals, returning from Temoaya, drunk, encountered a group of students from Comalco and got into a fight. Two students were injured in the fracas, one of them gravely, setting off a series of protests in other internados and demands that teachers and students throughout the country receive better protection from federal authorities. The governor of Mexico tried to pass the tumult off as a simple drunken brawl, but students would not be appeased without real guarantees for their safety.[63]

The response from students at Matlapa, San Luis Potosí, was typical of the response by students throughout the country. Noting their profound indignation over the "savage assault," they declared that "this proves once again that we Indians have enemies who will, at any cost, try to impede our efforts to educate ourselves." Undaunted, they promised to redouble their efforts against the reactionaries.[64] The response to the assault was thus as illuminating as the assault itself. Deeply committed to the internados and the opportunities they offered, a large number of indigenous students saw their community not as a specific indigenous village, but as a community of youths endeavoring to make a better life for the Indian.

This ethos was a sure indication that by this point many internados were succeeding in their missions. By the late 1930s there were 3,000 students in the internados (2,100 men and 900 women), a number that would remain fairly constant for the next decade.[65] In fact, absolute failure seems to have given way to moderate success, mostly due to the willingness of students to withstand the problems the schools faced. By 1940 the internados had graduated several classes of bilingual men and women who returned home as teachers, went on to the rural normal schools, or pursued a variety of careers within and outside of the state.[66]

It would be impossible to argue that the internados were ideal educational institutions, but in many ways they provided crucial opportunities for the thousands of young men and women who filled their classrooms.[67] These institutions provided the means for young indigenous individuals from poor villages to obtain their initial education, and eventually move on to the IPN and other institutes and become professionals, working as engineers, teachers, doctors, lawyers, and the like. According to a study conducted by Alicja Iwanska in the early 1970s, many were driven out of their villages and into the internados by a combination of poverty, political oppression, repressive labor recruiters, priests, and outside opportunities. They all had a great deal of initiative to begin with, but the internados figured prominently in facilitating their goals. Once in the schools, most returned home only once a year, some only once every two or three years. Though most of the intellectuals Iwanska studied had no desire to return to rural poverty once they escaped, and went on to become professionals living in the Federal District, those who returned home were in a unique position to ascend local political hierarchies.[68]

In Ixmiquilpan, Hidalgo, locals today remember the three internados founded during the Cárdenas sexenio more for the important transformations they foretold in the community than for their problems. Many of the Otomí activists who worked as teachers, anthropologists, and bureaucrats in the region between the 1950s and 1990s began their educational careers in these internados. Their decision to attend these schools reflected both the paucity of rural schools in the region and the fact that the internado seemed like the best means of securing a professional future. Several current leaders of the Consejo Supremo Ñhañhu (the INI affiliated indigenous organization in the region) began their education as students in internados that had been founded during the 1930s.[69] Professor Juan Ramírez Pedraza, who was both a student at the internado at Los Remedios in the late 1940s and later director at Los Remedios in the early 1970s, remembers the internados as great successes in their work of "*capacitación,*" declaring that they "completed an extremely important task" in producing several generations of professionals.[70] Ramírez also remembers one of the most important and unique features of the school. While bilingual education was not always officially endorsed, the internado employed a number of Otomí teachers, and created an environment where monolingual students could ease into their education in Spanish slowly by having a great deal of bilingual communication and instruction. As with other internados, the use of maternal languages was an essential part of everyday life, and a key reason why the school found many supporters.[71]

Student support was also tied to the fact that graduates were promised continued aid from the internados in pursuing their careers once they completed their studies. Graduates were often successful in demanding tools for their trades, scholarships for a further education, or minor bureaucratic or teaching appointments. Appropriating the language provided to them by the revolutionary state, these students claimed that after providing them with an education, the federal government owed them the opportunity to fulfill the work of the Revolution. Typical of this strategy, in 1938 a group of students at the internado in Caró who had finished four years at the school and could not pursue further studies without help because of their poverty, petitioned Cárdenas for scholarships to further their education. They asked for help because they were "committed to continue progressing to a level where we would be able to occupy a public office and where we could be useful to our nation."[72]

Though these demands were for individual advancement, they were also part of a larger strategy that indigenous leaders developed for demanding rights through the internados. Because of the mandate that the internados serve and accommodate themselves to specific ethnic communities, for the first time in over a century indigenous Mexicans could claim special privileges because of their ethnic identities.[73] Demands for Indian languages, the exclusion of mestizos, and scholarships for Indians could only be made in the context of the internado. There was nothing new in indigenous communities struggling with representatives of the federal state, but decisions by federal officials to respond favorably to these demands (and therefore deem them legitimate) marked a shift in Indian-state relations.

The specific demands that the internados respect cultural and linguistic traditions and promote the interests of local leaders were fulfilled in several noteworthy instances. Ignacio León, the child of Tarahumara notables and former student in the Casa, had remarkable success as the director of the Tarahumara internado in Tónachic. In spite of obstacles created by local SEP officials, León and his wife were able to build a harmonious relationship with communities throughout the sierra, which were said to have "total confidence" in his leadership at the school. Working under harsh conditions, he maintained high enrollments in the school, and by the early 1940s several generations of teachers educated in his school worked as teachers in the region. During Léon's tenure the same school was also the site of one of the early experiments in bilingual education undertaken by Maurice Swadesh.[74]

Similarly, the internado in Tlanepaquila, Veracruz, was able to become "the soul of the Indian communities and their environs," because of the close relationships between teachers and students, and their successful outreach in the community.[75] In another case, during the relatively brief period while the Yaqui internado in Vícam, Sonora, was under the direction of Juan Aguayo, the school became an important center of community life. It gained support because Aguayo taught Yaqui history, commissioned murals celebrating Yaqui culture, and used the Yaqui language in the school. Yaqui teachers were hired for the primary school, tribal affairs were administered through the internado, and a mothers' society was formed. Several educators also learned to speak fluent Yaqui, earning some allies in the community.[76]

Aguayo's story however, is starkly illustrative of the perils the internados often faced. Teachers in the region often displayed deeply racist attitudes towards recalcitrant communities,[77] and intracommunity conflicts in the area were severe. Its prominence made the internado at

Vícam a focal point in these struggles, which were made even more acute because of an ongoing dispute between community leaders and the state over what they believed was the woeful inadequacy of land reform.[78] In mid-1937, Aguayo became embroiled in conflicts with the local *jefe de colonias,* who organized a group of fifteen community leaders to protest directly to Cárdenas. They attacked the director as immoral, complaining that he insulted the local population, went around drunk in public, and stole much of the money sent to feed one hundred students (feeding only thirty-four students and using the rest for people not belonging to the school). They also accused Aguayo and the military commander of the zone (a Colonel Dosal) of misrepresenting the community to Cárdenas, complaining that "none of the individuals that Colonel Dosal brought to you represent these tribes . . . we deauthorize all of their actions."[79]

In spite of Aguayo's efforts to defend himself and his supporters as the true representatives of the community, the jefe de colonias ultimately prevailed in the duel of competing claims to authenticity. Aguayo's supporters proved less powerful than their enemies—individuals who were most likely concerned that the school represented a threat to their power in determining the division of land in the local reform, and who wanted to ensure that members of their clique controlled both school admissions and the resources of the school. Aguayo was replaced by a series of directors who were notable mostly for their abuses, and who proved ineffective at improving the situation. With conflicts festering, the DAI created a *Comisión Intersectarial* to study the Yaqui problem in early 1938, and took over all the schools in the region in 1939.[80]

These problems disrupted the pedagogical mission of the schools, but they did little to discourage the North American linguist Maurice Swadesh, who during 1937 and 1938 spent time studying the use of Yaqui in the internado.[81] A recent Yale Ph.D. who had come to Mexico to work for the DAI, during this time he worked in several northern internados, studying and promoting the use of indigenous vernaculars. After limited successes in Vícam and Tónachic, in 1939 he was granted the opportunity to establish the Academia de la Lengua Tarasca (aka the Proyecto Tarasco) at the internado in Paracho, Michoacán. Rooted in the principle that "literacy in the native tongue is the most effective means for the cultural development of Indian groups," the Proyecto Tarasco was the first large-scale effort to incorporate Indian languages systematically into the educational process.[82] Swadesh and his team of linguists, ethnographers, and teachers undertook a series of studies as a part of the project, conducting local grammar and lexicographic studies, dialect studies, studies of mono- and bilingualism, studies of social composition, and studies of economic and social life in the meseta tarasca. Their long-term goal was to integrate the use of local dialects and the national language in the school, but students would first learn to read and write in their own language.[83]

The Proyecto Tarasco took place at a time when a growing number of activists and rural pedagogues had been convinced that indigenous vernaculars needed to be used in the process of Indian education. Rural teachers in schools where Spanish was the only language used complained of a "linguistic battle" that destroyed the harmony of their schools and retarded the educational process. Carlos Basauri, Vicente Lombardo Toledano, and Andrés Molina Enríquez (in his role as spokesman for the Organización Nacional de Indios de la República) likewise publicly supported education in Indian languages. The influence of William Townsend, the American linguist and missionary, was also notable. Townsend (like Swadesh) believed that individuals should learn to read in their own language before they learned another. He believed that monolingual Indian students took upwards of six years to become literate if they were taught only in Spanish, whereas they could become literate in less than six months if taught in their own vernacular. Expanding on this proposition, the anthropologist Jorge Vivo noted that after first becoming literate in his mother tongue, "the very ability to read will give the Indian the ambition and confidence to continue in his studies until he learns the national language."[84]

Founded in an old church in 1935, the internado in Paracho had seen some success prior to the Proyecto Tarasco in spite of its location in the heart of a region divided by cristero-agrarista conflicts.[85] Teachers in the school had a reputation for dedication to their responsibilities, and had at one point even donated part of their own salaries to pay for music lessons for the students.[86] Most of these teachers would be retained during the project, but Swadesh was given authority to reorganize the school. He was also granted control of all the schools in the region, and extra funds to bring more teachers to the meseta tarasca.[87] He planned several years of work in the region, and a school that would both create a cohort of educated Tarascans and act as the forum for determining a standard Tarascan language based on a common agreement with representatives from the villages in the area. Swadesh was emphatic that the school had to be a harmonious place where students would learn in their own language without the threats and punishments so typical in Indian education.[88] Students in the school were taught primarily in Tarascan, while Spanish was gradually introduced. Formal Spanish was not taught until the second or third year, and as many texts as possible were provided in Tarascan.[89]

Swadesh also hired twenty young men and women who habitually used Tarascan, many of whom were graduates of internados or normal schools in the region. They were given a month of training in reading and writing Tarascan, based on methods designed by Townsend. They then began preparing texts in Tarascan, developed a system for teaching literacy, and installed a press in Paracho.[90] Hoping to foment a literary culture that would be shared by all communities in the meseta tarasca, native students and teachers trained in Paracho translated a variety of materials into Tarascan in 1939 and 1940, including dictionaries, grammars, and a series of pamphlets. These included pamphlets on the dangers of dirty water, care for a variety of childhood illnesses, warnings of the dangers of alcoholism, and information about the causes and cures of syphilis. They also translated a number of other pamphlets about agriculture and illnesses, one called "Legal Information Every Indian Needs to Know" (including the Constitution, Agrarian Code, and other key legislation) and the "Book of Tarascan Lessons." In order to further these efforts, Swadesh provided typewriters to establish presses in Indian languages in the normal schools.[91]

Observers were impressed by the work done at Paracho. Students and community members welcomed the work of the school, both because of its pedagogy and because the project gave local leaders the opportunity to obtain funds for improved roads, telephone service, irrigation, a doctor, potable water, a truck, and several purebred dairy cows.[92] Community leaders also responded enthusiastically to efforts to promote the use of Indian languages in the region, pressing for an expanded selection of classes in Tarascan, and more teachers who could speak the local vernacular. They also endeavored to enlarge the project's successes, petitioning federal officials on several occasions for continued efforts to train teachers in Tarascan, and for a growing body of publications in native languages.[93]

The project was eventually canceled in 1941, but the decision to end it was the product of high-level political struggles in the SEP, not a lack of support in the community. In fact, its proponents proudly claimed that the school showed that adults and children could learn to read and write Tarascan in a period of thirty to forty-five days, and in spite of its ignominious end Paracho would become a model for a series of programs in bilingual education after 1940.[94] This was a victory not just for Swadesh and his team of linguists, but for the myriad of indigenous communities that struggled to shape the internados during these years. In the short run SEP officials would prefer to ignore many of these demands, but in the long run they could not. Bilingual and bicultural education, introduced in limited ways in the internados, would ultimately become a core part of indigenous education in Mexico.[95]

Epilogue: The CEI in Ixtlán de Juárez

The varied experiences of the internados should warn scholars against using individual cases to make broad generalizations about their meaning and significance. Their successes and failures were invariably tied to particular circumstances, from the individual proclivities of their directors to traditions of local civic participation in educational institutions. However, individual stories can highlight social transformations in ways that are more effective than broad analyses of trends and tendencies. For this reason, this chapter ends with the story of the internado founded in 1937 in the Zapotec community of Ixtlán de Juárez, Oaxaca, the birthplace of Benito Juárez.

The revolutionary state was given to highly symbolic acts (often in the absence of systematic programs), and the internado at Ixtlán was no exception. Cárdenas described the school as an "act of justice for this pueblo,"[96] and appointed a Zapotec teacher named Silvestre Gómez Hernández as the school's first director. The school opened in a series of appropriated houses in the municipio in February 1937, lacking all but the most basic necessities, but officials promised a spectacular internado to honor the hero of La Reforma. An ambitious program of school construction began on 10 May 1937, with a plan that included offices, dormitories, workshops, houses for teachers and the director, gardens, various agricultural programs, pigs and chickens, and a twenty-five-meter swimming pool.[97]

As was all too common, problems began almost as soon as the survey stakes were put in the ground. The engineer commissioned to build the school, Maximiliano García, angered local residents when he arbitrarily claimed a number of local buildings and several hectares of community land for the school without first securing the agreement of the municipal authorities. In June 1937 Francisco Ramírez, Municipal President of Ixtlán, complained to Cárdenas about the invasion of lands by the internado.[98] He seemed to get García's attention, as the engineer immediately retreated from some of his more onerous demands and began working more closely with local officials. García concluded that the initial problems were due to the prejudices that people in the Sierra de Juárez harbored against the federal state, a result of false and unfulfilled promises in the past. He took the resolution to mean that the people of the region now believed in the promises of the Revolution. By contrast, local officials considered it a question of boundaries that had been resolved.[99]

Marking the conclusion of the original conflict, at the end of June municipal and school officials came together in a public ceremony to inaugurate the school and show their solidarity. Speaking at the gathering, Agustín García, personal secretary and brother of the engineer, addressed his "Zapotec brothers," in a speech filled with the flowery rhetoric of revolutionary redemption, as the "noble and virile race of bronze, the glorious Zapotec race." While accepting that there would always be those who attacked the Indian as "flojo," he praised both "the pueblo of Ixtlán and its authorities" and this "temple dedicated to the study of the sciences and arts" as proof positive that the Indian was anything but lazy.[100]

By early 1938 the school had a sizable complement of students, who seemed to be progressing adequately in their studies, but the building itself remained unfinished, and Maximiliano García's relationship with the municipal authorities was becoming increasingly strained. The workers who had been hired to construct the buildings, those men of the "noble and virile race of bronze" whom the school was intended to serve, were angry about the way García and his associates treated them, and were on the verge of laying down their tools. In March, fifty workers from the Agrupación Indígena Regional Benito Juárez signed a petition complaining about the construction process at the school. They claimed that García was abusive and incompetent, that his staff forced

Foundations for the internado at Ixtlán de Juárez. (AGN)

them to work too hard, and that he did not pay a wage on which they could survive. They demanded that he be fired, that the hours of work be reduced to those prescribed by federal labor laws, that wages be improved, and in a tactic that was reminiscent of indigenous attitudes toward internados in other parts of the country, they demanded restrictions against nonlocal laborers.[101]

Their demands were only partially fulfilled, leading to an escalation of conflicts in October 1938, when the new school director (Manuel Fernández Molina) and García were accused of fraud. At the time, the school building itself remained little more than a foundation. José Ochoa Rentería, the teacher who leveled the most serious accusations, managed to secure a transfer out of the school from Cárdenas after he complained that he could no longer stomach the constant intrigues

The photographs on this and the facing page show the construction of the internado. (AGN)

among the teachers.[102] It was also around this time that local municipal authorities took an increasingly active role in the school, repeatedly petitioning for funds to finish the buildings, criticizing the directors and engineers when they misbehaved, and constantly trying to protect their own interests. Even so, by 1939 almost none of the buildings were finished.

Fortune seemed to smile in April of that year, when Cárdenas himself promised to set aside funds for completing the internado, along with enough to build a hospital in Ixtlán.[103] His promises again went unfulfilled, and four and a half years later the internado remained unfinished. In December 1943, it still lacked electricity, and various classrooms could not be used because they had only walls. Nothing had been done about this in spite of repeated requests to the SEP and repeated promises that funds would be set aside for its completion. The congressional deputy from the region, Hermenegildo Luis, even

entered the fray on several occasions, but to no avail.[104] In the meantime, teachers and directors found themselves in fairly regular conflicts with municipal authorities over the lax morality and disorder they seemed to provoke.[105]

There is no evidence that the internado was ever completed to the satisfaction of local authorities, and it is almost certain that the ambitious plans first laid out in 1937 were long since forgotten by 1943, when local residents simply requested a roof and power for their school. Thus, in a physical sense, the internado seems to have been a failure, as symbolic in its unfinished walls as its architectural plans were in their vision. This, however, tells only part of the story. Another part is told by the constant attempts by community leaders to limit the power of the school to make demands of the community, while still endeavoring to see federal resources earmarked for its completion and provision. The internado was a unique institution, a forum where

Community members at the end of a day working on the internado. As the photo indicates, entire communities, men, women, and children, contributed to the work. (AGN)

indigenous leaders could make claims to the state based upon their oppressed status and glorious past, and they made every effort they could to take advantage of this opportunity. The very founding of the school conferred symbolic capital on their Zapotec identity, and they used this new currency with some success. Some of the buildings went up, some of the materials arrived, and some of the laborers were paid.

Beyond this, there is another story of the internado at Ixtlán that is not told by struggles over construction, the employment of local laborers, and the misuse of funds. As José Ochoa noted in 1938 even as he quit the school, in spite of intrigues and construction delays, the educational mission of the internado was progressing as planned. This was a common story. Funding problems suspended construction of internados throughout the country at various points, and while this was prejudicial to the interests of those employed in construction, it did not prevent the larger educational mission from continuing.[106] Throughout the country students pursued their education under trees, in churches, in private homes, and wherever safe spaces could be found.[107] Like-

Students from the internado. (AGN)

wise, students in Ixtlán took classes, developed skills, and pursued their perceived interests regardless of the problems and incomplete state of the internado. They successfully promoted their own careers, enlisting the support of anyone they could in obtaining both the skills and materials they needed for their trades once they had graduated from the school.

In February 1941, a student in the school named Pedro Pérez did what many students in internados did when they finished their studies — he wrote to SEP officials requesting that they either provide him with tools to ply his trade or permission to continue in the school for another year. Summoning up as much weight as he could, he spoke in the name of all the students in the school when he made this request.[108] The regime having changed, and the internados having lost priority, one might expect that his request went unfulfilled, but such was not the case.

Pérez's request made it to a high-level official at the SEP, who ordered that Pérez and the *"alumnos capacitados"* who had finished their programs be given the tools they requested, and that a sufficient budget be created so that this would not be a problem in the future.[109]

Pérez's successful petition revealed the complex mix of style and substance that was central to the story of the internado in Ixtlán. Students like him passed through the school and found it a suitable forum for pursuing their own interests. Along with their communities, they used the promises of the revolutionary state to secure their own needs, and were ultimately important beneficiaries of the school that was never finished. Indeed, the school, like the revolutionary state, would never fulfill all its promises, but if we only examine these failures we miss its larger impact. The very promises it made afforded local residents opportunities they had not seen before, and they would push them to their limits.

Pedro Pérez disappears from the historical record shortly after he successfully asserted his interests as an alumno capacitado. Others, however, grew increasingly prominent as public actors in the years after their education was completed. Empowered through education, work experiences, and ultimately the institutions created by the federal state, a new generation of young indigenous males used the skills (linguistic, political, and otherwise) gained in internados to challenge the limits and shape of revolutionary hegemony. Collectively, through accommodation, opposition, and negotiation, they appropriated the educational principles of the state and reconfigured them in an often successful effort to make the system work for them.[110]

3 Science and State Formation in the Departamento de Asuntos Indígenas

The Indian is not for the statist what he can be for the ethnologist, the unmixed remnant of the pre-Columbian races. More important than the blood, it is the economy that conjoins millions of mestizos and Indians in their political identity as an autochthonous mass, and which will make them the most decisive of all the elements that make up the nationality.
—El Nacional, *20 April 1937*[1]

Traveling the country during his campaign for election to the presidency during 1934, Lázaro Cárdenas was struck by the abject poverty he witnessed in Indian communities. In the seventeen years since a new Constitution promised justice for the dispossessed, almost nothing had been accomplished in many places. New federal agencies had seen few successes, proposals to study indigenous communities had largely gone unfunded, and the internados were in deep crisis. Acutely sympathetic to the plight of the poor, Cárdenas decided that in the face of these problems he would use his presidency to make unprecedented efforts to bring the resources of the executive to bear on the Indian problem. Speaking to the people of Chiapas on 25 February 1934, he made public his intention to create a new department devoted to applying the expertise of the social and natural sciences to the problems that haunted the lives of indigenous Mexicans. His "manifesto" bemoaned the suffering of the Indians, trapped in "dormant spirits, with semi-naked bodies," and promised to "convert them into men capable of intellectual development, and an active economic force struggling for the advancement of their race."[2]

Those social scientists and pedagogues who had been advocating such a step for years were heartened by Cárdenas's promise. Immediately after the announcement Cárdenas received a flood of proposals for the new agency. Many saw this as an opportunity to substantially expand rural education under the consciousness-raising mandates of Educación Socialista. Others took a more authoritarian tone, calling for compulsory military service for Indians. Eulogio R. Valdivieso and

Andrés Molina Enríquez, of the Organización de los Indios de la República, also chimed in, calling for an agency directed by an "Indian or Indo-mestizo" and charged with the task of passing legal reforms in order to create special codes to reflect the needs of Indian communities. They also proposed a new Museo de los Indios, separate from the Museo Nacional, where the professors would be of indigenous origin.[3] Cárdenas passed over these proposals though, in favor of one from Moisés Sáenz, who since the failure of Carapan had been working in Mexico's diplomatic service. Sáenz's experience in rural education, his professional credentials, and the ideas he had developed while conducting a series of ethnographic studies in the Andes, made him the ideal architect of an agency that would draw upon the most modern scientific approaches to the Indian problem. Throughout 1935 he worked closely with the new administration assembling the framework of the agency that would be founded as the Departamento de Asuntos Indígenas in January 1936.

Sáenz took advantage of this opportunity by first calling for an entirely new approach to the Indian question. Arguing that the apostolic, inconsistent, and poorly designed programs of the past had resulted in a "*fracaso trágico,*" he suggested that the new agency adopt a comprehensive program of social and cultural elevation — but this could be no simple program of assimilation. He began his proposal by emphasizing that the problems faced by indigenous Mexicans were distinct from those of other rural peoples. "There exists in Mexico an Indian problem with its own characteristic nature, different from the campesino problem in its social and economic aspects, in its requirements, its urgency, and the methods needed to attack it." He argued that Indians (two million of whom did not speak Spanish) were an "extra-social class," and that the most remote lived in a world completely independent from Mexico.[4]

Sáenz divided the Indian population into two discrete groups. The first lived in regions where the process of acculturation had made it "more difficult every day to find 'pure' Indians," making "the separation of the Indian and the mestizo often impossible." In these parts of the country he envisioned a program that would treat all campesinos similarly, where limited rights would be enjoyed by all. In "genuinely Indian regions" (defined by vast linguistic and cultural differences from the national mainstream) however, Sáenz believed that residents should not really be considered Mexicans. While he rejected the notion of creating reservations, he did envision an agency that would undertake concerted efforts in these areas, because residents of these regions were "not in the category of full citizenship." Sáenz suggested that in the most serious cases the DAI be given exclusive jurisdiction in these areas so that economic, social, educational, cultural, and legal issues could be addressed in a concerted fashion.[5]

Sáenz described these communities as desperately poor, illiterate, and ignorant of many of the factors that typified modern life, but unlike the assimilationists (and his own earlier writings), he did not advocate the simple introduction of modern practices. Rather, he believed that the communities of these regions lived a spiritual and religious life that made them distinctly non-Western. Identified with the soil, pantheistic, and deeply spiritual, Sáenz argued that "above all we must recognize that the Indian is an oriental, opposed (in his view of the world) to the European." Those Indians that fit into this "oriental" category could not be helped through traditional programs, because neither simple incorporation nor socioeconomic emancipation could resolve their problems. These were communities that had turned profoundly inwards because of poverty and exploitation, not unlike a variety of European cultures in the not-so-distant past. "Full stomachs" were necessary to resolve this crisis, but beyond this Indians needed a gradual program of social, spiritual, and economic emancipation.[6]

As a part of this gradual approach, Sáenz called for a program that respected many aspects of the lives of indigenous communities. Recognizing the importance of traditional power structures in indigenous communities, he advised that "we should give preference to *naturales* in the educational process, making use of the knowledge that they already possess (which is in many cases very refined and effective, notwithstanding its empirical characteristics)." He encouraged efforts to preserve religion, legends, arts, music, and all aspects of spiritual life, believing that "the religious problem will better be resolved through positive methods based in substitution of the new orientation, than through suppression and persecution." Priests should be removed, but temples left open, and Indians should not be impeded from celebrating their devotions. Rather than suppressing fiestas, Sáenz recommended an approach that would minimize excesses and promote cultural programs, propaganda, and expositions sponsored by the state. Noting that socialism was a type of religion, and that the Indian had communist vestiges in his religion, he believed that this effort was plausible.[7]

Sáenz framed these practices around treating Indians as "potential citizens of Mexico, as that is what they already are. We should make them capable *(capacitar)* of exercising the functions of free men . . . participants (in the nation) with the responsibilities and privileges of all full Mexicans." Rooted in the Indigenista tradition of infantilizing indigenous peoples, in this view citizenship was not an inalienable collection of rights, but was instead a privilege conferred upon those who could demonstrate a capacity for modernity. However, Sáenz overtly rejected the tradition of treating Indians like children, claiming that all practices rooted in this ethos were destined to fail. Declaring that the DAI needed to treat the Indian as a potential, even an "incipient citizen," he noted that "the Indian may be maladapted, but he is neither a minor nor much less an imbecile. Any program rooted in a belief in the inferiority of the Indian (and paternalism is one of these) will have poor results." His answer to paternalism was an agency that would respect local traditions and practices, and treat indigenous peoples with dignity.[8]

Once Indians "blossomed" into full citizens, Mexico would inevitably become a more unified nation. This was the ultimate goal of the DAI, as Sáenz wrote:

> The logical end for the Indian is to make him a Mexican. To imprison him theoretically or practically on "reservations," is to condemn him to a sterile life, and ultimately extinction. I have never believed in the romantic, childish illusion promoted by those who wish to "Indianize" Mexico through a poetic return to prehistory. I believe in the Indian as a part of the Mexican. To me, the exotic Mexican Indian seems as incongruous as the *criollo* who identifies with all things foreign. Like a few others, I hold Indian values in high esteem, but precisely because I hold them so high, I want to give them a more concrete place in Mexican life. Should this be considered a conquest of the Indian? Perhaps. But it is a life-giving conquest, not a conquest of death. Winning over the Indians will give us the possibility of permanently insinuating them into Mexico's idiosyncrasies; steeped in the pulse of their emotions and sensibility, illuminated by their illusions, and in the dark blood that will forever

> run through the veins of the mestizos. Their contributions will enrich the Mexican. If we appropriate the Indians, we will make them both more Indian and naturally, more Mexican (for "Mexican" is, by definition, in part Indian).

Thus, while recognizing a plural society, the goal of the DAI as Sáenz envisioned it was to diminish heterogeneity in the interest of ameliorating poverty.[9]

He called for an agency with a minimum of bureaucracy. Most of its agents would be teachers, agronomists, doctors, or investigators working in indigenous communities. Economic questions would take precedence, as the agency would endeavor to resolve land and water claims, improve methods of cultivation, and establish small-scale agricultural credit. Schooling should also focus on improving living standards through improved cultivation and artesanal production. Overall, these programs would focus on "the protection of the Indian and his values, the elevation and improvement of his standard of living, and the assimilation of Indian groups into the Mexican family." As such, the DAI would promote "a reinterpretation of their sensibilities and culture," intended to promote harmony between indigenous cultures and the national community.[10]

Unlike past programs, these efforts had to be "integral," based in a combined focus on "biological, economic, cultural, and emotive life." Agents needed to focus not only on economic and social issues, but also on "aspects of interior life and the development of the personality." This was to be the scientific mandate of the agency, which would develop a series of new practices under the auspices of "Indian sociology," or the "social anthropology of Mexico's Indian groups." Even as the agency implemented a variety of federal programs, its agents would gather information about indigenous economies, communal use of land and forests, the economy of their industries, and their techniques, as well as producing statistics about hygiene and health. This scientific data would in turn help the agency design more efficacious programs.[11] Whereas in the past most scientists had studied the Indian as "an anthropological curiosity, but not as an element of the national population," under this practice the Indian would be treated "as a man of today, an incipient citizen." As such, this new science would be indispensable for the successful and rapid resolution of the Indian question.[12]

Sáenz believed the agency needed several hundred employees and a budget of $2,166,170, to be divided among five departments: Economic Affairs, Social Education, Hygiene and Health, Juridical Issues, and Inspections and Social Investigations. Most of the employees would work for the first three departments, and be assigned to one of ten regional offices that could specialize in local issues. A larger group of experts (including agronomists, economists, doctors, lawyers, teachers, carpenters, and tradesmen) would promote agricultural, industrial, social, and cultural improvements throughout the country. The Juridical Office, with fewer than ten employees, would promote legislation in favor of Indians and protect them in the legal system,[13] acting "like a true attorney and agent for the Indians." The Office of Investigations and Inspections would be the section responsible for conducting studies of Indian life, particularly their economy, demography, and biological mores. This office would also conduct censuses and critique the results of the department's other programs. It would have no formal employees, but a variety of agents from other sections would contribute to its efforts, and it would have a $30,000 budget to undertake research projects at the discretion of the director.[14]

Founding the Department

Sáenz's plan was conceptually ambitious and called for a significant commitment of resources. He would encounter resistance on both counts. As for the latter, he would be repeatedly forced to revise his budget during the fall of 1935, eventually reducing his proposed budget for the department to a little over $500,000 (plus another $400,000 in start-up costs). His scaled-down version of the agency would employ a group of *procuradores,* agronomists, doctors, and engineers in the task of investigating problems and petitioning other government agencies for their resolution, leaving the DAI with little power to actually implement programs in the countryside.[15]

Sáenz ran into even deeper trouble for his larger conceptual view of the department. Wary of any program that would "fatally separate the Indians from the general mass of our population, and make them a caste apart,"[16] Cárdenas chafed at the suggestion that the agency (and "Indian sociology") treat some indigenous Mexicans as distinct from the national community.[17] Cárdenas had a much simpler view of the

Indian problem. He believed that the Indian was a backward proletarian, possessed of a number of vices (alcoholism, fanaticism, isolation, etc.), and continually exploited by a variety of class enemies, but open to redemption.[18]

Cardenismo thus sought a delicate balance, characterizing Indians as primitive individuals who needed aid from the state, but who were simultaneously part of the national community. In the founding documents of the agency Cárdenas made this clear, stating that "it would be practically impossible to define with precision who should be considered Indians."[19] As a class, Indians (like the rest of the rural poor) were oppressed, backward, and in need of vast amounts of aid, but their cultural otherness was really only a product of exploitation. Indian proletarians had been essential actors in the nation's past, and were essential to the future. Declaring that "the only thing the Indian lacks has been the possibility of obtaining instruction and adequate nutrition," Cárdenas claimed that "there is a civic sentiment in the Indian masses, in many ways of a superior quality than that we have seen in other peoples; they are not people who oppose improvements, they are not conservatives; it is misery and ignorance that impedes their evolution."[20] This view justified Cárdenas's aggressive efforts to extend federal authority throughout the country, a process he explained as necessary to disrupt the traditionally exploitative social arrangements in rural Mexico.[21]

As a concession to Sáenz's original plan, Cárdenas admitted the scientific importance of sociology, ethnography, and anthropology in setting the agendas to be undertaken by the DAI. He even went as far as hiring an anthropologist as a part of its permanent staff, a move that Sáenz had not requested.[22] Nonetheless, Cárdenas was emphatic that the mission of the department would not be scientific, but "active and concrete in its goals, and in the techniques used for their realization." Advocacy duties would also take precedence over scientific investigations.[23] The DAI would study economic and social conditions only inasmuch as these studies could increase the effectiveness of other state agencies and develop practical solutions to improve living standards.[24] Aside from limited concessions to regionally sensitive programs and a vague commitment to protecting the use of Indian languages,[25] the DAI would principally work to help indigenous communities press their interests before the state without the interference of outside exploiters, and promote a program of rural development not unlike those that had largely failed to make headway for nearly two decades.[26]

Cárdenas revealed a great deal about his priorities with his choice for the director of the new agency. He chose Graciano Sánchez, an agrarista leader and former teacher originally from Tamaulipas.[27] Sánchez certainly did not represent the marriage of social science and action that Sáenz envisioned, having no experience as a scientist of any sort. He did, however, fit some very important criteria for Cárdenas. He was a loyal ally, having reputedly assassinated the occasional political enemy of his patron, Emilio Portes Gil.[28] Furthermore, after his stint as a congressional deputy from Tamaulipas, Sánchez had worked for the Departamento Agrario, where between 1934 and 1936 he successfully supplanted local agrarian leagues in several states with groups allied with the Cardenista Confederación Campesina Mexicana (CCM).[29] Sánchez made numerous enemies in these struggles, but successfully worked towards the Cardenista dream of building a centralized national network of campesinos allied with the state. The choice of Sánchez thus signaled a very specific direction for the DAI; social science would serve the state, but as a poor cousin to political mobilization.

His would not be an easy task. Enjoying an annual budget of only $400,000 and a staff of sixty-nine when it opened in January 1936, the department had virtually no power to carry out any programs on its own.[30] The budget was barely enough to cover basic administrative costs, let alone pay for political organizing, social action in the countryside through the Brigadas de Penetración Cultural Indígena, and the presidentially mandated residence for poor Indians to stay in when they came to the Federal District.[31] As Cárdenas himself acknowledged, a department of this size could really only act as an intermediary between indigenous communities and the ministries that had the power to implement social reforms.[32]

As the rural agents of the DAI, the twenty-two procuradores hired during 1936 were charged with conducting ethnographic studies of the economic, social, and cultural conditions of Indians, promoting agrarian and other claims before the state, and generally acting as organizers and interlocutors within and between communities.[33] Sáenz had imagined that these agents would play a limited role as advocates for indigenous communities, but in the final design of the program they were supposed to combine all the skills—economist, agronomist, doctor, lawyer, engineer—that were essential for dealing with rural poverty. Situated as the key intermediaries between the Indian and the state, the entire success of the DAI rested on their shoulders.[34] Yet twenty-two agents could not possibly cover the entire country. During the first year there were only two procuradores in Chiapas, one in Veracruz, one in Puebla, and none in Mexico or Quintana Roo.[35]

Often undermined or attacked by local power brokers, the procuradores could make problems public, petition authorities, and even negotiate agreements, but their power to actually effect change rested on moral suasion and shame, not enforcement.[36] Their meager training likewise meant that they were unlikely to possess or develop the regionally specific knowledge that Sáenz believed was essential to the department. Some made this situation worse by abusing the little power they possessed, yet many seem to have taken their responsibilities seriously.[37] In their first year, procuradores brought 7,216 requests to federal agencies, mostly concerning *ejidal* limits, grants, expansion and restitution, irrigation, water rights, and colonization. These actions increased in 1937–38. Even as the number of procuradores remained virtually the same, they forwarded 11,309 requests in twenty-seven regions during the year.[38]

These efforts had significant results. Their complaints resulted in changes in 272 ejidal authorities, 140 actions against judicial authorities in favor of Indians and campesinos, and 264 actions against *guardias blancas*, in many cases resulting in their disarmament. Their efforts also led to 4,859 interventions granting land and water to ejidos, and 34 grants of water rights to specific Indians and campesinos. Two hundred and one conflicts with the Banco de Crédito Ejidal were also resolved in favor of ejidatarios. Even so, these were relatively minor accomplishments for a department charged with overseeing the redemption of millions of indigenous peasants, and many observers were not impressed by the accomplishments of the DAI. As of April 1937 the DAI still employed only twenty-three procuradores to attend to the needs of between five and six million Indians in twenty-two states, one territory, and 1,260 municipios. "Due to these circumstances," Sánchez claimed, "it has not been possible even to visit all of the Indian pueblos, much less to study their economic, social, and cultural situation."[39]

This sorry state of affairs came to an end just a few months later, when in January 1938 a broad set of new responsibilities was assigned to the agency. The most significant change came with the transfer of authority over most aspects of Indian education (including the internados and the Misiones Culturales) from the SEP to the DAI. Sánchez promised that materials, food, and nutrition in the internados would be improved, and that students would be given a role in the management of funds in the schools. He also promised more aggressive efforts to establish co-ops and experiments in student management, setting up the CEI Fray Bartolomé de las Casas (Ixmiquilpan) as a model. In order to pay for these efforts, the budget of the agency was increased fivefold, to over two million pesos. During the next eight years funding for the DAI would grow steadily, peaking at four million pesos in 1946.[40]

The events that followed this transfer of power were the subject of a great deal of controversy, but by all accounts they did not reflect well on the DAI as benefactor of the Indian. Sánchez saw the takeover of the internados as an ideal opportunity to solidify the regional political networks that he had been developing through both the CCM and the DAI, and quickly abandoned most of the pedagogical and social scientific agenda of the agency in pursuit of this endeavor. In his view, students and teachers in the internados needed to be loyal to the regime, and act as political agents of Cardenismo in the countryside. In keeping with this ethos, he insisted that his new employees join the DAI's syndicate, give up the seniority they had earned at the SEP, and avoid any actions that could be interpreted as criticizing the department.[41]

Within months of the transfer, several school directors complained to Cárdenas that the DAI had completely undermined the mission of the internados, and that the change "has been a disaster."[42] Sánchez had suspended all ethnographic, medical, and economic investigations, destroyed student self-government, and had created new teachers' councils that they complained were "made up of people who have no understanding of the Indian's personality." The men who Sánchez had placed in charge of these schools, they lamented, "are truly an affront and danger to the work of Indian redemption." Indian students had been forced to flee numerous schools, only to be replaced by mestizos who had converted the institutions into centers of political agitation.[43]

As of August 1938, internados in Rincon Chamula (Chiapas), Bolaños (Jalisco), and El Domo, in Ixmiquilpan (Hidalgo) had been temporarily closed. Sánchez had also dismissed eight directors, put a number of students and teachers into jail, and placed much of the personnel and the directors of San Gabrielito and Paracho under suspension. Others were driven to resign, including the directors of Pequetzén and Matlapa.[44] Expressing a common sentiment, residents of Cuidad Valles in San Luis Potosí called Sánchez's actions a "criminal maneuver directed against the education of the Indian tribes."[45]

To be sure, Sánchez did not fire all of the directors. Many seem to have been most angry about losing their seniority in the DAI's syndicate, and some of the agitation by teachers seems to have been an effort to be reassigned to relatively more secure positions in the SEP.[46] Yet there were some fairly egregious cases of abuse under Sánchez, one of the most notable involving the internado El Domo in Ixmiquilpan. Students and teachers in the school found themselves in conflicts with the DAI almost immediately upon the school's transfer from the SEP. They complained in June 1938 that the internado had been in the hands of DAI for six months, and that their buildings were falling apart, that many students were sick and lacked medicine, and that the DAI was generally abusing the school. In a letter to Cárdenas, they lamented that the employees of the DAI "have absolutely no interest in us."[47]

Matters were made worse when Sánchez's inspector in the region, the Russian-born Alejandro Wladimir Paucic, responded to their requests by attacking several teachers, and according to the students, disrupting life at the school. As conflicts between the teachers, director, and the inspector boiled over, several asked that Paucic be removed. On 7 June 1938 the leader of the local teachers, Fidencio Zavala, complained not only that their requests for materials were systematically denied, but that all Paucic cared about was undermining the school's union.[48]

Just days later another DAI inspector expelled thirty-six students and imprisoned the school's director, causing a wave of protests in Ixmiquilpan and at other internados.[49] Many of those students who were not jailed fled the school, finding themselves far from home in a countryside in which they were strangers. This in turn led to more protests at schools all over the country.[50] Sánchez remained intransigent in the face of the protests, claiming that the internado's director, Juan Peña y Peña, had been dismissed for poor conduct, that the personnel in the school had refused orders from the department, and that the students were not expelled but had simply abandoned the school.[51] Disappointed by these results, Pantaleón Torres, writing on behalf of the expelled students, asked Cárdenas to intervene directly in the conflict "because the DAI expelled us for purely political reasons, while Spanish students enjoy benefits and guarantees."[52]

Torres's complaints did not help him in the short run, but they formed part of a growing chorus of attacks against Sánchez that ultimately resonated at the highest levels. At the beginning of 1939, after only a year of overseeing the internados, Sánchez left the DAI to head up the newly created Confederación Nacional Campesina (CNC). As a close ally of Cárdenas, his departure was not explained as a failure, but his replacement at the DAI suggested otherwise. The man chosen to replace Sánchez, Luis Chávez Orozco, was a scholar and a teacher who believed that indigenous peoples in Mexico should be respected as autonomous nations within a larger Mexican community. As such, Chávez Orozco was likely to bring an entirely different set of priorities to the Indian question than had his predecessor. He was also likely to respond favorably to the demand that the department be more responsive to local needs and concerns. Most importantly, for Sánchez's enemies in the internados and elsewhere, Chávez Orozco offered a respite from the top-down political organizing of the past year and a chance to return to a more nuanced educational program.

The Experiment with Cultural Pluralism

Much like modernizers throughout the West during this era, men like Cárdenas and Sánchez took it as axiomatic that human civilization was evolving from a collection of localistic folk cultures into national (even international) communities defined by class and ideology. They believed that even without their efforts, the Indian would inevitably disappear. However, the man that Cárdenas chose as the new head of the DAI was among a number of individuals who were increasingly uncertain about the wisdom of this view. When they looked at the national population they saw that, contrary to all predictions that the Indian was bound to gradually disappear, the Indian population was growing, and indigenous languages and cultures were flourishing. By 1939, 3 million Mexicans spoke nearly fifty Indian languages. The single largest group included 670,595 Nahuatl speakers, but almost forty other languages also enjoyed a vigorous existence. As the anthropologist Julio de la Fuente noted, it appeared that Indians were proud of their languages, and they had no interest in abandoning them. As would later become evident, the Indian population was growing relative to the rest of the population, leading some to conclude that far from being assimilated, they were the most vital sector of society.[53]

Indigenistas had long since given up viewing the Indian as a racial other, but they lacked an adequate framework for explaining the persistence of Indian ethnicities. It was this problem that motivated several individuals, including Moisés Sáenz, Vicente Lombardo Toledano, and Chávez Orozco, to turn to the Stalinist theory of oppressed nationalities as a means of explaining the continued diversity of the nation. Mexico, they decided, was not one nation but many, each with a right to self-determination based upon their distinct histories, geographies, and cultures. More importantly, they concluded that these differences did not present a problem for the future, but were instead a source of strength.[54]

These were radical conclusions, even more so since these individuals generally relied on patronage from the DAI. At the highest levels of the SEP and DAI, officials had only reluctantly supported programs that respected the cultural diversity of indigenous peoples, and even then did so with much opposition from those who feared balkanization.[55] Likewise, many of those officials who supported the use of Indian languages continued to believe that they were primitive tools, and that they should only be used in schools as a bridge to a monolingual Spanish education.[56] Chávez Orozco, however, took an entirely different view on these issues. Contrasting his vision sharply to Sánchez's shortly after taking over the department, he publicly asserted that indigenous languages constituted one of the great resources that aboriginal peoples possessed. He also promised expanded efforts to prepare natives as teachers, and a program that would be much more sympathetic to indigenous peoples' right to protect and preserve their own cultures.[57]

These were the key issues addressed by the Primera Asemblea de Filólogos y Linguistas, which met in Mexico City during May 1939. Organized by the Anthropology Department of the IPN and the DAI, it was attended by a number of prominent Indigenistas, including Daniel F. Rubín de la Borbolla, Miguel Othón de Mendizábal, Luis Alvarez Barret, Alfonso Caso, Rafael Ramírez, and delegates from sixteen Indian communities.[58] Like Chávez Orozco, the delegates were strongly influenced by the theory of oppressed nationalities, and committed to promoting autonomous organizations. They also called for the use of local vernaculars and local administration, and for practices that placed economic decision-making power in the hands of local indigenous peoples—privileging individuals who were steeped in the "customs and psychology" of their regions.[59]

The meeting also produced a series of resolutions that called for a new direction in Indian education. Dismissing two decades of failed efforts to incorporate the Indian through the rural school, the delegates declared that Indian communities should never be treated the same as those that spoke Spanish. They argued that the "shock" teachers and inspectors experienced in these communities resulted in false prejudices, which in turn produced inappropriate and unscientific programs grounded in the belief that Indians were inferior. This prejudice doomed Indian education, and needed to be eliminated in favor of a perspective that did not simply link cultural differences to cultural inferiority. If, instead of eradicating differences in the interest of assimilation, educators created programs that respected cultural diversity and sought to provide real opportunities for progress, they would find that "every ethnic group has the same possibility of arriving at a 'civilized' state."[60]

The mother tongue, they argued, reflected both a linguistic and psychological system, and was always the best means of education. Indian languages, the delegates argued, were not primitive means of communication, but reflections of the different worlds that indigenous Mexicans lived in, and were the only effective means through which educators could understand their students. They thus called for the publication of dictionaries, grammars, and literature in indigenous languages, as well as programs that would give preference to teachers who were native speakers of those vernaculars.[61]

That these demands were made so publicly was a function of the change in leadership at the DAI, as was the fact that Maurice Swadesh would have the opportunity to put them into practice in the following months in the Proyecto Tarasco (see chapter 2). Swadesh's role at the congress and in Paracho, along with the importance of William Townsend's ideas, signaled an important shift in Indigenismo. Incorporation in one form or another had always been an important mandate of SEP programs. Foreign investigators like Franz Boas and Frank Tannenbaum had been actively involved in these programs, but their influences had traditionally served nationalist ends by suggesting the possibility of assimilating the Indian. Such was not the case here. Townsend and Swadesh openly challenged assimilation, and by extension, Mexican nationalism. They were repeatedly attacked for this, and Chávez Orozco took a considerable risk when he named Swadesh the director of the Consejo de Lenguas Indígenas at the DAI and gave him authority over the Proyecto Tarasco. In later years the "foreignness" of Swadesh's ideas would become the very basis for discrediting his work.[62]

Though he did not attend the congress, during this period Sáenz also endeavored to undermine some of the foundations of Mexican nationalism. By the late 1930s he emerged as perhaps the most public advocate of the pluralist reconceptualization of the nation, exhorting Cárdenas both privately and publicly to discard the incorporationist ethos that had animated social and educational projects since the 1910s.[63] His 1939 opus, *México Integro,* marked the final stage in his transformation from advocate of assimilationist rural schools in the 1920s to pluralism. While he continued to believe in a larger national community informed by principles of economic and social justice, by 1939 he unambiguously denied the need for that community to be completely unified or homogenous.[64]

Taking his impressions of Carapan to their logical conclusion, *México Integro* described the country as a collection of isolated regions. Sáenz used regional motifs to allow for a wide variety of practices within the national culture, based not in the primitive/modern hierarchy but instead on the view that these differences were imposed by time and space. He argued that regional cultural differences (products of a combination of Spanish feudalism and Indian regionalism) made the country "truly a living panorama of peoples and cultures." Mexico was a "grand symphony," the product of regional geographic variations and different traditions of mestizaje. Going further, he proposed that "the modern tools of unification—schools, education, mechanical civilization—should be used with great caution, because the risks of standardization and mechanization can be as grave as the risks of isolation." Though he believed in an essential *mexicanidad* (a rebellious attitude, a love of color, corridos, retablos, and the like, and melancholia, all rooted in the Indian past), he asserted that each Mexican cultural tradition had discrete local origins, and that only foreign tourists could generalize them into simple national practices.[65]

The book described a diverse series of Mexican scenes. Images of life in Quintana Roo, rancheros in San Luis Potosí, Tarascans in Janitzio, and the Sierra de Puebla collectively described the diversity of the country not as a problem, but as its wealth. The Totonacas he described in the Sierra de Puebla were democratic, self-governing, and capable of keeping mestizo exploiters at bay. Describing Oaxaca, he commented that Mixtecos and Zapotecos, "vigorous and secure in themselves," were well situated to preserve their eight hundred local cultures even as they "confront the Mexico of the highways."[66]

He concluded that education could create harmony among Mexico's peoples and bring modern practices, but should not seek to destroy the local cultures. Schools should be democratic, and encourage community participation based in both general principles and local particularities. He remained committed to the civilizing mission, but argued for a considerable program of social action to accompany it. This program could not be based solely on European civilization, but had to be attuned to indigenous interests and cultures. "The stereotypical phrase 'incorporate the Indian into civilization' should be changed to 'incorporate civilization to the Indian.'" Rejecting segregation and paternalism, as well as the idea that Mexico should be an Indian paradise and Nahuatl substituted for Spanish, he called for the incorporation of the Indian into the "Mexican family," based on the principle that the Indian was "a real and important factor in the integration of Mexico." Mestizo Mexico "must be integrated with all of the ethnic, cultural, and spiritual elements of our heritage."[67]

This, he argued, could only be achieved through a program that accepted diversity. Local systems of government, like councils of elders and other institutions, need not be eliminated, but could instead be used in the process of integration. Local practices had been "created through centuries of experience," and acted as the foundations of dignified collective existence. There was no reason to eliminate these institutions; in fact their elimination would be deleterious to the interests of all involved. He concluded that the federal government had to allow for "the coexistence of two entities, the Mexican and the Indian."[68]

Sáenz had clearly left the nationalist mainstream, but in the climate of the late 1930s this did not signal his political demise. Having established his scholarly credentials through more than a decade of careful research, all the while cultivating a friendly relationship with his political patron, Sáenz had a limited opportunity to challenge the precepts of Cardenismo without ending his own career. In fact, even as he published *México Integro,* Sáenz assumed a prominent role as one of the key organizers of the Primer Congreso Indigenista Interamericano (PCII), convened by the DAI in Pátzcuaro, Michoacán between 14 and 24 April 1940.[69] The last of a series of important Indigenista congresses held in Mexico during the Cárdenas sexenio, Pátzcuaro represented a key moment in the convergence of anthropological knowledge and state formation in Mexico.[70]

Sáenz and Chávez Orozco set the tone for Pátzcuaro, where a growing number of Indigenistas, working through newly created institutions (the Escuela Nacional de Antropología e Historia and Department of Anthropology at the IPN were both founded in 1939), presented research that challenged many of the precepts of the incorporationist paradigm, and proclaimed the rights of indigenous peoples to their own cultures and languages.[71] Encouraged by the privilege Indigenismo seemed to have gained in this forum, and inspired by the host of foreign researchers who were then working in Mexico, some would even go so far as to use the congress as an opportunity to call for the right to "self-determination" for Mexico's indigenous peoples.[72] Their claims represented a limited form of pluralism — limited by the fact that most Indigenistas retained the authority to determine which indigenous communities deserved autonomy and which did not, and which Indian traits were positive and which were not. Nonetheless, Pátzcuaro gave the claim of a right to self-determination based upon cultural plurality a legitimacy that it had never enjoyed in Mexico.[73]

Jorge A. Vivo, a member of the Consejo de Lenguas Indígenas and a researcher at the Instituto Panamericano de Geografía e Historia, used his presentation to suggest that some indigenous cultures should indeed be treated as separate nationalities in Mexico based on their population, territory, history, language, and culture. Though his schema denied most groups autonomy (some because of their high levels of mestizaje, and others because of their need for government tutelage), Vivo argued that self-government should be considered as an alternative for more "advanced" Indian cultures.[74] He argued that groups like the Mayas could "constitute strong nations in the near future" based on cultural and economic factors. More importantly, he asserted that

Indians had an absolute right to elect their own representatives and officials, to conduct their affairs in their own languages, to design their own social programs, and to control their own organizations.[75]

In other presentations Alfonso Villa Rojas and Luis Alvarez Barret dismissed past incorporationist practices and called for a system that would consider the "dignity, sensitivity, and morality of the Indians," and recognize the real value of indigenous cultures and traditions. Based on his work among the Tzeltals, Villa Rojas argued that educational failures in the region were not the product of deficient "mental structures," but rather the lack of teachers who understood local social structures and attitudes. Alvarez criticized SEP programs because they "are based in the principle that the only thing that distinguishes an Indian campesino from a mestizo or white campesino is their inability to speak Spanish. They never take into account differences in customs, mentality, and tradition." He argued that for Indian children the process of learning Spanish was not simple, nor did it lead to assimilation into a Mexican culture. In most SEP programs Indian children used Spanish mechanically, like an instrument. They also tended to become adults who understood neither Spanish nor their mother tongue particularly well.[76]

Alvarez did not believe that Indians generally rejected modernity. He noted that in spite of continued language differences, Indians were driving cars and tractors, engaging in commerce, and visiting state capitals. Claiming that these indicators showed Indians were able to integrate themselves into the national life without total cultural and linguistic immersion, he concluded that Indian cultures did not reject modern ways per se. However, he noted that the indigenous Mexicans who embraced these markers of modernity did not simply replicate the values and practices of the mestizo mainstream, because their personality, customs, and "rhythm of life" differed from those of non-indigenous Mexicans. Alvarez believed that any efforts to eliminate the backwardness of the Indian economy had to avoid a "closed, intransigent, uncomprehending attitude" towards this difference between Indians and other Mexicans. Indigenistas needed to embrace "the positive aspects of their culture, their decorative arts, their ancient agronomic experiences, their original conceptions of justice, liberty, and the human personality." Ultimately, these "essential elements of Indian life" had to be embraced in educational programs if they were to succeed.[77]

This tendency was also seen in a series of presentations that decried the influence of outsiders on indigenous arts in Mexico. Past efforts to improve Indian arts were attacked for distorting their essence, and several speakers called for concerted efforts to preserve popular arts. In contrast to the earlier efforts by Indigenistas like Manuel Gamio, these presenters focused on preserving specific regional cultural practices and celebrating local cultures as part of a complex and varied developmental process. Likewise, they pointed out the problematic nature of the idea of a single national culture, and instead identified Mexico's Indians as a collection of different, yet valuable, cultures, which should be supported and encouraged rather than stamped out in the interest of nationalization. To these ends, Alfonso Pulido Islas called for the creation of Conservatorios Regionales de las Artes Populares Indias, where experts in regional arts would teach locals their own artistic traditions. Alfonso Caso proposed museos regionales where degenerated work could be displayed next to genuine articles.[78]

The Nationalist Counterpoint

Pátzcuaro was a triumphant moment for cultural pluralists, but not an uncontested one. Cárdenas had no sympathy for the pluralists, and in what has ironically become the most important historical memory of the PCII, began his address to the delegates by explicitly attacking both racists and advocates of the theory of oppressed nationalities. He did not mince his words, asserting that the Indian was neither a child nor a race apart, but "a member of a social class taking part in the collective task of production."[79] "More than through skin color, particular forms of political organization, or artistic manifestations," he argued, the Indian was defined by "his position as an oppressed class."[80] This placed the Indian within his nationalist narrative, and prescribed a program of emancipation that would be the same as that for the proletariat of any country, allowing for unique local needs.[81] Most famously, he stated:

> Our Indian problem is not that of making the Indian "stay Indian," nor of Indianizing Mexico, but in Mexicanizing the Indian himself. If we respect his blood, and turn his emotional powers, his love of the soil and his unmistakable tenacity to account, we shall root the

> national feeling more firmly in all, and enrich it with moral qualities that will strengthen the spirit of patriotism, thus asserting Mexico's personality.[82]

With these words Cárdenas evoked the long-held nationalist sentiment that the incorporationist ethos was far superior to the North American tendency to treat Indians as separate from the mainstream.[83] He could have been accused of ignoring the actual needs of indigenous peoples, but Cárdenas found support at the congress from what might have seemed an unlikely constituency: the indigenous delegates he invited to Pátzcuaro. Invited in spite of the fears of Cárdenas's own Secretary of Foreign Relations that they were incapable of contributing anything to their own improvement, delegates like the Otomí and Mixtec leaders Edmundo Domínguez and Adrian Plácido López used this forum to make demands that emphasized their sympathy for the Cardenista agenda. They wanted schools, lands, roads, health programs, and all the implements of modernity, from plows to gasoline lamps and radios. None of the Indian delegates from Mexico suggested that they wanted to live outside the mainstream.[84]

In April 1940, *El Maestro Rural* published a series of articles on the Indian problem that echoed these views. The articles asserted that each different Indian culture in Mexico simply represented levels on the same universal continuum. In fact, they claimed there were 5.5 million mestizos who were as socially, culturally, and economically backward as the Indians, and that for this reason "we should not consider Indians as a special group and treat them separately from mestizos who live under the same conditions."[85] This reiterated Cárdenas's point that Indians, along with the rest of the rural and urban poor, were members of a single proletariat. As a class, Indians (like other rural poor) were oppressed, backward, and in need of vast amounts of aid, but their cultural "otherness" was only a matter of economic and social problems.[86]

This interpretation of the Indian question found adherents not only because it was straightforward and fit easily into the nationalist agenda, but also because it offered a clear vision for the creation of a more egalitarian society through state intervention. Many members of the intelligentsia recoiled at the ideas that pluralists articulated in the late 1930s, accusing them of isolating Indians from the benefits of civilization and denying the nation the unity it needed. This was the reason that pluralism not only offended hispanophiles and conservatives, but leftists as well.[87]

Luis León suggested that these *"indianistas"* simply wanted to incite Indians to "ignite a caste war, expel the whites from our country, and create a racial hecatomb."[88] José Pavia Crespo argued that cultural diversity was a problem in that it allowed authorities to abuse legal statutes to exploit, demand payments from, and jail Indians because of their isolation and lack of contact.[89] Elena Torres, long known for her feminist activism, rejected the claim that "any ethnic group, no matter how small, has the absolute right to preserve their own language," because it allowed colonial powers to perpetuate the inferior position of native populations, who could not speak the language of power.[90]

Some attacked the very existence of the DAI, suggesting that the department betrayed the best traditions of Mexican history by setting the Indian apart, and treating Indians like children, rather than providing the things they really needed. In one case, an editorial in *Gráfico* accused the DAI of treating Indians as icons for tourists instead of incorporating them into the mainstream.[91] These attacks were sure indications that, while they had managed to secure some privilege within the state because of their scientific credentials, pluralists had not won the hearts and minds of the Mexican intelligentsia. Telling, perhaps, was the fact that Sáenz's *México Integro* was not even published in the country during the 1930s. As for Swadesh and Townsend, their foreign provenance, along with the evangelical mission of the Summer Institute of Linguistics, made them easy targets for accusations of imperialism.[92]

La Población Indígena de Mexico

One of the defining qualities of most of these attacks was that they were launched by nationalist intellectuals with little experience in ethnographic research. Furthermore, they were leveled at Indigenistas who had come to care more about the problems indigenous Mexicans faced than about the larger nationalist project. As such, these critiques could have been dismissed for their fantastic quality, for their failure to take into account the real needs of living Indians in their desire to imagine the nation. If the nationalists were to deflect this criticism, they needed an intellectual buttress, an evidentiary basis for arguing that their point of view was as ethnographically sound as that of the pluralists. They found just that with the 1940 publication of Carlos Basauri's three-volume *La población indígena de México,* the most substantive effort to produce ethnographic knowledge on the Indian undertaken during the Cárdenas sexenio. It was the product of joint efforts by the SEP and DAI to provide a detailed picture of Mexico's Indian population, and was principally intended to provide rural teachers with the means to understand their students and facilitate their incorporation.[93] While vaguely emancipatory, the goals of the study were clearly oriented towards developing more empirical knowledge about the nation, so as to facilitate both social reform and control.[94] Unlike the Proyecto Tarasco, *La población* utilized the social sciences principally in the service of the state, not the people.

In a sharp divergence from the work that was then ongoing in Paracho, most of the research was done not by experts, but by a diverse group of educational inspectors, school directors, and rural teachers. Though compiled by a small clique of experts at the SEP and DAI, most of the data for *La población* was drawn from their responses to a forty-eight page questionnaire composed by Angel Corzo, a long-time teacher, administrator in the DAI, and expert on the Indians of Chiapas. The surveys revealed the fundamental intentions of the project by explicitly stating that their goal was to gather data on Indians in order "to consciously promote their transformation," elevating them to the same level as mestizos. Teachers were told to observe a series of markers and place them into preselected categories, privileging some social and cultural practices as important and neglecting others as marginal.[95]

The questionnaires had teachers evaluate communities according to a fairly standard but detailed set of categories, including history, geographic distribution, population, language, anthropology, economy, social structure, and material and spiritual culture.[96] The questions explored a number of psychological issues, requiring that teachers gather information on the role of religion and belief systems, as well as social and sexual practices. The questionnaires also spent a great deal of energy on vice. Surveys asked about crime, but focused mostly on alcohol. They asked what community members drank, if there were cantinas and pulquerias in the community, if drinking was essential to community life, if women drank, if they produced alcohol, and if they believed drinking helped them understand Spanish. They also asked if the subjects drank only on fiesta days, and if they drank to excess or in moderation. Other questions asked if degeneration from alcohol could be seen in the community, and if the respondents found deformed, idiot children.[97]

As a whole, the surveys were overwhelmingly concerned with the slow process whereby Indian communities entered the modern world. In this they were informed by a series of desires that ran directly counter to the pluralists. While individuals like Sáenz, de la Borbolla, and Chávez Orozco were arguing that indigenous cultural systems had to be understood in their totality, Corzo's surveys used a series of simple markers of modernity to evaluate how far along the road to progress Indian communities had traveled. Respondents were asked if Indian communities had mail service, a church, a school, modern medical facilities, roads, if they knew about the larger political entities in which they lived, or had much interaction with outsiders. They were asked to evaluate whether or not the communities were open to outside influences, and about community attitudes towards whites and mestizos. The march towards modernity was also measured through questions that asked if members of the community had been in a car or train, seen a plane, heard Victrolas, knew how to read a watch, or used motorized corn mills, candles, gasoline lamps, or sewing machines. Likewise, surveys asked if residents smoked factory-made cigarettes.[98]

The minutia of the surveys—a vast array ranging from questions about individual sexual proclivities to smoking preferences—would ultimately produce the reality they sought to describe. The wealth of information gathered on culture, economic practices, consumption habits, and vice could only be coherently interpreted through a lens that used each one of these measures as an indicator of where these communities stood in the process of national integration. And even though the categories did allow for cultural peculiarities among Indians, these practices were understood as holdovers to be destroyed in the interest of progress or preserved out of context for the national good.

More importantly, certain features built into the surveys offered explanatory frameworks for why rural teachers might struggle in the communities they served. This can be seen in the attention paid to community dysfunction, fanaticism, and alcohol (three age-old signifiers), but was also powerfully conveyed by the inclusion of a series of psychological questions. Rural teachers with absolutely no training in the fine arts of Freud and Jung were asked if their clients were moody, pessimistic, or given to emotional outbursts. Respondents were asked if the Indians they observed were "slothful, irritable, impulsive, given to quarreling." They were asked if there was a sentiment of cruelty in the community toward women, children, or animals. They were also asked if people in the community toward were "vengeful, rancorous, perverse, or reasonable and understanding."[99] Whether or not community members really possessed these qualities, these questions gave outsiders the power to interpret shouts, insults, and threats from local authorities as reflections of poor mental health.[100]

As a result of the surveys, recalcitrant groups like the Lacandon, Otomí, and Huichol were rendered as primitives, bewitched by evil spirits, and often crippled by violent or perverse social and sexual practices.[101] By contrast, among those communities where teachers and other federal officials had seen some limited success, as with the Tarascans of the meseta tarasca, the story was altogether different. As a community with clear ties to one of the great preconquest civilizations, the Tarascans were "a strong and prosperous nation," "extremely industrious and hard-working," and practiced a healthy social life. Descriptions of their social conventions were admiring, and included no mention of violence.[102]

As a whole, the ethnographies in *La población* provided all the evidence that nationalists needed to describe Mexico as a single hierarchical community. The similar types of data and methods of collection produced an image of the country that suggested all Mexicans were on the road to becoming a single community. Indigenous communities were simply at different points in the path. Basauri confirmed this by using them to formulate a description of the Mexican nation that divided the entire national population into seven different "evolutive stages," from the most primitive, including the Seri and Lacandon, to the relatively small group that constituted modern Mexico. Confirming the SEP's original mandate for the study, this created a model for unifying the nation based on the gradual introduction of modernity to primitive areas. Having placed each culture in their stage, he suggested the next logical step that should be taken in promoting their redemption, and also held out the possibility that—through a long and carefully orchestrated process—all Mexicans might one day be modern.[103]

Similar tendencies were also evident in the portions of the study that delved into physical anthropology. In keeping with common practice, racial characteristics, including cephalic and nasal indexes and skin color, were determined for each group in the study. Furthermore, in the interests of scientific detail the researchers measured endemic illnesses, average pulse rates, blood pressure, and temperature.[104] Yet the conclusions they drew from this evidence were sharply different from those reached in the past, and completely in accord with the interests of the Cardenista state. Basauri used the measurements to conclude that with the infinite mixing and variety in Mexico, it was impossible to do accurate racial typing. He argued that instead of being used to classify race, physical anthropology should really be used for biotype, physiology, and psychology.[105]

Drawing on the measurements done for the study, *La población* explicitly repudiated the view that Indians were a racial category, along with the theory of racial degeneration. At a time when representatives of the state in other nations were increasingly obsessed with racial degeneration, Basauri described it as a "vulgar pseudoscientific concept,"[106] and as he did elsewhere, denied that degeneration had any connection to race. Rather, he argued that degeneration was rooted in the physical misery Indians lived in and poor diets they ate, and was not inheritable. Though Indians may possess a degenerated culture, he claimed, "this is not to say, in any manner, that there exists a degeneration that affects the entire Indian population."[107]

Basauri's statement here perhaps reflected his own journey through race as a concept. He began as an earnest advocate of racial mestizaje and the use of racial measures (like cephalic indices) during the 1920s and early 1930s, but by the time he was appointed chief of the SEP's Departamento de Educación Indígena, he publicly rejected the idea that the term *Indian* had any measurable racial content. Whether this was simply a cynical effort to reposition himself to suit the needs of the Cardenista state or a genuine repudiation of his past priorities, he did commit himself to a position that rejected racial determinism in *La población.* Specifically attacking the notion that degeneration was an inherited abnormality that affected the Indian's *"germaplasma,"* he argued that "the genotypical characteristics of the race are of high biological value," and that decadence was a simple and reversible phenomenon caused by environmental conditions.[108] Proof of the Indian's value could be seen in the constant growth of the Indian population, and the numbers of Indians in the surveys who had abandoned their isolation.[109]

Adopting a practice that was increasingly popular outside of Mexico, Basauri also drew heavily on the psychological evidence gathered in the surveys to offer a diagnosis of the Indian personality. Psychology here offered clear explanations for Indian poverty, and had the added benefit of being more strictly scientific than either cultural pluralism or Boasian ethnography.[110] He noted that the standard markers of intelligence (perceptions, attention, memory, imagination, ideation) were poorly developed in the Indian. Instead, indigenous Mexicans showed an "affective indifference," and "little love for life," coupled with moments of intense emotions, "diverse manifestations of cruelty," religious sentiments, and an exalted eroticism. Their everyday lives passed with little expression, but in explosive moments, "the Indian grows angry and assaults, wounds, or kills with true cruelty." Basauri also noted enormous sacrifices for their fiestas, and that "when there are grudges between two villages or two families over the boundaries of lands or property rights, aggressive and bellicose fights are very frequent. Rapes and other sexual assaults are also common."[111]

Unlike the pluralists, who would have attributed many of these phenomena to cultural conflict, Basauri simply saw individuals who were so crippled by poor nutrition, oppression, and psychological abuse that they could not see their own best interests.[112] His psychologically and socially crippled subject showed a remarkable resemblance to the individual described a few years earlier by Samuel Ramos (1934) and later by Octavio Paz (1950). Psychology had the ambiguous result of defining an Indian emotional pathology, while simultaneously describing a personality type that encompassed most Mexicans. Science thus defined the Mexican not as a racial type, but as a series of deficient psychological complexes. Indians, and by extension most rural Mexicans, had an "abnormal mentality." They were impulsive, cruel, indifferent, ambivalent, and discordant. These problems were rooted in alcohol, an incomplete diet, and historical, social, and economic factors that for centuries had shaped their psyche. Moreover, these problems were also signs of a long history of class exploitation, the phenomena through which Cardenistas typically defined the national past and present. More than simply deracializing the Indian, this united all members of the folk into a single category, and suggested that the ethnic differences that divided Mexicans were ephemeral. As such, it suggested that Mexico was not simply evolving towards a single national community, but that in fundamental ways it was already one nation.[113]

Basauri could certainly have tied the psychological complexes he saw to race, as was fairly popular in Europe at the time. Investigators in Mexico were familiar with racial psychology, and several had been exposed to these ideas in depth in Europe. Yet even as they drew from psychology, Mexican social scientists rejected racial psychology in describing the mental state of the Mexican Indian.[114] This decision reflected one of the central needs of science in revolutionary Mexico. While the recalcitrance of Indian communities in the face of the state might be explained in a variety of ways, from cultural conflict to backwardness, it could not be explained as a product of impermeable alterity.

Conclusion

The year 1940 was an unusual one for Indigenistas. During that year federal officials struggled to present two distinct and ultimately irreconcilable visions of the Indian—the member of an oppressed nation and the slowly assimilating primitive. The latter vision had the advantage of being the one preferred by the president, but this did not mean that pluralists could be easily silenced. In the unique context of the late 1930s, when social scientists gained an unusual amount of privilege—even autonomy—to develop their own solutions to the Indian problem, pluralism found a large enough group of adherents that it briefly became the guiding vision of a number of government agencies. The most important of these was the DAI, where pluralist ideas informed not just the planning for the PCII, but the Proyecto Tarasco, the Congresos Regionales Indígenas (the subject of the next chapter), and the internados. After 1940 Indigenista social scientists would often lack the capital (symbolic and otherwise) to act as important voices in public policy, but between the founding of the DAI and the PCII, individuals like Sáenz, Julio de la Fuente, Luis Chávez Orosco, Jorge Vivo, and Daniel Rubín de la Borbolla effectively used the social sciences to challenge the very vision of the nation that their patrons articulated.

It may seem anachronistic to describe the late 1930s as a pluralist moment, given the fact that even the most radical pluralists of the day remained firm advocates of a Eurocentric science, and advocated integrating the Indian into some form of national society. Yet the use of the term pluralism remains nonetheless appropriate. These Indigenistas took the radical view that the nation was made up of a plurality of cultures, and called for self-empowerment, the inclusion of locals in decision making, and ultimately even recognized the right of indigenous peoples to self-determination. Based on their experiences in indigenous communities they concluded that assimilation would not work, and that the only hope for a more equitable future lay in respecting cultural differences, and working only gradually and in limited ways to create a larger community that could supersede those differences.

Of course, critiques of the very concept of ethnographic authority, the capacity of science to find solutions to the problems of poverty, and of modernity as a whole, were not generally components of these debates.[115] The pluralism seen in Mexico since the 1970s has been linked to a deeper critique of the role of "experts" in diagnosing the other, a feature of contemporary debates that distinguishes the past from the present. Activists in the 1930s offered critiques of oppression, abuse, and the "unscientific" application of government programs, but they believed in the capacity of science to cure society's ills. Chávez Orozco, Sáenz, and others saw profound local differences, but also believed that many of those differences were the legitimate concern of the state. The pluralists of this generation believed that the state had both a right and an obligation to undo the poverty, exploitation, inequality, and injustice they saw in the countryside, whereas today many see the state as an ideological construct that inevitably reproduces relations of domination and subordination.

This tension between respecting difference and solving problems was one of the ambiguities that Manuel Gamio confronted when wrestling with the pluralists' claims. Believing that the differences between indigenous Mexicans and the mestizo mainstream were more a function of poverty than cultural distinctiveness, he observed that the nationalities that the Stalinist theory of oppressed nationalities had been created to describe (all of them Soviet Republics) all possessed certain similarities, at least in what Gamio considered their "level of culture." Mexicans, he believed, suffered from such gross cultural, economic, and social inequalities that the theory was not relevant.[116] Gamio's assertion deserves critique for his ethnocentrism, but at the time it represented a serious challenge to Mexican pluralists. More than attacking pluralists for undermining the nation, Gamio offered the very reason that nationalists needed to deny indigenous Mexicans a right to self-determination. Indians needed help from the state, they needed to be more Mexican.

4 Empowering the Masses at the Congresos Regionales Indígenas

We want real things, promises which are fulfilled. We are tired of sending our complaints and requests to one department or another, and getting nothing. — *Otomí leader Edmundo Domínguez, April 1940*

The era of farce and vain promises is over. — *Governor Trujillo Gurría of Tabasco to the Chontal Congress, December 1939*[1]

Indigenistas always framed their projects in ways that made the political empowerment of the Indian an important goal. From Teotihuacán, to the Casa and the internados, they promised to make their charges into "social leaders" who could renovate the Indian community from within. Before 1934 however, these priorities rarely translated into a systematic practice, in part because Indigenistas relished the power conferred by their status as interlocutor between the silent Indian and the revolutionary state, and in part because the political needs of the Mexican state had never favored the transformation of Indians from wards of the state into political actors.

Lázaro Cárdenas found this arrangement unacceptable. From the time he ascended to power he led a very fragile coalition, one in which his control of the country was based on savvy politicking, egalitarian social reforms, and constant efforts to maintain and enlarge his political constituency through popular mobilization. Cárdenas envisioned a corporatist Mexican state; one that created spaces for those sectors of society which had previously been excluded, and which established official channels for oppressed and unrepresented groups to communicate their demands to the state and receive the benefits of modernity. From the state they would receive lands, water, sanitation, schools, and all of those other markers of modernity that Cardenistas valued. In return, they were expected to defend the state from attacks by foreign and domestic enemies.[2]

Cárdenas built these coalitions through workers', agrarian, and women's organizations, which in turn held a multitude of public congresses during his presidency to mobilize their members. In these forums, agents of the state and representatives of popular sectors came together to publicly negotiate the shape of the revolutionary state. These events offered limited opportunities for subaltern Mexicans to articulate their needs based on their class, professional, or gender identities, along with excellent opportunities for the state to direct popular mobilization. Some events, like the Primer Congreso Obrero Campesina Indígena, which took place in Oaxaca in 1934, even claimed to represent indigenous Mexicans, though Spanish was their lingua franca, and few actual Indians were ever made participants beyond playing a supportive role. As such, the impact of these initiatives on indigenous communities was negligible.[3]

The Cardenista state needed a mechanism for building alliances with indigenous Mexicans, some means through which federal officials could gradually extend the power of the state into indigenous communities while simultaneously finding new sources of support. In 1936 Cárdenas turned this task over to Graciano Sánchez and the DAI, ordering the agency to organize a new kind of congress, where delegates would be brought together at the expense of the state, fed, clothed, and treated with a dignity they had never before seen. Rather than simply being told about their needs, delegates would have the opportunity to empower themselves. They would make federal bureaucrats sit and listen while they "gave voice to their words," without the interference of caciques, landlords, priests, and the other outsiders who had traditionally silenced and exploited the Indian. Implicit was the promise that once Indians made their needs public by speaking for themselves, the state would satisfy their demands. Cárdenas would ask for only loyalty in return.[4]

The Congresos Regionales Indígenas began with a meeting of 720 Otomí delegates in Ixmiquilpan in late September 1936. It was followed by seven major and many more minor congresses during the following four years. Hundreds of delegates attended most congresses, including 184 at the Segundo Congreso Regional (Tarasco) in Uruapan, Michoacán, in December 1937, and 800 at the Tercer Congreso Regional (Azteca), in Tamazunchale, San Luis Potosí, during March 1938. Another 600 attended the Congreso Regional de la Raza Mixteca, celebrated in Tlaxiaco, Oaxaca, in May 1938. Four hundred attended the IV Congreso Regional Indígena in Ixtlahuaca, Mexico, during September 1938, and 900 attended the Chamula congress in Las

Casas, Chiapas, May 1939. In October 1939, 332 attended the Huasteca congress that met in Tantoyuca, Veracruz, and Tancanhuitz, San Luis Potosí, and 130 came to the Chontal congress in Villahermosa, Tabasco, during December 1939.[5] In these forums delegates were given wide authority to vent their grievances and garner immediate aid from sympathetic officials. Some even saw their demands published in the press and broadcast nationally by radio.[6]

Creating the Framework

From their inception the congresses were envisioned as unique spectacles, where "genuine representatives of the Indians" would articulate the needs of their communities without outside interference.[7] Delegates were elected in popular assemblies held in all communities of over fifty inhabitants that met the criteria set for each congress. The rules mandated that they be elected democratically, but that delegates be chosen because they were members of the designated ethnic community and habitually spoke the local dialect. Officials from the DAI were also explicitly ordered to convince the communities that they should "designate their most characteristic representatives to be spokesmen for their ambitions, needs, and problems."[8]

These rules were meant to produce delegates who could speak for their entire community, but given the deep internal divisions in many indigenous communities, it was likely impossible that most delegates could speak on behalf of their entire village. Moreover, the very nature of the congresses required that delegates possess qualities that would have made many of them unrepresentative of their communities. Delegates needed to be able to communicate their needs to the assembled officials, and while problems could be expressed orally in indigenous languages, petitions to the congresses (and in some cases, presentations) had to be written in Spanish. For these reasons, local assemblies were asked to select at least one delegate who was bilingual, a requirement that limited the pool of potential candidates considerably. More importantly, these elections were overseen by DAI representatives who, while ordered to merely serve "as auxiliaries to the communities in presenting their grievances, initiatives, and presentations," would play a significant part in the selection of delegates and the composition of petitions, complaints, and presentations.[9]

For at least a decade federal bureaucrats had been consciously cultivating young males to act as representatives of the state in indigenous communities, and the mandate that at least one delegate from each community be bilingual gave these individuals a considerable advantage in being selected as delegates. Among the delegates were numerous young bilingual teachers and administrators who had attended the Casa, the internados, and other schools.[10] Federal officials sought to empower these young men as "representatives . . . before the Mexican nation," and made every effort to situate these young men in this role at the congresses, and in the organizations that were created in their aftermath. Women, while granted the privilege of becoming social leaders on a limited basis through the internados and rural normal schools, were excluded entirely.[11]

Beyond ensuring that the delegates were entirely male, the rules dictated that they were mostly young.[12] Though we cannot be certain of the ages of delegates at the other congresses, Julio de la Fuente's breakdown of the delegates to the two sessions of the Huasteca congress is instructive, and likely reflects the larger trend. In the two events he observed that 22 percent of the delegates were age twenty and younger, 51 percent were between twenty-one and thirty, 23 percent were between thirty-one and forty, 14 percent were between forty-one and fifty, and only 10 percent were between fifty and seventy. Similar numbers were recorded at Tancanhuitz.[13]

De la Fuente undoubtedly saw these age breakdowns as illuminating, given that many Indigenistas believed that young members of indigenous communities found modernization more appealing, and that deep factional cleavages could already be seen in those indigenous communities where modernity had made inroads. As he noted in his presentation to the PCII, generational changes in indigenous communities were undermining traditional social hierarchies; young people were rejecting traditional marriage patterns and were less disposed to obey the elders, because "the youths can counter them with their new cultural contacts." De la Fuente worried that these changes had a deleterious impact on the quality of life in the Zapotec communities he studied, but was nonetheless pleased that these changes offered youths "liberation from mystical ideas," the opportunity to change local political structures (such as *mayordomía*), and the opportunity to benefit from the increased presence of outsiders in their communities.[14]

At the apex of age-based hierarchies, older men were more likely to be invested in maintaining traditional forms of local autonomy, and opposed to incursions by the federal state. Revolutionary programs thus appealed to younger, poorer, and more alienated males, who could use the state to fight generational conflicts and ascend to power in their communities. Young people, Rubén Novelo Gil observed, "are the elements that could help the teacher in his struggle against the dominant savagery, as they are the least attached to their antiquated customs." In contrast, he described the older generations as "refractory to progress," in particular because of their tendency to oppose the efforts of rural teachers.[15]

The Public Spectacle

In some ways the congresses were very much like any number of other populist events during the Cárdenas sexenio. Delegates were often outnumbered by the representatives of federal agencies and popular organizations, who saw the congresses as ideal opportunities to educate Indians as to their own interests. Hoping to "create in the Indians a sentiment of civic solidarity, and awake in them a sense of responsibility," these agents of modernity gave presentations and showed films about health, hygiene, nutrition, modern agricultural methods, and national and international events. In some cases these efforts were profoundly paternalistic, as in the explanatory pamphlet *The Indian Problems of Mexico,* or the instructional film *Authentic Mexican Dances.*[16]

These presentations ensured that much of the time at these events would be structured by organizers, placing the delegates in a passive role and leaving them with few means of interacting with the process. They could be silent, abandon the theater, shout down the presentations, or cheer. Most of these responses were out of the question though, since the selection process had ensured that the majority of the delegates had a vested interest in supporting the proceedings. Not surprisingly then, reports indicated that the speeches made by bureaucrats and organizers were met with "Viva!" and loud applause, at times so frequent or thunderous that it drowned out the speeches. Photos taken at the Tarascan congress in Uruapan affirm this, showing the 184 delegates heartily endorsing "the work of the revolutionary government of Lázaro Cárdenas" through a show of hands. In another instance, delegates loudly cheered resolutions that gave thanks to Cárdenas for his work on behalf of indigenous Mexicans, and even drafted a special letter congratulating him for the nationalization of the oil industry.[17]

There was nothing remarkable about these speeches, as most reflected long-standing, paternalistic approaches to the Indian. The next stage of the congresses, however, was unusual. All-knowing federal officials were told to silence themselves and listen as hundreds of delegates rose and expressed their own needs in their own words.[18] A representative of the president and the DAI presided over these plenary sessions, and they were governed by parliamentary procedures, but no time limits were placed on the speeches given by the delegates. This was intended to create a context where delegates could "speak about whatever they wish, with absolute liberty, and be attentively listened to by representatives of the federal authorities."[19]

In light of a long history in which Indian voices had been silenced, organizers made free speech a central goal of these events. Each congress's *Memoria* devoted several paragraphs to affirming that Indians explained their problems and suggested potential solutions with complete frankness, and "without reticence, without fears, without suspicions, or misgivings."[20] Generally delegates were allowed to speak in whichever language they felt most comfortable. Moreover, in some cases the interference of non-Indians in the deliberations of the congresses was prohibited so that they could freely denounce the authorities, foreigners, rich mestizos, politicians, and rural teachers who abused them. Explaining that none of the organizers would be permitted to participate in the discussions (except for giving the information for which they are asked and listening to the proceedings), one article explained that these rules guaranteed that the debates and discussions were authentic, and allowed "voices which have been constrained for centuries to be lifted up."[21] These were the first times that Indians spoke in "their own voice, without third persons to disfigure and occlude the great truth of their misery."[22]

Press reports indicated that ninety-three delegates took advantage of this opportunity to speak in Ixmiquilpan.[23] Similar reports from

Tamazunchale told of fifty delegates bravely rising before the assembly to speak.[24] Describing his impression of these speakers, the anthropologist Jorge A. Vivo commented:

> The phrases of the delegates were lively. The ideas were expressed without fear. The protests were virile. The secular timidity of the Indian was shown to be a myth of the past, because all of the delegates courageously detailed their lives, their miseries, and their needs . . . in this environment of freedom.[25]

And what did they use this opportunity to say? Reports from Ixmiquilpan, Uruapan, Tamazunchale, and elsewhere indicated that delegates told of their misery, but overwhelmingly demanded roads, schools, telephones, and other modern conveniences, along with protection from their exploiters. These Indians believed in and were struggling for their own "redemption," aficionados of those things that would allow them to "march in unison with all other elements of Mexican society."[26]

Otomí leader Daniel T. Casas's speech in Uruapan epitomized this idea. In a presentation that was credited with "synthesizing, with precision, the aspirations of the Indian masses of Mexico and revealing their noble and sincere character," Casas (speaking Nahuatl) stated that the Indians "have a true desire to incorporate themselves into civilization and to be factors in the progress of our nation." Arguing that it was simply a lack of opportunities that kept his Indian brothers impoverished throughout Mexico, Casas declared that "the Indian feels the Revolution, he has a great yearning for progress and desires to help the Revolution, because in turn the Revolution benefits the Indian." The memoria of the same congress repeated this sentiment, declaring that the Indians in the region "already have a vision, more or less clear, of their responsibility in the class struggle," and that they were ready to be "converted into productive factors for their country."[27] These words affirmed Cárdenas's explicit goal for the congresses, namely that by allowing delegates to freely express themselves, they would assure their own transformation into "active members of the nationality."[28]

These speech acts however, did much more than this. In a society that had traditionally silenced indigenous speech, these were highly disruptive acts by their very nature. In both subtle and obvious ways they undermined both the state's claim to paternalistic authority over the Indian, and the deeply embedded racism of Mexican society. The very act of having a voice, and using that voice to inform the state as to real issues, invested the speaker with rationality, especially when high government officials sat for hours and listened to petitions and complaints from the delegates. It challenged onlookers to look away, assert that these were not real voices, or reconstruct their own sense of the primitive and the modern. The mouths that spoke, as evinced by the photos, nationwide radio broadcasts, the press reports, and the official record, were in fact long-silenced Indians.[29]

Delegates disrupted a series of narratives about the savage, premodern, and isolated Indian through their words and deeds. The silent, passive Indian, so often rendered as a feminized other who "patiently awaits the benefits of the Mexican Revolution," was transformed into an active agent. These individuals were literate, engaged with the state, desired progress, and had an obvious capacity for self-improvement. These delegates had transformed themselves from objects of study and social reform into genuine political subjects. It was a performance in which the Indian was simultaneously the modern citizen and a member of a clearly defined ethnic community.

On the other hand, the congresses empowered these Indians to speak for themselves, but they did not empower all Indians to speak. They could dissent, but only as long as they accepted the overarching goals of "modernization," national integration, and an expanding corporatist nation-state, values that delineated the "limits of the possible" within which they spoke. Those who expressed their desires through more aggressive means, such as boycotting and deserting schools, refusing to participate in revolutionary social programs, or violent confrontations with revolutionary authorities, were represented in very different ways. The very act of resisting or failing to recognize revolutionary authority made communities such as the Cochimis and Guaycuras of Baja California "nomads and savages." In relying on this traditional dichotomy, Indigenistas made clear distinctions between those who spoke at the congresses and the barbarians who murdered agents of the revolutionary state. The federal state created an opportunity to call for certain rights, but those who claimed those rights had to speak within the idiom created by the state. As Judith Butler argues, "there is only a taking up of tools where they lie, where the very 'taking up' is enabled by the tool lying there."[30]

The Ethnic Question

One could conclude from the preceding discussion that the goals of the congresses were similar to those of institutions like the Casa del Estudiante Indígena. Though the national community they would join was more clearly defined by class than in earlier forums, the congresses were nonetheless informed by the nationalist desire to create a common linguistic, cultural, political, and geographic brotherhood. Graciano Sánchez, Lázaro Cárdenas, and his agrarista stalwarts saw them as opportunities to connect the Indian (as proletarian) to the state. Although the congresses were organized for specific ethnic communities, Cardenistas usually treated ethnic consciousness as a transitional phenomenon, a bridge they could use to build nationalist consciousness in the Indian masses.[31]

This was an ambiguous undertaking, and would only become more so as time passed. Cardenistas believed that as young indigenous males became more aware of their ethnic brothers, they would also ultimately become more aware of their class brothers. In this they rather simplistically replaced the notion of race with ethnicity, and endeavored to build solidarity in ways that were similar to earlier incorporationist projects. Yet to many individuals working within the DAI, ethnicity and race were two very distinct concepts. Race, like class, was a broad and all-encompassing category that denied the particular in favor of sweeping images of internally undifferentiated groups, whereas ethnicity referred to the diverse linguistic, cultural, and kin communities that inhabited the countryside. As was discussed in chapter 3, during the preceding two decades the ethnographic research carried out by these individuals undermined sweeping generalizations about the Indian population, both as a racial other and as a unified set of folk practices. Their work also suggested that educational, economic, social, and cultural programs needed to be tailored to given communities, accommodating to local ethnic identities rather than eradicating them.

While it was important that they publicly assert their loyalty to the state, some organizers and delegates clearly believed the congresses could be an excellent opportunity to promote a new level of ethnic consciousness among indigenous Mexicans. They did not deny the importance of class in understanding indigenous peoples, and neither would they overtly challenge the nationalist agenda, but a significant number of the Indigenistas at the congresses clearly believed that indigenous communities needed to be treated differently than campesinos and workers. This strategy was invariably oriented to creating larger cultural affinities and power structures that could act both in concert with and against federal authorities. Even if the promotion of ethnic affinities did not challenge the nation, they nonetheless would create another layer of power directly oriented to protecting the interests of a community that defined itself as parallel to the national polity. As with programs in Soviet Russia, these efforts did not have to deny the geographical boundaries of the nation and the legitimacy of the federal government in order to make a place for ethnic autonomy. If successful, the permanent commissions created in these congresses would promote the use of Indian languages and indigenous rights, as well as focusing on the cultural autonomy (or at least the specificity) of given communities.[32]

Julio de la Fuente's comments on the Huasteca congress are instructive in this regard. At the congress he was impressed to find campesinos who, in spite of the ridicule they suffered at the hands of local mestizos, were rightly proud of their linguistic and cultural traditions. Encouraged by the sense of collective interest he saw at work, de la Fuente commented that "the pailomlábksi, or representatives, have a clear idea of the need to organize to defend themselves better." Even though few spoke more than rudimentary Spanish, they were not "backwards Indians." For their part, delegates showed their ethnic pride by requesting that federal officials offer new sources of funding for their regional dances and popular festivals.[33]

De la Fuente may have been reluctant to voice these views prior to 1939, but he found sympathetic ears among his superiors once Luis Chávez Orozco took over the DAI. Chávez Orozco provoked subtle changes in the ideology of the congresses, as populism was downplayed, and self-empowerment and ethnic specificity emphasized. In his own remarks to the Huasteca congress he made this clear. Moving the focus away from the role of corporatist organizing, he stated that "the redemption of the Indian does not have to be exclusively the work of the state, but also fundamentally the conscious action of the Indians themselves."[34] He also stressed that "the redemption of any class or social sector has always been the result of the conscious and dynamic action of that very class or sector."[35]

Chávez Orozco repeatedly used the notion of self-empowerment to clothe a pluralistic perspective by drawing on the Cardenista demand for popular power to justify his claims. His use of self-empowerment was rooted in a belief that indigenous Mexicans needed to determine their own destiny, and he promoted mechanisms to relocate power to the local level. Seizing on the fact that the congresses drew delegates from specific ethnic communities, he pressed them to develop "a perfectly clear consciousness of their racial and cultural unity."[36] Arguing that the lack of unity (and even intense conflict) among ethnically similar communities had traditionally facilitated exploitation by outsiders, he declared that delegates needed to develop specifically Indian institutions. He believed that these organizations should be created and managed by indigenous leaders drawn from the communities they represented, because mestizos and whites could not fully understand or appreciate their needs. As a concession to Cardenismo, Chávez Orozco suggested that "empowerment" would be only a means of "incorporating the Indian spirit, as valuable as it is, into the life and progress of Mexico," but his underlying intentions remained opaque.[37]

Reading the Spectacle

Given that the congresses were linked to the promise of large quantities of federal aid, it should not be surprising that in spite of all the efforts to ensure that they were forums for Indians alone, non-Indian voices entered the public records of the congresses from a variety of sources. Political bosses, merchants, labor organizers, agraristas, rural teachers, inspectors, and other bureaucrats aided in presentations, worked as organizers, and sometimes even attended congresses as delegates. Some did so out of an earnest belief that they knew how best to help the Indian, but others did so in a cynical effort to monopolize the benefits Indigenismo conferred, adopting the moniker "Indian," while it was being privileged by the state.[38]

The language requirements necessitated that teachers and DAI employees (typically procuradores) played a central role in every stage of the congresses.[39] At the local assemblies federal officials set the agenda, influenced discussions, and created the limits on the debates by ordering that "matters of a political or religious character should not be dealt with."[40] Teachers also prepared the delegates, sometimes claiming that the "insufficient grade of culture" of local Indians necessitated their intervention. Convinced of both the "chronic ignorance" of the local campesinos and committed to their mandate of "bringing the revolution into the community," many rural teachers could not have imagined allowing voices other than their own to be heard in the proceedings. The likely result was that many delegates were close allies or protégés of rural teachers.[41]

Local organizers, often politically powerful leaders, endeavored to use their connections to monopolize the events for their own political and economic ends.[42] In Ixmiquilpan, the merchant Marcos Galindo (who operated one of the largest businesses in Ixmiquilpan) and Vicente Ordoñez (in whose house Cárdenas stayed during the congress) were members of the organizing committee.[43] The committee also included Agustín Olvera, Graciano Sánchez's local henchman and later a congressional deputy.[44] Olvera had a violent reputation; his men repeatedly invaded ranchos in the region to assault, extort, and insult local campesinos, refusing to allow them to peacefully cultivate their fields. He was also implicated in the murder of the local agrarian leader Manuel Hernández in 1935, an act allegedly committed on orders from Sánchez.[45]

Sánchez did little to stop Olvera. In fact, he seems to have protected him in spite of his abuses because he was an important ally in his efforts to have his friend Javier Rojo Gómez elected governor of Hidalgo. Their efforts to mobilize support for Rojo Gómez through the congress led to accusations that they rigged the delegations to include "candidates who were accomplices of the rich and the politicians," and that the delegates were not "genuine representatives, but politicos in league with Rojo Gómez, exploiter of the proletariat."[46] These complaints were to no avail, as Rojo Gómez closely accompanied Cárdenas at the congress, and used his connection to the *mandatario* to boost his credentials. Press reports singled him out as the "candidate of the workers and campesinos of the state," and reported his prominent place in the presidential entourage. For his part, Agustín Olvera was one of the few local leaders to greet Cárdenas directly as he disembarked from his car in Ixmiquilpan.[47]

The Primer Congreso Indígena del Estado Chiapas, which took place in Las Casas, Chiapas, in May 1940 and drew eight hundred delegates from three hundred Indian communities,[48] experienced conflicts similar to those at Ixmiquilpan, though in this case the conflict was between the DAI and state-level officials. DAI officials had a tense relationship both with the state's governor, Efraín Gutiérrez, and the chief of Chiapas's Departamento de Protección Indígena, Erasto Urbina. Preparations for the congress revealed these fissures, as Urbina clashed with Ángel Corzo, the DAI's top local official, and it rapidly became clear that the congress would involve a struggle over control of the indigenous population of the state.[49] When Urbina sensed that Corzo had little respect for state authorities, he complained to Gutiérrez that the congress was being used simply to mobilize "all of the enemies of the state government." More than this, he argued that Corzo was bringing in outside mestizo agitators to dominate the proceedings, undermining his efforts to ensure that only Indians from Chiapas attended.[50]

In spite of these conflicts the congress went ahead as planned, and was hailed by Chávez Orozco and Corzo as a "transcendental success," especially because of the spirit of empowerment delegates voiced against mestizo exploiters.[51] Gutiérrez, however, was not so pleased with the work done by these DAI functionaries. He was infuriated by Chávez Orozco's failure to meet with him upon arriving for the event, and incensed by the attacks launched on him by Corzo, Chávez Orozco, Ramón G. Bonfíl, and other DAI functionaries. Responding to Chávez Orozco's claims that Chiapas had failed to help its Indians, he asserted that "the government of the state has distributed land, not only in the Indian zone, but in all of the state." He noted that he had also built roads, campaigned against alcohol, and supported education.[52] Local officials further claimed that the delegates "rejected the sterile and ill-intentioned efforts" of federal bureaucrats, who had tried to undermine their support for the state government.[53]

While the record is silent on the matter, these conflicts undoubtedly gave individual delegates the leverage to push their claims to state and federal officials in ways that would have otherwise been impossible. Subaltern Mexicans have historically pressed their claims strategically when elites were divided, as they clearly were at Las Casas. More broadly, the congresses represented an opportunity for delegates to press their interests before federal and state officials in return for the promise of loyalty. At Ixmiquilpan, for instance, Rojo Gómez imagined that the congress would be an excellent opportunity to solidify political patronage networks to secure his election as governor. However, the mandate that the congress bring in genuine representatives of Otomí communities necessitated that this process include new actors, that some of the traditional networks be enlarged, and that certain struggles be carried out by proxy. Delegates could use the promise to support Rojo Gómez to extract concessions from federal bureaucracies, which they did en masse, based on the fact that their ethnic identity gave them a right to speak and make demands.[54] Delegates may have simply been the "campesino masses," but the "Rojo–Gomista caciques" needed to deliver certain results in order to garner their support.[55]

This need underscores the fact that the congresses were not simply staged forums in which nonindigenous outsiders could promote their own interests through their indigenous clients. They were instead contested political ground where regional political elites, federal bureaucrats, local bosses, and indigenous delegates competed for the right to represent the Indian. At their worst these struggles generated considerable bitterness, as when members of the Indian community of Chinonamel, Veracruz, complained that the delegates they obediently sent to the Tamazunchale congress in March 1938 "were the object of ridicule on the part of the mestizos."[56] However, at their best these struggles produced real opportunities for indigenous activists and material benefits for their allies.

For his part, Sánchez did deliver some results. At the Otomí congress he announced efforts to introduce potable water in a number of communities in the region, and also immediately sent clothes (shirts and pants) for the delegates and their communities, where the inhabitants were reputed to be naked or dressed in rags. By December 1936 Sánchez had distributed twenty thousand pieces of clothing to the Otomí residents of the region.[57] Sánchez also announced that internados would be founded in Ixmiquilpan and Actopan, that the Comisión Nacional de Irrigacíon would begin a project in the region, that new Brigadas de Asistencia Médica y Social would be established in the area, and that agrarian petitions would be immediately resolved.[58] Delegates to later congresses were granted similar material concessions from the government, including agricultural equipment, skilled teachers, machetes, shovels, axes, hammers, and plows.[59] This was the explicit promise made at the congresses: make your needs public, speak for yourselves, and we will give you what you demand.[60]

The Petitions

The congresses offered several means for delegates to make these demands. They might be one of the lucky few who actually addressed the assemblies, gaining the attention of federal officials or others who could offer help. They could also go directly to the high-level officials who attended the congresses, presenting their needs orally in private audiences. More often however, they would use the local assemblies that preceded the congress to compose a petition to be presented to federal officials on behalf of the entire community. Thousands of delegates chose this option, making this the only definitive expression of the vast majority of participants. Speaking for the tens of thousands of indigenous Mexicans who could not attend, the petitions provided the appearance of absolutely "authentic" Indian voices.

Three hundred and three pueblos in thirty municipios presented 1,155 formal petitions and complaints in Ixmiquilpan. Smaller numbers were presented at later events, but their numbers were typically in the hundreds.[61] Most petitions were anonymous, and they had to be submitted in Spanish, which made them vulnerable to manipulation. Yet their sheer numbers and the diverse forums in which they were composed militated against any single controlling interest emerging out of them. Instead, they revealed the interests of the wide range of actors who struggled for control of these events. The net result was a cacophony of texts that provided multiple simultaneous renderings of the Indians' needs and interests.

As confirmation of their importance, the petitions presented in Ixmiquilpan and Uruapan were published as part of the memorias of these congresses. In lieu of publishing the petitions of the Tercer Congreso Regional in 1938, Sánchez opted to simultaneously broadcast the demands made by the delegates across the country by short- and long-wave radio, giving the first truly national forum to indigenous voices.[62] Explaining his decision, he claimed that as a whole the petitions presented in Tamazunchale raised identical points to those made in Ixmiquilpan and Uruapan, in that they asked for land grants, restitution, amplification, agricultural machinery, schools, infrastructural improvements, and the provision of water to villages.[63] In affirming the just nature of these petitions and broadcasting them across Mexico, Sánchez both revealed a class of progressive Indians and suggested that the simple resolution of these claims was tantamount to the resolution of the Indian question.[64]

Demanding Admission to the National Community

In July 1936, just two months before the Ixmiquilpan congress, residents of the Otomí village of El Gundhó, in the municipality of Ixmiquilpan, pleaded with the president to reopen a school that had been closed because of low attendance and nonexistent community support.

> We are campesinos, who will help us? Citizen President of the Republic, General Lázaro Cárdenas, Sir: we have aspirations to leave the state of intellectual backwardness in which we find ourselves. Perhaps because we are adults, it will not be easy for us to acquire the indispensable knowledge that people use for living well, eating well, and acquiring the resources that we need to improve the environment in which we live, but even though it is impossible for us, we desire it for our children. Tomorrow, they will be the future of our beloved nation, which will be created through the school.[65]

Four years later, when he gave "voice to the word" at the PCII, Otomí delegate Edmundo Domínguez took a different tone, but made very similar claims. Declaring that after centuries of exploitation and misery, he could not trust politicians and the promises they made, Domínguez bemoaned:

> We want real things, promises fulfilled. We are tired of sending our complaints and requests to one department or another, and getting nothing. . . . We need good houses with more than one room, so that we need not sleep with the dogs, chickens, and other small animals. . . . We believe these conditions are the reason for our many illnesses. . . . We want more water wells and more canals to irrigate our lands, for if we do not have water our small herd of sheep which provides the wool for making our clothes will die. . . . We want the promises made to us this time to be kept. We are dedicated to helping the government, but now we do not want words and promises. We want the government to give us effective help with schools, more

cooperative stores, plows for our lands, canals to irrigate them, and, in the end, we want the means to resolve our own problems so that we can improve our lives.[66]

His words were heavy with exasperation, but as with the residents of El Gundhó, the revolutionary state had little to fear from Domínguez. He wanted programs that officials had already promised, and he wanted an end to empty promises. Framed more as a right than a privilege, these were just the types of demands that Cárdenas wanted to fulfill. In this, they were very much like the myriad requests for schools, teachers, and associated resources made in the congresses.[67]

The organizers of the congresses had no doubt about the meaning of these claims and the petitions that accompanied them. Directed to a variety of state agencies, including the DAI, the SEP, the Departamento Agrario, the Secretaría de Gobernación, the Secretaría de Defensa Nacional, the Secretaría de la Economía Nacional, the Secretaría de Comunicaciones y Obras Públicas, and the Departamento de Salubridad Pública,[68] their contents were summed up as a series of demands for "social, cultural, and economic improvements."[69] While they established that delegates were assertive and unwilling to trust the promises of federal officials, they also created an image of an Indian who was engaged in a proactive relationship with the revolutionary state, often demanding the icons of progress that Cardenistas loved so dearly.

Though invariably strategic and often critical of the inaction of past administrations, these kinds of petitions invited the federal government to establish its authority in the community. Because of the absence of designated authorship, they also suggested that the entire community was behind the request.[70] Many called for specific programs administered by the Departamento de Salubridad Pública, including aid in procuring potable water, doctors, veterinarians, nurses, and sanitary brigades for improving hygiene. Petitioners also repeatedly noted the inadequacy of federal efforts in alleviating infant illness and mortality, the lack of medicine, and the failure of past administrations to provide treatments for specific illnesses.[71]

The petitions that addressed economic questions often expressed similar desires. A large number called for projects that would create national markets and facilitate development in Indian regions.[72] Requests for roads, bridges, the dredging of rivers, electricity, telegraph lines, and telephone lines were all understood as part of a desire to integrate Indian regions into the national economy and promote development.[73] Petitioners requested specific material aid, increased credit opportunities, and agricultural aid from the Banco Nacional de Crédito Agrícola and Banco Ejidal.[74] Delegates likewise showed their desire to utilize the institutions of the Cardenista state to improve their material lives in their requests for federally supported land and forest cooperatives, price supports and subsidies, and enforcement of the minimum wage. Many included specific requests for tools like windmills and plows, to "increase our industries." In these requests petitioners often cited the symbolic and legislative programs of the Revolution, calling for action from the federal government under Article 27 of the 1917 Constitution or the Agrarian Code.[75]

Federal officials were pleased by these requests, taking them as confirmation of a modernizing spirit in the Indian.[76] They similarly believed that educational demands were intimately tied to a desire on the part of Indian communities to be a part of the modern nation. As José Hernández Mota (the procurador assigned to San Luis Potosí) stated at the Tamazunchale congress, "there exists among the Indians a manifest desire for progress, made patent by the numerous requests for schools."[77] These petitions commonly included requests for the construction of a number of different kinds of schools, the appointment of teachers, money for educational materials, scholarships for students, desks and tables, gas lamps, typewriters, radios, sewing machines, sporting equipment, and libraries.[78]

Like those petitions focusing on health care, these requests had a common sense quality, and were perhaps most noteworthy for the desires for the benefits of the modern Mexican state that they expressed. This is even more evident in those educationally oriented petitions that contain a nationalist component. For example, the village of El Guayabal asked for "an album of portraits of national heroes, a gasoline lamp, the national flag, and a watch for use in the school."[79] Others also requested books of national heroes. Combining a desire for material benefits and symbolic markers of the national culture, these petitioners were ideal proto-citizens.

The total absence of any petitions that defended Catholic institutions and beliefs would have also pleased Cardenistas. Numerous requests called for the federal government to intervene in struggles between "backwards" and "progressive" elements in the community, and others asked federal authorities to grant exemptions from cargo contributions for "profane fiestas."[80] Additionally, specific symbols of the Catholic past were aggressively attacked. At Uruapan the villages of Patamban and San José de Gracia asked "that the chapel of San José be ceded to the Indians for use as a granary, in view of the withdrawal of the (Roman Catholic) sect." Other attacks included a request that "the church of Chilchota be ceded for establishing in its place the offices of the Comisario" and a request from San Jeronimo Purenchecuaro for a clock to be put into the local church tower.[81] Represented as the unmitigated demands of Indian communities, these requests left no doubt as to the revolutionary credentials of the solicitants. They were, of course, extremely divisive issues in the communities from whence they came.[82]

This is one of the interpretive challenges facing any reading of the petitions. Anonymity created a unified voice, but it also allowed non-Indian voices to play a powerful role in requesting federal largesse under the guise of being Indian. Requests for nationalist icons (flags, portraits of national heroes) were probably initiated by rural educators, as were the petitions that called for increases in the salaries of rural teachers. Similar assumptions could be made of the requests that teachers be given arms for their personal defense. On the other hand, expressions of anticlericalism may not have been simply manipulations by teachers and other officials. Anticlericalism, the desecration of sacred objects and the closing of churches, had long been a feature of local agrarian struggles in indigenous communities. Some factions adopted agrarian and anticlerical beliefs out of convenience, and others out of conviction, but in any event these expressions offered marginal members of communities opportunities to make strategic alliances with federal and state officials, especially in regions that had been centers of cristero violence during the late 1920s.[83]

As with all petitions, one can never be sure of the reasons that members of the community signed, but we tell an incomplete story if we focus on outright resistance to the exclusion of those who selectively supported federal programs. Indigenous Mexicans have a long tradition of strategically adopting the language of power in order to promote their interests, and the revolutionary period was replete with examples of communities that cooperated with officials in return for help in pursuing land and other claims. This suggests that the inclusion of teachers' demands in the petitions may have reflected an accommodation between the community and its teachers rather than outright manipulation. Thus, rather than dismissing these demands, we would be wise to recall the deep divisions in these communities, and interpret them as the demands of a faction that wanted to claim the popular voice. They may have been a minority, but they parlayed their willingness to align with the revolutionary state into new forms of authority.[84]

Keeping the State at Bay

In their letter to Cárdenas in July 1936, the residents of El Gundhó ended on a note that departed from the supplicating tone of most of the text. Noting that most of the teachers they had seen in their school were poor or unable to live under the conditions they faced, they asked that Cárdenas name Camerino Gonzaga, a resident of the nearby village of Remedios, as director of the school. They wanted him because "beyond having the sufficient capabilities for the job, (he) is a person who is admired, and who understands poverty well enough to be the type of effective educator our communities demand."[85] In specifically designating Camerino Gonzaga, they chose to blend an effort to exercise power over personnel into their request for a school. Gonzaga was probably a relative or friend of one of the village authorities, but he was also from a small Otomí community in the same municipality, was familiar with local customs and culture, and likely spoke Otomí. All of this suggested that he could create a school that met their needs.[86]

The request for Gonzaga is suggestive of the ways that local authorities embedded competing claims in their petitions to the congresses. They requested that their communities benefit from federal programs, but simultaneously demanded that power, as much as possible, remain localized. Delegates repeatedly favored solutions that, while legitimizing federal authority, carved out spaces for local self-determination under the umbrella of federal authority. Demands for autonomy, conflicts with local elites, and internal political struggles were often woven into the petitions, even when they were phrased in a language that outwardly affirmed the goals of the revolutionary state. Did Edmundo Domínguez not ask for the "means to resolve our own problems" even as he demanded aid?

Even when they seemed to support national integration, petitioners did not envision the elimination of local autonomy, especially when it came to control of local resources. Delegates made more requests for concessions in local land and water conflicts than any other issue. A large number requested the establishment, improvement, or demarcation of the boundaries of ejidos. These requests included the following: access to and control of timber and water resources, reductions in land taxes, and the donation of animals and equipment. Illustrative of these concerns, the Ixmiquilpan congress saw thirty-eight requests for land grants, fourteen for restitution, and thirty-five for enlargement of existing ejidal parcels. "Definite possession," along with "immediate resolution" of these conflicts was a regular feature of these petitions, demonstrating a clear desire on the part of petitioners to make themselves the arbiters of their own destiny.[87]

Some requests demanded a more powerful role for local leaders in the administration of federal programs. Under a discussion called "the economic problems of the Otomís and ways of resolving them," delegates to the Ixmiquilpan congress passed a number of resolutions that did this. They called for educational programs that promoted Otomí popular culture, asked for special schools for their children, demanded that their teachers speak Otomí, and that they be well trained and paid. These resolutions were echoed in other congresses, where delegates demanded that teachers learn local dialects, that authorities in Indian villages be Indians, and that communities be allowed to name their leaders without outside interference.[88]

Delegates also frequently demanded benefits that in later decades would be associated with multiculturalism. Beyond articulating a right to self-representation and education in indigenous languages, they demanded more local control over resources like land, water, and forests, and that certain programs be reserved for indigenous youths exclusively. They also repeatedly demanded the removal of corrupt officials and the dispossession of "outsiders." They asked that educational reforms consider local needs, that teachers be "qualified," and that unpopular or unqualified teachers be removed. Furthermore, they requested guarantees of continued support from the government, demonstrating their sophisticated understanding of the regular modus operandi of postrevolutionary governments. Selective engagement was the rule.[89]

Cardenismo emphasized the right to self-representation, particularly when it came to condemning corrupt and abusive officials, and during this era indigenous leaders took advantage of this opening to attack officials for inaction, oppression, drunkenness, and even incivility.[90] The congresses became an important forum for such attacks, as petitions often targeted specific individuals for their unfair treatment of Indians, calling for action against unpopular or abusive officials, removal of local officials who sided with *hacendados* against Indian groups, and protection from "rural guards," "white guards," and *pistoleros*. Several also requested changes in judicial, agrarian, and ejidal authorities, and guarantees of security. One of the most detailed examples of these requests comes from the Ixmiquilpan congress. At this event specific complaints were leveled against twenty-eight rural teachers, ten municipal authorities, seven local deputies, three agrarian authorities, four white guards, and twenty-four others.[91]

Abuse by hacendados, unfair taxes and rents, and other arbitrary impositions of authority also generated numerous complaints. These included requests for the suppression of the *alcabalas*, other "inhumane impositions," and exemptions from ejidal contributions. Some also sought the means to force local authorities to guarantee the personal safety of community members "so that they can dedicate themselves to their work," or asked for the resolution of disputes and guarantees against oppression, land takeovers, and other forms of abuse. In some cases they also asked for new titles or copies of the original land titles from the AGN, and official declarations renouncing illegal or unfair land takeovers.[92]

Ironically, many of these types of petitions requested an intensification of federal power as a means of securing liberty. Appeals for arms for local defense, detachments of the federal army, and the appointment of procuradores and judges all called for the rule of law in regions where federal authorities were spread too thin. These appeals created the impression that far from resisting the imposition of federal authority in indigenous regions, delegates saw the state as the only effective mechanism for securing justice in their communities. It was a reluctant concession, as many petitioners preferred obtaining the means whereby they could defend themselves, but in lieu of arms for their own defense they asked that federal authorities undertake this responsibility, affirming the national state as the final arbiter of local conflicts.[93]

Such was clearly the case when Eliseo Rosas, secretary of the Comisión Permanente del Congreso Regional Tarasco, sent a series of requests to Cárdenas in November 1938. Always claiming that he spoke for the majority of the inhabitants in the region, Rosas's petition on behalf of Uruapan and the surrounding sierra called for a number of things that would increase the authority of the federal state in Tarascan communities and integrate those communities more effectively in the national communities. Requests for potable water, a Centro de Higiene in Charapan, the extension of telephone and mail service in the region, and increased agricultural credit all affirm this desire, as did Rosas's specific requests regarding the extension of the road system in the region. He claimed that "the resolution of the project for the national highway is urgent for the majority of Indian communities . . . it would be of great utility for the agricultural and touristic development of the region."

Yet Rosas also embedded some clearly local concerns in the petition, suggesting that integration to the national community would not cede total control to the state. In his commentary on the educational needs of the region, he requested that Cárdenas provide teachers who possessed the "sense of responsibility needed to discharge their duties." Similarly, Rosas noted that definitive title to forest resources and the technical means of exploiting them had yet to be provided, and claimed that "the economic tranquillity of the Indian communities of the sierra depends on possession of their own forests, and the utilization of this wealth."[94] Rosas thus blended demands that affirmed local control over forest and land resources and local oversight of educational institutions with others that expressed a desire to be part of the national community.

The Indian and the Indigenista

The desires expressed by delegates became even more opaque when, rather than presenting individual petitions, they composed a single synthetic petition to present to federal officials. This was the case in the Primer Congreso de la Raza Chontal, which took place in Villahermosa, Tabasco, in December 1939. At the Chontal congress, 140 representatives of Chontal, Zoque, and Zotzil communities produced a collective petition that fused all voices into one. Victor Zapata Frías, a mestizo merchant who lived in Villahermosa, played a prominent role in the congress as the representative of the Cooperativas de Sombreros y Petates, and tried to use his role to act as the intermediary for the Indians in the region. Not surprisingly then, some of the very specific requests made at the congress reflected his interests. The petition included requests for improvements in local infrastructures and industries (including telephones), teachers and machines for making sombreros, the dredging of local rivers, and a concession from PEMEX to move goods to market along their rail line.[95]

Another key organizer, a teacher named Guadalupe Concha who was an expert in sewing, also saw her interests forwarded by the congress. Federal officials immediately granted sewing machines for making sombreros to five communities, and gave her a stipend to travel to these communities and teach people to use them. A further two thousand pesos was granted for purchasing more sombrero-making machines, along with three hundred plows to use in Tabascan communities, and a gas lamp for each school. In granting these concessions, federal officials were able to please the delegates from the communities that would benefit from the machines, the teacher who was able to expand her work, and merchants like Zapata Frías who could expand their businesses in the process.[96]

These results united the "Indian" and the "Indigenista" inextricably, but it would be a mistake to suggest that they eliminated indigenous voices from the petition. At Villahermosa, Concha and Zapata Frías's demands were mixed with a series of other demands that did not reflect their concerns. There were several requests for hygiene centers, maternity and infant care centers, potable water, sports equipment, ejidal loans, and "definite possession" and "immediate demarcation" of ejidos for Tabascan ejidatarios.[97] More importantly, delegates demanded an Escuela Vocacional de Agricultura para Indígenas in Tabasco to serve the Chontales, Zoques, and Zotziles exclusively, and the reorganization of the Escuela Regional Campesina in Jalpa de Méndez. They also asked that scholarships reflect the cost of living in Tabasco, and that "Indians be given preference in the granting of scholarships." Further requests asked that the land pertaining to the existing agricultural school in the region be reduced to thirty hectares so that it did not prejudice the interests of local ejidatarios, that the SEP give special preference to Indian regions for construction of "good schools," and that those schools be granted "the complete complement of school materials and capable teachers who will teach them in their own language."[98] None of these concerns pertained directly to economic development. Rather, they suggest that petitioners wanted a certain amount of control over the implementation of revolutionary programs.

Though it is impossible to know with certainty, it seems likely that the assemblies that preceded the regional congresses focused mostly on local concerns, as is reflected in the petitions that can be directly attributed to Indian delegates. This is not to suggest that delegates did not have a larger vision of their problems, but rather that they prioritized specific local concerns when given an opportunity to address the state. This phenomena was placed in particularly high relief at the Tercer Congreso Regional, where delegates had the advantage of being able to make special appeals to Ignacio García Tellez, the Secretario de Gobernación, who attended the congress on Cárdenas's behalf. Over two days, García Tellez received petitions from ejidatarios and residents from twenty-five communities in the region. While officials at the congress made long presentations on alcoholism, women's rights, the need for teachers, hygiene, and credit, the campesinos who spoke to García Tellez echoed only some of these concerns. They made nineteen requests related specifically to land and water issues, generally for delineation and amplification of ejidos, resolution of conflicts over land (one which had been pending for eight years), irrigation, regulation of the rents, and animal use on common lands. They made twelve requests related to education, only three of which actually requested teachers, while the others requested construction, repairs, and school materials. A further nine requests centered on the security of Indian communities, requesting arms for defense, and for guarantees that assassins would be eradicated and communities be allowed to live in peace. Four requests for loans and bank credit were made. Further requests included several for the termination of fees at the civil registry (three), the suppression of municipal fines, and end to forced work details and other fees (such as coffee exportation fees) (four), requests for "Indian authorities" and the removal of outside authorities (three), and one request for the creation of a peasants union. Contrary to Graciano Sánchez's claim that delegates demanded programs attacking "alcoholism and other vices," not a single request to García Tellez asked for the regulation of alcohol, or attacked the church. There was talk in Tamazunchale that all of the homicides committed in the area were committed by drunken campesinos, but this nonetheless did not make forced sobriety a popular demand.[99]

As happened on several other occasions, some of these indigenous delegates were also participants in another congress that took place in

Tamazunchale that month, the Primer Centro de Educación Popular.[100] Beyond the claim that both represented indigenous interests, the two congresses identified the key concerns of the Indian community in strikingly different fashions. Not surprisingly, delegates to the Primer Centro defined the region's social problems in terms of educational deficiencies, and called for the "culturization of the working masses."[101] Rural teachers at the congress, such as Professor Rubén Rodríguez Lozano, Director of Federal Education in the region, prioritized local needs in the following order: teachers needed help in their educational mission, taxes on alcohol had to be raised so as to place it out of the economic reach of the working classes, the regulation of churches had to be completed, alcabalas had to be eliminated, and local authorities had to be forced to minimize fees charged to small holders of livestock, lands, and agricultural fields.[102]

Rodríguez Lozano betrayed his didactic approach to these issues by folding his own concerns into popular demands in a highly incongruous way.[103] There is no evidence that local groups, whether agraristas or fanatics, ever prioritized antialcohol campaigns, and suggestions that alcohol be taxed out of the reach of workers smacked of paternalism.[104] Moreover, the petitions he presented were rooted in a "class"-based concept of Mexico's social problems, and focused on the need to elevate peasant consciousness.[105] This vision was reiterated by another teacher at the congress, Fernando Castellanos, who assured Cárdenas that "throughout our sessions one could see a united and constant endorsement for the constructive and class-based politics of your government." His petition also created a "united" voice, merging all the demands made at the congress, from calls for higher salaries for teachers to arms for local ejidatarios, into one petition. This was similar to the results of the Chontal and a few other congresses, where delegates "unanimously" endorsed a range of federal programs, from federal labor legislation to prohibitions on the fabrication and sale of alcohol.[106]

In this, Rodríguez Lozano and Castellanos were not unlike a host of rural teachers, engineers, military officers, and bureaucrats, who used their power as literate interlocutors to mix their own interests into the demands of indigenous activists. It was an uneasy relationship, open to abuse. As villagers pressed their thumbprints to petitions, most could not have known with certainty what those petitions requested. It was not, however, simply a manipulative relationship. Most had to include some popular demands in their requests, a fact that is confirmed by the overlapping demands that were evident even in Tamazunchale and Villahermosa.[107]

Placing the Congresses in Context

The weaving of popular and elite agendas in the indígena congresses offers a glimpse of the opportunities created for popular groups under the umbrella of Cardenismo. The important role of teachers and other federal officials might confirm the arguments of those who view Cardenismo as ephemeral, imposed from above, and characterized by political manipulation.[108] Yet the congresses were much more than this. The congresses acted as forums in which federal and local officials, merchants and teachers, the leaders of popular organizations, and the indigenous delegates themselves competed over resources, control of federal largesse, and the right to represent key political constituencies. As such, the congresses may be best understood as multivocal public spectacles, moments of "paper-thin" hegemony, where members of subaltern groups "adopt(ed) the ideological terms of reference of the elite" in order to gain a relative degree of privilege.[109] While it is true that agents of the state created the terrain for these events, the process through which they came to do this was part of a long history of contestation, as were the forums themselves. Indigenous actors could not control the forum, but they influenced the congresses and their outcomes in important ways. They ultimately produced a state whose influence was very uneven, because the results of these negotiations varied from place to place, and were invariably linked to local histories, the strengths of local institutions, and geographic, cultural, and economic factors.[110]

In this sense, the congresses were integral to the process through which federal officials endeavored to create what William Roseberry referred to as a "common discursive framework," the legitimate procedures whereby popular groups express both consent and dissent.[111] In local assemblies—forums marked both by democratic procedure and federal oversight—a new generation of young men became representatives of their communities. Even where the forums were a sham, the act of assuming the role of representative of the community before the state had an impact on the delegates' position within the community. Cardenismo empowered these actors because they were social leaders, a category based in part on a notion of democratic representation, but more importantly on the modern values of the leader. It emphasized bilingualism and biculturalism, and a desire to destabilize traditional sources of power.

The Cardenista state promised protection against exploiters and the material benefits of modernity, but in return required some degree of political allegiance. In order to ensure the success of the program, the men empowered in these forums needed to be able to deliver loyalty, or at least control in their home communities. They needed to be authentic: they had to "be Indian." They had to speak Indian languages, wear Indian garb, and have clear connection to the tillers of the soil. They also needed to be modern, a category they could enter simply through their participation in the congresses. The combination of these attributes was an act of signification—they could be both Indian and modern, possessors of the country's past and subjects capable of exercising rights in a modern political framework.[112]

The limited evidence that remains from these congresses suggests that many of the men who came before the state in these forums were the very same individuals who in later decades acted as mediators between federal and local power. The names of several men who went on to become powerful caciques are found among those that survive from the Ixmiquilpan congress.[113] Similarly, delegates at the Las Casas congress included the young followers of Erasto Urbina, who was head of the Departamento de Protección Indígena in Chiapas during the late 1930s. In the years after the congress these young men slowly ascended to positions of power in their communities. Their power was enhanced by the department's 1939 decision to deal only with bilingual leaders, and they ultimately became the key brokers between their communities and the state. Having started as scribes, by the early 1940s they were union officials, the heads of agrarian communities, leaders of local branches of the PRI, and representatives to the CNC.[114]

Perhaps no one used these forums more effectively than Ignacio León, who attended the Casa, taught in an internado, and presided over Tarahumara congresses in 1940, 1944, and 1945. Over two decades León and fellow Casa alumnus Patricio Jaris became key intermediaries between their communities and the state, using the congresses and other forums to promote their interests in ways that were previously impossible. They repeatedly supported democratic processes at the village level through their positions, and demanded that each community in the Sierra Tarahumara be allowed to elect its authorities without outside interference. They also insisted that Tarahumara be taught in schools, from the primary level to the normal school. Their work in the internado was particularly notable, where in spite of budget crises, epidemics, water shortages, and generally unhealthy conditions, they planted an orchard with six hundred trees, had a productive workshop, and gave all students a musical and military education.[115]

León and other delegates could be credited with subtly recasting the terms of Indian domination in the congresses, transforming themselves, their communities, and ultimately the state in the process. Yet we must also guard against the temptation to celebrate their strategic manipulations of the language of Indigenismo as entirely successful. The actors who spoke at the congresses, like the indigenous activists who petitioned federal officials throughout the country during these years, did so from an extremely disadvantaged position. Likewise, the sympathetic federal officials who responded to their demands were constrained by a series of factors that often undermined all efforts at reform. In order to illuminate these challenges, and the burdens that local activists often faced, this chapter ends with the story of the struggle between Pablo Baez and Cirilo Jacinto, representatives of the Indian community of Huatlatlauca, Puebla, and Miguel, Manlovio, and Modesto López Alonso, the local strongmen.

As the official representatives of the community of Huatlatlauca (Pablo Baez was also the president of the comité ejecutivo of a ranchería in the municipality), Baez and Jacinto were like many of the young men who attended the congresses during these years. Literate, educated in certain legal questions, and eager to mobilize the federal state to defend their interests, these young men spent several years trying to displace the López Alonsos, who operated with the protection of state officials. At various times they accused the López Alonsos of employing seventy-nine gunmen to terrorize their community, demanding arbitrary contributions from all Indians, charging excessive fees in the civil registry and for the services of priests, manipulating ejidal parcels, murdering agrarian authorities, and preventing ejidatarios from working their land. "Their acts," claimed Baez and Jacinto, "contravene an order and a presidential resolution that (the land) is our right and inalienable."[116] In 1938, after being forced to flee their homes and branded as thieves, they demanded justice entirely in the revolutionary idiom of constitutional rights and privileges.[117]

Baez and Jacinto repeatedly wrote to the DAI and Cárdenas, provided documentation of the abuses of the López Alonso brothers, and even visited Cárdenas and Graciano Sánchez personally. However, their efforts yielded nothing. Lamenting in April 1939 that their petitions to the DAI and Departamento Agrario had seen no results, they complained that in spite of personal assurances from Cárdenas, "disgracefully, professor Sánchez did not comply with your orders, Mr. President, and the situation in which we find ourselves is the same as we have denounced in the past."[118] Increasingly desperate, they mobilized the language of citizenship and class by citing specific constitutional protections to which they were entitled, but they also appealed to Cárdenas as a patron by noting his "history of working for the social revindication of all the disinherited classes of our beloved Mexico."[119]

Cárdenas was not immune to these demands. Not only did he visit with Baez and Jacinto, he pressed a series of agencies into action, and repeatedly asked state officials to resolve the situation favorably. In this, he responded to Baez and Jacinto much like he had responded to congress delegates; when they shrouded their demands in the language of revolutionary modernity, he endeavored to use the resources of the state to meet those demands. However, a demand for plows, radios, and other material concessions was ultimately much easier to fulfill than demands for the extension of federal authority into local conflicts. As had happened in Ciudad Las Casas, Ixmiquilpan, and other congresses, local power brokers were often too powerful for the procuradores and other representatives of the Cardenista state to overcome.

There is no question that Cárdenas wanted to supplant these traditional sources of exploitation, but his ability to do this was limited both by the resources of the state and the need to avoid further civil unrest. In the case of Huatlatlauca, the local political boss, Refugio Ortega, repeatedly contradicted Jacinto's and Baez's claims, declaring that the region was in peace.[120] More than this, the governor of Puebla, Maximo Avila Camacho, was simply too powerful to force into an accord with Jacinto and Baez. In response to Cárdenas's specific request that they be allowed to live unmolested in their communities, he refused. Claiming that they were simply fugitives trying to elude justice for crimes they committed in 1934, he declined to meet any of their demands.[121]

It was here that Cardenismo met its limits in the starkest terms. Cárdenas could plead with Avila Camacho, he could write letters to officials in a variety of agencies, but his power to take action on the ground was always limited by his ability to gain the compliance of local officials. In this case, Cárdenas was involved in a struggle with a powerful conservative family, and he lacked the political capital to force them to comply with his orders. As Cárdenas's later acquiescence to the choice of Manuel Avila Camacho as his successor suggests, he had to tread very carefully in his efforts to supplant traditional power blocs. In some cases, when the congresses elevated new authorities to positions of power in indigenous communities, he was able to force changes, if only in limited ways. In the case of Baez and Jacinto, there was nothing he could do. The failures of Jacinto and Baez thus revealed the limits inherent to the revolutionary state, and in the project of hegemony itself. Local leaders could adopt the revolutionary idiom, but absent mechanisms that could enforce Cardenista efforts, the use of that language was at best futile, and at worst fatal.

5 Indigenismo in the Shadow

Tata Lázaro, do you remember the hospitals, the schools, and the lands that you gave us? The hospitals are now cantinas, the schools are occupied by soldiers, the lands belong to the newly rich.—Members of the Yaqui Council speaking to Lázaro Cárdenas, after 1941[1]

If the marriage of social science and populist politics seen in the regional congresses represented a triumph for revolutionary Indigenismo, many of the organizers nonetheless feared that the delegates would get a meal, a new shirt, and maybe a plow, but little else. Even worse, delegates might simply facilitate their own exploitation by tying themselves more closely to a fickle state. Indigenistas needed a substantial commitment to the work begun at the congresses, a mechanism that could ensure that at least some of their successes would be preserved. Even better, if they could take the progress made at one of the events and expand it with the cooperation of a variety of federal agencies, they might provide a model for the revindication of Mexico's indigenous peoples.

It was with this in mind that the DAI founded the Comisión Intersecretarial de Estudio y Resolución de los Problemas Social del Valle de Mezquital (Hidalgo), based in Ixmiquilpan, in early 1937. Given the well-known indolence of the population, the Valle de Mezquital was a risky selection, but its proximity to Mexico City and its symbolic importance as the site of the first congress made it a propitious choice. The Comisión would focus on the municipios de Ixmiquilpan, Actopan, Tasquillo, and Santa María Tepeji, overseeing a region that comprised approximately thirty-five hundred square kilometers, with a population of about thirty-six thousand Otomí. Unlike the more famous Yaqui and Mayan land grants, it would rely not on grand gestures and political rallies, but would instead be based on a methodical effort to integrate economic planning, ethnographic data, and egalitarian reforms into a massive effort to transform the lives of the valley's residents. It would survive in one form or another for almost two decades, as succeeding generations of experts endeavored to transform the lifestyles of residents of the valley. Its experience was also a microcosm of the larger demise of revolutionary Indigenismo. Born of a promise made on a late September day in 1936, the Comisión would begin with great optimism and activism, and end in a quiet death as cronyism, penury, and failures to understand local conditions undermined its efforts.[2]

A Laboratory of Revolution

Sixteen different federal and state agencies invested $1.25 million [all amounts in pesos] in the Valle de Mezquital between 1937 and 1939, not including their own bureaucratic and personnel costs. These investments ranged from minor efforts to organize cooperatives and study the prevailing social and economic conditions in the valley, to large-scale investments by the Banco de Crédito Ejidal and massive medical programs that vaccinated most of the inhabitants. The Comisión itself was originally made up only of officials from twenty federal and state agencies, but by 1939 representatives of campesino and Indian organizations in the valley, including delegates from the Comisión Permanente del Congreso Indígena Otomí, were also given a voice. Each member, regardless of their origin, had "voice and vote on every issue" in the meetings, which were held every fifteen days.[3]

The initial efforts of the Comisión began in December 1936, as the Departamento Agrario, Banco Ejidal, Comisión Nacional de Irrigación, Departamento de Trabajo, Departamento de Educación Física, Departamento de Salubridad Pública, and Departamento Forestal undertook projects in the valley. Simultaneously, a Comisión de Penetración Cultural was installed in the municipal offices in Ixmiquilpan, staffed by experts in textiles, obstetrics, and sewing, and charged with "teaching all of the Indian women how to dress, as they live completely naked."[4] Land expropriations got underway by February 1937, supplemented with funds from the Banco Ejidal for intensifying cultivation, developing agricultural species that would be well suited to the region, expanding livestock raising, and improving local industries. Construction on a new internado in Orizabita also began in January 1937.[5]

By 1939, Luis Chávez Orozco, president of the Comisión, reported significant progress on indigenous interests in the valley. Investigators were exploring the possibilities of taxing pulque, the means for stimulating *ixtle* cultivation and sombrero production, and the ideal forms of agriculture in the valley. The Secretaría de Defensa Nacional reported the construction of barracks for local defense, and efforts to prepare the Otomís in the valley for military service. Other federal agencies had established consumption and production cooperatives, along with sanitation, immunization, and disinfection (of seeds and people) campaigns. Land claims had been resolved, and banking agencies had lent $259,000 to producers in the region. Fruit trees had also been provided for cultivators in the valley, along with irrigation and potable water. SEP officials reported that they had constructed several new schools, implemented health care programs, distributed clothes and provisions, and even organized trips to Mexico City for local children. In addition to these accomplishments, federal and state agencies had constructed roads and telephone lines, and improved infrastructures throughout the region (for full details, see Appendix B).[6]

Evaluating its efforts in the valley at the PCII in 1940, the Comisión Nacional de Irrigación declared them an unprecedented success, going so far as to claim that the most significant differences between barbarism and civilization in the valley were tied to the presence of irrigation systems. Whereas in nonirrigated regions the Indians lived like "beasts," in the irrigated areas the residents were clothed, lived in stable families, and worked bountiful fields. Their homes were larger, alcoholism had declined, children went to school, and the way of life was increasingly modern. Arguing that the irrigated region was now even producing its own distinct physiognomy, the presentation stated that "among them, one can observe living, intelligent eyes, that announce the awakening of this poor race that has been dejected and enslaved since the Aztecs." The presentation claimed that twenty thousand Indians had benefited from the Comisión's work, and the value of agricultural production had increased by over eight million pesos.[7]

These promising results were based on a relatively simple program. Though they employed a bevy of experts in the valley, for the most part the Comisión simply oversaw a massive infusion of aid and the administration of a host of already existing revolutionary programs.[8] It had not worked in Carapan nearly a decade earlier, however, and neither would it work in the Valle de Mezquital. As happened in many other regions, the promise of agrarian reform, education, and economic emancipation proved illusory. Local elites corrupted the process by ensuring that the reform often did not benefit those most in need. Lands proved inadequate or the reform lacked the long-term infrastructural assistance that was needed. Irrigation did in fact benefit some, but most were the dubious beneficiaries of canals filled from Mexico City's *aguas negras*, poisoning residents even as they irrigated their fields.[9] Beyond these failings, the programs administered through the Comisión were often short-sighted or ill-suited to local needs, and locals themselves often neither wanted nor could they make sense of federal largesse. Typical of these failures, only six local residents took advantage of the prenuptial exams offered by Salubridad Pública, a practice that eugenicists saw as essential to public health, but that local residents likely found intrusive and offensive. Stifled by impenetrable barriers between residents of the valley and their erstwhile benefactors, many of the programs undertaken by the Comisión proved ephemeral.[10]

In just two years the work of the Comisión was transformed from an optimistic undertaking into a troubling series of failures. After an immediate jump in agricultural production during 1937, in each succeeding year a declining number of ejidatarios cultivated less and less land, prompting new investigations into alternative forms of agriculture and economic development.[11] Similarly, in spite of massive investments in health care and education, a hospital for the region had yet to be built in late 1939, and residents of many communities in the municipality of Ixmiquilpan continued to complain that their schools remained closed or lacked adequate teachers.[12] The projects undertaken in the internados and cooperatives faced severe difficulties and even capital shortages, leading to scathing criticisms that the Comisión benefited only demagogues and tourists. One group of critics claimed that the wool textile cooperative in El Nith taught workers a foreign technique that was inferior to the one used by Indians, and even used wool of French provenance when perfectly good material was available locally. They also complained that too few workers were employed in El Nith to improve the local economy, and that their salaries were lower than factory-employed textile workers. Worse still, the thousands of pesos invested in the cooperative had not gone to Indians, Indians did not benefit from the new housing and other construction, and efforts to promote the use of ixtle in local weavings did not even use local materials, but ixtle imported from San Luis Potosí.[13]

Assessing this work during the early 1940s, Manuel Gamio lamented that in spite of over a decade of work, most people in the region remained "in the same low biological, economic, and cultural level." Even more seriously, other critics noted that most of the thirty thousand hectares of newly irrigated land in the valley had not gone to Otomí residents, but to mestizos or white landowners. Otomí ejidatarios had even been displaced from irrigated land. As a result of these failures, the Comisión was reorganized into the Comité Coordinador del Valle de Mezquital in 1943, and given the mandate to provide nineteen thousand hectares of newly irrigated land to fifteen thousand Otomís. Though the new project sought to empower Indians, there were no campesino or Indian representatives on the committee, which by 1944 had a total budget of $3,296,772.57 (expenses almost equal the total $3,698,392.36 assigned to the DAI).[14]

Given a wide variety of responsibilities to oversee initiatives in education, health, infrastructure, and development, but few coherent directives, the Comité functioned no better than its predecessor. Most seriously, it made little progress on the crucial question of irrigation, as the vast majority of its budget was devoted to repairs of existing systems rather than new projects.[15] At the top, it was deadlocked by conflicts between the former governor of Hidalgo, Javier Rojo Gómez, and Professor José Reyes Pimentel of the DAI. According to one member, the problem was that Rojo Gómez favored aggressive social action, and the "reactionary" faction led by Pimentel acted only to obstruct efforts by other members. Whatever the reason, the result was a lack of well-defined programs and objectives, and the Comité accomplished little. Work on the irrigation projects in the valley was regularly interrupted due to lack of funds, leading to flurries of complaints from local leaders. By 1945 irrigation projects had ceased altogether.[16]

Other efforts in the valley proved similarly doomed. As director of the Instituto Indigenista Interamericano (III) (founded in 1942), Manuel Gamio promoted a number of ill-fated projects in the Valle de Mezquital during the 1940s. He provided radios for residents to listen to cultural and social programs in Otomí and Spanish. In a project that was reminiscent of his attempt during the 1920s to introduce the fabrication of talavera-style pottery in Teotihuacán, he tried to introduce the production of oriental-style carpet weaving. In order to sell these rugs, and slow the out-migration of skilled weavers to regions where markets were better, he constructed a tourist kiosk on the Mexico–Laredo highway.[17]

Appraising the results of two decades of work in the early 1950s, Gamio lamented that in spite of massive irrigation systems, a variety of schools, a hospital, and the millions of pesos dedicated by President Alemán, valley residents still lived much as they had in the 1920s. The projects undertaken by the Comisión were now generally ignored, the valley was still hampered by poor communications, and it remained one of the greatest regions of poverty and *incultura* in Mexico. Comparing these failures to somewhat analogous projects in Matamoros, Tamaulipas, Gamio was shocked by the differences. The work in Matamoros had been generally successful, whereas little had changed in the Valle de Mezquital. Both regions were arid, both regions were initially impoverished, yet the differences in the results were striking. Gamio could only explain this through reference to the indigenous culture of the Mezquital, which he concluded remained poorly understood and acted as a continuing barrier to all efforts to improve life in the region. Many of the cotton workers in Matamoros had lived in the United States, and did not "possess ideas and cultural traditions of autochthonous origin." They had acquired healthy lifestyles, measured by the fact that they ate wheat and meat, wore shoes, lived in modern houses, appreciated modern medicine, and had learned to use modern agricultural tools, machines, and methods.[18] By contrast, in the Valle de Mezquital, monolingual Otomís predominated. Here even the rich lived at a standard that was inferior to the level afforded by their economic possibilities. In the face of this recalcitrance, Gamio undertook ever more intricate analyses of the "miserable Otomí population" of the valley. Assisted by UNESCO and the Rockefeller Foundation, his new projects were designed to develop better knowledge about the intimate lives of the residents of the valley, which could in turn be used to "transform and correct" their belief systems. Still locked in a view that measured the evolution towards modernity in much the same way as he had in Teotihuacán more than thirty years earlier, Gamio's continuing efforts would not see propitious results in the Valle de Mezquital.[19]

Residents of the valley were likely frustrated as well, having lived through three decades of imperious and self-serving behavior on the part of revolutionary officials, but they had no international agencies to which they could turn. By this time the Valle de Mezquital had become a prototypical example of difficulties involved in trying to alleviate the poverty of indigenous Mexicans. A whole series of projects, undertaken under the leftist ideology of Cardenismo, the more conservative values of Avila Camacho, and finally the growing influence of modernization theory in the late 1940s had done little to improve the lives of Otomí villagers in the valley. Rarely consulted as to the implementation of these projects, Otomí residents of the valley by and large remained hidden in their houses, windows facing away from the street, distrustful of outsiders.[20]

Decades later, little had changed. When developmental projects were funded in the valley, the money provided usually lined the pockets of local officials, caciques, businessmen, and mestizos. Lands that received irrigation wound up in the hands of the powerful, while for most the only means of escaping poverty was migration. Most of the pueblos in the region would have schools by the early 1970s, but attendance rates were low, and poverty in the valley was among the worst in Mexico. The two words, "miserable" and "Otomí," seemed inextricably linked to state officials then, and remain so to this day.[21]

The Decline and Fall of the DAI

Regrettably, the troubles in the Valle de Mezquital were mirrored by larger developments. Hobbled by a growing debt and rising opposition, Cardenismo went into retreat in 1938, and Manuel Avila Camacho's election to the presidency signaled the end of the linkage between populism and Indigenismo. After 1940 problems with *charrismo* and corruption in state agencies grew more acute, and reforms in the Agrarian Code made expropriation more difficult, reducing the pace of reform to a trickle. Support for the ejidal sector dried up and the state increasingly promoted privatization and the concentration of land holdings. At the same time, many of the political organizations and federal bureaucracies built by the Cardenista state (marketing and credit agencies, cooperatives, agricultural aid agencies) were divested of their emancipatory content and transformed into mechanisms of pacification and control. Nationalism and social reform lost their place of privilege, replaced by the pillars of modernization theory: order, economic stability, and capitalist accumulation.[22]

Immediately after the presidential election, Luis Chávez Orozco's short tenure as chief of the DAI came to an abrupt end. He was replaced by Isidro Candia, formerly the governor of Tlaxcala.[23] Candia was reputed to come from humble origins, having "suffered punishments and pains analogous to those that hold down our Indian brothers,"[24] but unlike Chávez Orozco he had no reputation for intellectual or social scientific proclivities. Instead, he was principally a reliable ally for Avila Camacho, whose vision for the DAI was much different than his predecessor's. Although the department's budget continued to grow, (from $3,038,373.34 in 1941 to $4,031,064.77 in 1946, an expansion of 31 percent), compared to other agencies charged with similar tasks the DAI fell considerably behind. During the same period, the budget for the SEP grew by 259 percent. Given the well-publicized knowledge that the number of monolingual Indians was growing relative to the population as a whole, this could only signal a significant shift in priorities.[25]

DAI procuradores continued to press thousands of claims before the state, forwarding over 12,600 cases in 1941. According to Candia, a "good percentage" of requests were decided in favor of the Indians. The numbers, however, did not support his claims. Sixty-four cases against the Departamento Agrario and 118 against the Oficina de Pequeña Propiedad were resolved in favor of ejidatarios, but only 22 percent (326) of the 1,488 cases filed against other federal dependencies were resolved favorably.[26] At the same time, growing numbers of procuradores seem to have used their office for illicit gains. Reports of procuradores abusing their authority, assaulting their enemies, and empowering themselves increased.[27] In one especially egregious case Benjamin Méndez, the man who served as procurador for the DAI in Tetela de Ocampo, Puebla, was able to establish a *cacicazgo* (he was known as the *regidor* of the *ayuntamiento* of Tetela) that lasted from the mid-1930s until the 1950s. Working in conjunction with the Subalterno Federal de Hacienda of Tetela, he exercised total dictatorial power over the municipio, murdering or ordering the murder of five people over the course of fifteen years, and stealing goods worth thousands of pesos. The villagers' repeated requests to the DAI, SEP, and other authorities for his removal yielded no results.[28]

Throughout the federal bureaucracy, Avila Camacho's ascendance signaled serious problems for leftists. Cardenista political stalwarts were neutralized or eliminated. Vicente Lombardo Toledano held on, but was forced to abandon many of his earlier priorities. Moisés Sáenz did not live to see the purge, dying suddenly in Peru in late 1940. Others, including Sánchez, Francisco Múgica, Rojo Gómez, and Chávez Orozco, increasingly found themselves out of style. The simple accusation that one was an advocate of "soviet doctrine" could be very dangerous, at one point even threatening the career of the avowedly nonleftist Manuel Gamio.[29]

For his part, Angel Corzo (official mayor of DAI) made every effort to ingratiate himself with his new bosses in Los Pinos. Although his own past included more than a few promises of adherence to leftist principles, in February 1941 he launched a series of salvos attacking several colleagues for their leftist sympathies and declared himself dedicated to eliminating "all exotic communist theories" and "soviet agents" from the department. Chávez Orozco, who was forced out of the DAI shortly thereafter, and Ramón Bonfil, who "defended the thesis that the Indian nuclei in Mexico constitute nationalities, which must be respected, and that a Union of Mexican Indian Republics should be created," were particular targets.[30] Corzo continued his struggle against the "pernicious foreign influence of communism" in the press, publishing a series of articles advocating the assimilation of Indians into the national mainstream.[31]

More than a simple act of self-preservation, Corzo's accusations were yet another reminder of the fickle relationship between the federal state and the social scientists who acted in its service. Activists were always at the mercy of the presidential administration, and found themselves in peril when their programs came into open conflict with the interests of those at the highest levels, or when administrations changed.[32] Twenty years earlier, Manuel Gamio had received widespread public praise for his work in Teotihuacán,[33] only to find himself out of fashion when Obregón left the presidential office. After the DA was closed in 1925, Gamio briefly held on to a position in the SEP, only to see the one million pesos he was promised for ethnographic research evaporate. Gamio was even forced to leave the country briefly when, in retaliation for accusing others of official malfeasance, he was charged with stealing money and valuable objects from the National Museum.[34] Events in 1941 struck a familiar tone. No suggestion of pluralism, self-determination, or special rights would be tolerated by a state that now favored theories of unilinear modernization and economic development. Those who advocated expanded attention to the relationship between indigenous peoples and the state found themselves trapped in institutions with limited budgets and little support.[35]

Sensing these shifting winds, barely four months after Avila Camacho assumed the presidential chair Jeremías Lópes Chiñas, the secretary general of the Federación Indigenista Revolucionaria Oaxaqueña (FIRO) (a popular organization created in the late 1930s to mobilize Indians), told his members that they could no longer count on state support, and that they should focus their energies on "constructive acts that demonstrate the progressive aspirations and moral structure of the aborigines." He warned members that they should "ask superior authorities for help and collaboration; but do not ask or hope for everything from them, because they have other promises and preoccupations."[36] Under the new administration, Lópes Chiñas believed the FIRO should "carry out any effort that benefits the nation, region, or community." They would fight fires, maintain canals, combat plagues like malaria, syphilis, and other epidemics, work to found hospitals, and vaccinate children. Similarly, they would "execute personal acts that dignify the Indian as a morally superior being" by condemning drunkenness, punishing laziness, and reading to the community. Downplaying any hint of ethnic self-determination, López Chiñas also suggested that the FIRO concentrate on reminding Indians that they had benefited from a number of white benefactors in the past, including the Catholic friars.[37]

The early 1940s also saw an end to most of the specialized programs that had typified the previous decade. Typical of this tendency, in November 1942 two highly placed SEP officials, Alberto Terán (head of the Dirección General de Enseñanza Primaria en los Estados y Territorios) and Dr. José G. Parres (chief of Enseñanza Agrícolas), declared that the Indian problem should not be conceived as a unique issue requiring special solutions. "In reality, there is no isolated 'Indian problem,' distinct from the other problems of the country. . . . The correct approach when speaking of the Mexican population, is not to distinguish between Indians, mestizos, and whites, but only to simply refer to Mexicans." Taking their cue partly from nationalists and partly from social scientists, they argued that since the races were not truly different from one another, federal agencies should not conserve the Indian, treating him like a "picturesque element in the national life," a folklore for tourists, but that they should instead Mexicanize him. They also noted that there really was no single Indian community, but more than fifty Indian dialects, which if preserved would doom the nation to perpetual strife. "We should make one Mexico, not a variety of Mexicos." Advising against special schools for a caste, class, or race, they suggested that the schools controlled by the DAI be reintegrated into the SEP, creating one system of national education focused on promoting mestizaje.[38]

Activists across the political spectrum had reasons to deny a specific Indian problem in the years after 1940. Fearing that pluralism would undermine broad social movements, many leftists folded the Indian question into their conception of class struggle. Important sectors of the Mexican Left remained opposed to bilingual education and ethnic organizations into the 1970s, arguing both that ethnicity was a form of false consciousness, and that Indians were not worth organizing because they were anachronistic pawns of the bourgeoisie.[39] On the Right, the elimination of programs specifically designed for Indians appealed to regional elites by offering them an opportunity to return to their traditional practices without much federal oversight, declaring the Indian question solved. They argued that given the massive reforms completed by the Cardenistas, no further federal action was required to eliminate exploitation.

The most immediate example of this tendency came in efforts to undo the work of the Proyecto Tarasco. By 1941 the school had developed a strong reputation for its work. It employed eighteen teachers, along with eight indígenas capacitados who lent their services without remuneration.[40] The first signs of trouble came in early 1941, when the teachers at the Proyecto Tarasco were publicly accused of being communists. Several weeks later, the DAI announced that it was suspending the project, as its work was completed and the pedagogy practiced in the school — which "consist(ed) in the utilization of the cultural reserves of the Indian, his language, of his own specific values" — was no longer in accord with the educational principles favored by the government.[41]

This decision evoked strong responses from local residents, who complained to a variety of federal agencies. Congressional Deputy Ramón Berzunza Pinto, who was visited by a delegation from thirty-two Tarascan communities, protested that teachers assigned to the project knew the region well and spoke Tarascan, knew their customs and traditions, and worked tirelessly. He argued that the project had been an incredible success, and that the DAI had suspended the Proyecto Tarasco without examining its records. It had, he claimed, proved that bilingual education was not only possible, but was the most efficient method of education for Indians. Education in Tarascan, he claimed, had "enlarged the Tarascan's body of knowledge, and has made it possible to make them understand important issues." As a result the school had inculcated a true patriotic sentiment, helped locals understand the Mexican constitutional system, awakened a desire for a better life, and made important progress in eliminating the inferiority complex that afflicted the local population. More importantly, the project inspired confidence in teachers and the government because it showed that the government respected their particular traditions and *buenas costumbres,* and only wanted to elevate their lives.[42]

Berzunza Pinto complained that the DAI added insult to injury by not only ignoring these successes but also ordering the return of many of the objects which were now community property, including a printing press, a mimeograph, a dictionary, and literature in Tarascan. According to Berzunza Pinto, this course of action revealed a shocking level of incomprehension about the emancipatory nature of the project. It also showed "a lack of respect for the traditions of the Indians, which in the end might unleash renewed discontent and a loss of confidence on the part of this race towards the authorities of this country."[43] These were threatening words, but Angel Corzo, who launched several attacks against the school from within the DAI, and his superiors in the DAI were unmoved. Efforts to have the SEP or INAH take over the project were unsuccessful. Some bilingual education would continue on an ad hoc basis, but it would be nearly a decade before federal agencies again pursued any systematic attempt to promote education in indigenous languages.[44]

Once the project came to an end, serious problems quickly emerged in Paracho. When the DAI decided to change directors at the school in January 1942, the municipal president of Paracho protested, claiming that the work of Professor Antonio D. Luna, then director of the school, "has been substantial and beneficial for this region" and that his loss would "prejudice the interests of the Indians."[45] The new director immediately implemented significant changes, expelling a number of students and jailing others for not respecting his authority.[46] More protests followed, as leaders from a number of local organizations complained that the ineptitude of the new administration was an insult to the "labor completed by Lázaro Cárdenas for this Indian race."[47] Conflicts between students and the new director escalated until June 1943, when the school was engulfed by a student strike over accusations that the director was abusing and physically assaulting the students.[48] They proved unable to remove the director from his post, but ended their strike when the DAI promised to send plows, sewing machines, gasoline lamps, and fishing equipment to a number of local communities, and the director agreed to respect the student society at the school.[49]

Similar problems were seen in other internados during Candia's tenure at the DAI, as programs that once focused on increasing popular participation and scientifically informed social policy became simple mechanisms for promoting patronage networks. The number of internados under the DAI dropped from its high in the late 1930s of thirty-three to twenty-nine in August 1941, and under Candia they were divested of their former missions. They were first transformed into Escuelas Vocacionales de Agricultura (1941), and then into Centros de Capacitación Económica (CCE) and Centros de Capacitación Técnica (CCT) (1942), where they were to focus on technical education, assimilation, and an almost strictly economic mission. By the end of 1942 the DAI operated seventeen CCE (these included Paracho, Los Remedios, Matlapa, Guelatao, Vicám, and Tonachic), two CCT, and eleven Misiones de Mejoramiento Indígena. In spite of a budget of $2,444,476, many still lacked land, teachers, equipment, or regular student attendance. Some also saw significant cuts, with scholarships eliminated and facilities reduced.[50]

The other programs Candia pursued at the DAI showed similarly broad tendencies. One of Candia's pet projects, the "Continental Tribute to the Flags of America," was typical. Planned as a massive parade to take place during the week of 6–12 October 1941, it was a classic nationalist and assimilationist demonstration. As a part of the parade, Indians from all of the nuclei of the continent were to carry flags as the representatives of every country in the Americas in celebration of the discovery of the Americas. It revealed Candia as an individual who preferred the imaginary Indians of a Rivera mural to living subjects who demanded respect for their unique cultures. Pátzcuaro and the respect for indigenous cultures had become a distant memory.[51]

Similarly, the DAI was also an important participant in the *Casas y Familias Modelos* program, implemented in the Valle de Mezquital in 1941. Reputed to be the brainchild of Avila Camacho himself, the program was typical of the shift in policy after 1940. Implemented in the Otomí community of Alcalá, in the municipio of Temoaya, Hidalgo, the program aimed to produce model communities and families to serve as examples for other poor Indians to follow in their efforts to improve their lives. In a direct repudiation of past practice, the model neighborhood with eleven Indian families created by the project was made up of community members who already had economic resources. They were placed in simple but clean houses, with public services, medical care, a motorized corn mill, and a sewing workshop.[52]

This practice would have rankled those who earlier argued that the most "uncultured" Indians needed the most direct intervention from the state, but it was supported by Manuel Gamio. Taking his cue from Avila Camacho, he argued that this was the best way to undertake such an effort. He also suggested that planners recruit Indians who had lived in the United States as "culturizing agents" in these communities. No longer slaves to a diet of maíz, chile and frijol, migrants were familiar with meat, eggs, and milk, and had replaced their primitive huaraches with shoes. Building on these advances, Gamio suggested that they be taught to eat products derived from soybeans, and that they be given access to consumer cooperatives so that they could purchase products at moderate prices. Even more, Gamio suggested that they be given access to another important aspect of American consumer culture, the installment plan.[53]

Always aspiring to please his patrons, Gamio made the best of these developments by suggesting ways to improve efforts at the DAI, while endorsing its general overall program. Others, however, grew increasingly vocal in their criticisms of the department after 1941. Amid growing complaints that the department had "*fracasó*,"[54] a Consejo Técnico Consultivo was assigned to evaluate the department in 1942, made up of Alfonso Caso, Ramón G. Bonfil, José Galvez, Guillermo Bonilla, Alfonso Fabila, and Daniel de la Borbolla. Their report confirmed the worst. The department's budget was a mess, resources were not being used to resolve the problems faced by indigenous peoples, employees were acting arbitrarily and sometimes coercively against Indian communities, and the DAI as a whole lacked a clearly defined mission.[55]

Several months later Genaro Vázquez, Cárdenas's close ally and a prominent Indigenista, launched an even more scathing attack. He lamented that since the purges, this jewel of Cardenismo was marred by a shortage of personnel with the technical training and aptitude to apply its program over great distances. Too much bureaucracy, changes in political elites, and a lack of concrete methods and goals were crippling the department. This was made even worse by the frequent transfer of employees who had developed an expertise in a given region, which undermined effective work on the ground. Vázquez was also disturbed by the growing tendency to treat "the Indians like a uniform mass, implementing a uniform program and activities for all," which he claimed was a result of the fear that designing specific programs for specific ethnicities would incite caste war. Calling this an utterly false prejudice, Vázquez asserted that efforts at simple incorporation for Mexico's "Indian nationalities" could not reduce inequality. Instead, he called for a major effort at economic empowerment, with education and social reform as secondary and tertiary issues.[56]

Wise though they may have been, neither Vázquez's nor the Consejo's suggestions were implemented within the DAI. By this time the department was under attack from a variety of opponents, including those that wanted to have its educational programs returned to the SEP, those who felt that the DAI undermined national unity, those who cynically argued that Cárdenas had resolved the Indian question, and those who felt the department had to do more to fulfill its mandate. Candia limped on as chief through 1946, but several years of ineffective labor ended with Miguel Alemán's decision in December of that year that the functions of the DAI would be better served by other federal agencies. He announced that as of 1 January 1947 all matters pertaining to the study, education, and aid of Indians would henceforth belong to the SEP. Typical of the moment, once these responsibilities were relocated to the SEP, no special provision for Indian education was made.[57]

Though they did not lament the passing of an agency that for the previous six years had been characterized by its irresponsibility and lack of scientific orientation, many Indigenistas nonetheless expressed surprise and consternation that the federal government had abandoned any specific program of Indian redemption.[58] Alemán also faced a flood of angry protests from hundreds of indigenous communities, and considerable international opprobrium for his decision to close the DAI.[59] He attempted to mitigate these criticisms by founding the Instituto Nacional Indigenista (INI) under the leadership of Alfonso Caso (former head of the INAH) in 1948. It would resume some of the duties of the DAI, but in a considerably stripped down version, focusing principally on academic investigations and limited work in education, justice, and health.[60]

Though some older Indigenistas had high hopes for the INI,[61] its limited budget and responsibilities reflected a much-diminished interest in the Indian question. Caso had a daunting task in finding support, as he had to contend with a reaction against Indigenismo at the highest levels. By the early 1950s the INI initiated a series of projects in Las Casas, Chiapas, under Gonzalo Aguirre Beltrán and then Julio de la Fuente. Later centros would be established in Chihuahua, Oaxaca, Yucatán, Nayarit, Guerrero, Michoacán, and Puebla. Still, the INI would have to wait until the Echeverría administration in the early 1970s before it was able to enjoy an adequate budget. The neglected child of a conservative state that did not support radical agendas, during the 1950s the INI did little more than promote clinics, schools, the popular arts, and social welfare. Empowerment, as it had emerged in the congresses, internados, and organizations of the 1930s, was jettisoned altogether, and a program whereby a paternalistic state simply instructed the Indian became the norm.[62]

Divested of its nationalist mandate, social science took on an international dimension in this period. Major projects, as in the study of the Tarascans undertaken by Ralph Beals in 1940, and later efforts in the Valle de Mezquital, increasingly relied on funding from institutions like the Rockefeller Foundation, the University of California, and UNESCO. During this time the functionalist researchers associated with the University of Chicago and their Mexican students (including Julio de la Fuente and Alfonso Villa Rojas) increasingly dominated institutionalized anthropology, widening the gap between social science and nationalism. Under their influence, in a very short span of time anthropologists were transformed from nationalist visionaries into technocrats who used their expertise in specific locales to resolve limited concerns, working as part of international teams with only limited support or interest from the state. Ironically, it was in this context that the INI began using indigenous languages much more extensively in their programs, as a limited number of social scientists (many of them foreign) and indigenous activists crafted programs more suited to local needs without much supervision from above.[63]

The Persistent Savage

The demise of the DAI was in part due to its failure to transform the countryside, but on another level it was a product of the larger failure of Indigenismo to resonate broadly in Mexico.[64] Like its antecedents in the SEP and DA, the DAI attempted to supplant older images of the Indian with new nationalist symbols, but as long as contrasting images of the Indian remained more popular, their power would be limited.[65] Roland Barthes observes that myths and symbols need to seem like common sense, accessing deeply held values without doing so overtly, in order to be compelling. This would always be one of the most serious obstacles Indigenistas in the DAI and elsewhere faced. Their remade Indian was so far from the lived experiences of most Mexicans, so removed from the common sense wisdom of Mexican society, and thus so clearly ideological, as to appear flimsy in the face of deeply embedded beliefs and everyday practices.[66]

The DA and the DAI were the products of a commitment on the part of the central state to prioritize the Indian as a national problem and a national icon, but were never widely supported outside of fairly narrow circles. Just as Diego Rivera's murals often offended the sensibilities of urbanites, hispanophiles responded to folk arts with disdain, and Lázaro Cárdenas's trips to Indian villages became objects of ridicule,[67] outside of the DAI it remained common to believe that Indians were profoundly inferior, degenerate, corrupt, lazy, and perverse, "a heavy burden that impedes our nation from making rapid advances on the road to progress."[68]

Major figures like Manuel Gamio, Carlos Basauri, José Palacios, Pablo González Casanova, and Luis León could call racial prejudice an unscientific myth, deny that Indians had "atavistic instincts," or were "primitive and savage,"[69] but their claims were often ignored outside of Indigenista circles. Even at the height of the DAI's influence, confrontations between federal officials and indigenous peoples were generally interpreted in ways that reinforced the racial alterity of the Indian. Press reports regularly decried the "savage customs" of Indian communities, describing these peoples as "refractory to all civilization."[70] Typical of this tendency, in June 1938 Eduardo Pallares described a confrontation between federal officials and Indians in the state of Mexico in terms that left no doubt as to who was responsible for the conflict. Pallares concluded that the violent assault on federal agents "has shown us the black chasm that is the soul of the uncivilized Indian," and used the incident as evidence of the profound naiveté of the government's perspective on indigenous issues.

> We are not talking about some psychologically strange evil-doers from the community. We are talking about the community as a whole, including the elderly, women and children who, indignant because a detachment of soldiers stopped them from carrying out criminal activities in the woods, treacherously attacked them with sticks and stones, and left these unhappy men in a state of agony. All this for men who were only trying to do their duty, and undertake civilizing work, putting a limit on the idiotic destruction of the forest.
>
> The Revolutionary authorities live completely in a mystical age with respect to the soul of the Indian and his capacity to evolve spiritually. The Indian's advocates believe he is a good being, hardworking, peaceful, capable of indefinite progress, docile and humble; that he needs only instruction and money. Others claim we need to leave Indians in full liberty to live their own lives, to organize, to enjoy the land, to form cooperatives, and to become a forceful element in national life. All of this is either pure mythology with political ends, or errors produced by clumsy, ingenuine, and ignorant idealism. The social reality that many revolutionaries know and confess to in private is completely different. The ethnic and historical reality is that the soul of the Indian is, in many of its aspects, primitive, savage, and on occasions horribly savage. The life that they live, the crimes they commit, the inertia in which they vegetate, their resistance to transforming themselves into civilized beings, the vices that wear them out, the filth that surrounds and characterizes them, their tendency to incest, all demonstrate that the great masses of Indians, although made up of human beings who are worthy of

respect and merit protection, nevertheless continue to represent the primitive, the barbarous, and that which remains at the margins of a civilized and cultured existence.

Pallares concluded that the only solution to this problem lay in disciplining Indians, making them obedient to federal authorities. "The Indian should be treated as what he is, a being who is for the most part primitive, and who offers great resistance to the work of social assimilation." Calling on the military to do this work, he wrote that "many of the soldiers in the National Army come from the countryside; they are Indians snatched away from the land where they were born. Military discipline, life in the barracks, has transformed them in a brief time . . . the military regimen has beneficially incorporated them into civilization." This, in his opinion, was the only way to rid them of their "atavistic instincts."[71]

In a society that had only recently come through a period of profound fratricidal violence, it should not have been surprising that Indian communities were places of violent conflict. Moreover, the reports of assassinations and political intrigues that fill the SEP archives indicate that educators and the populace in general understood that the struggle for social reform remained a violent one. There was, however, a quality to these descriptions that made this violence different. Whereas other violent incidents may have been political maneuvering, this was an emotional primitive, a precultural and feminized Indian, possessed by a violent blood-lust, an irrational will to destroy. Secondly, this was not violence carried out by thugs, but the actions of entire communities. These were the primal screams of people whose minds were clouded by fuzzy primitive logic.[72]

Pallares created a good deal of controversy for the "racial prejudice" he showed in his article, but it was more likely Pallares, and not the Indigenistas who criticized him, who represented the more popular point of view on the issue.[73] In spite of all claims to the contrary, outside of Indigenista circles theories of racial inequality remained popular during the 1930s. Many critics of Indigenismo continued to believe that the effects of degeneration, particularly those connected to alcoholism and malnutrition, were passed from generation to generation, leading to irreversible degeneration in the "human organism." Some saw an Indian made irredeemable through sexual practices, or crippled by a diet so insufficient that it could produce "neither strong and resistant organisms nor brains capable of elevated thought."[74] An essay that appeared in *El Universal* in 1937 typified this view, arguing that children "born of this sick organism" inherited the illnesses and weaknesses associated with alcoholism. "Generation after generation has been decaying as a result of these factors, and for the most part the miserable economic, moral, and physical state of our Indian races is due to the vice of alcoholism."[75] Other common racializing explanations for degeneration lay in the inherited results of disease, malnutrition, and "premature sexual unions."[76] Like Clorinda Matto de Turner, who decades earlier argued that a vegetarian diet caused brain swelling, these interpretations started with the assumption that nothing associated with Indian life was useful, and concluded that the product of this lifestyle was beyond saving.[77]

One of the most serious challenges to the project of the DAI came from the ascendance of the Mendelian theory of eugenics in Mexico during the mid-1930s. Prior to the 1930s most advocates of eugenics in Mexico had adopted a neo-Lamarckian stance, but after the Sociedad Eugénica Mexicana para el Mejoramiento de la Raza was founded in Mexico City in 1931, Mendelian eugenics became increasingly popular. Across Latin America eugenics took an increasingly negative view on heredity, race, and gender during this time, abandoning practices that Nancy Leys Stepan identifies as "soft heredity."[78] Reflecting this trend, a 1936 editorial in *Excelsior* declared:

> It is true that some governments have promoted one or another methods promoting Indian regeneration, but this has always been principally a tool of electoral oratory. What is clear is that the overwhelming majority of the primitive races remain in the same condition that they were in a century ago, without showing any improvement.
>
> The Indians, with rare exceptions, are proof that the theory of environment cannot be sustained by scientific criteria. The environment has no effect on the Indians, who oppose all efforts to improve them with an overwhelming inertia. This is why the resources devoted to Indians have proved sterile, although we must recognize we have never seen effective efforts, and they were never undertaken with constancy and intelligence. The unsociable condition of the Indian race makes any concrete efforts very difficult. The Indian race

> feels an ancient terror, and together with a disconcerting meekness, this makes them wary of anything that seems foreign to them. Their polytheistic ideas, which no one really understands, undermine efforts at regeneration. They consider themselves happy hidden in the canyons, as far away as possible from the pernicious influence of the cities, and engaging in commerce with the whites only when it is indispensable for their material subsistence.
>
> The Mendelian theory of inheritance serves as a basis for vigorously opposing the humanitarian work of the Government. The norms of the contemporary Indians have been passed from parents to their children as a sacred trust, and it is no simple task to remove these obstacles.[79]

This view represented a serious challenge to Indigenistas, who responded vocally to these types of claims. Based on his experiences at Teotihuacán, along with his work as a demographer at the Secretaría de Agricultura y Fomento, Manuel Gamio repeatedly exhorted Mexicans to discard their racist beliefs. In part he did this by continually reminding his readers that cultural evolution and improvement had been seen throughout the country, but he also specifically addressed the underlying racist assumptions of his critics. In broadly circulated essays he claimed that the racial and linguistic markers traditionally used to define the Indian simply could not be applied with any meaning to Mexico's population,[80] and that racial identity meant nothing in terms of "mental capacity, and receptivity to education and the elevation of living standards."[81] As for the value of ethnic classifications, Gamio concluded that anthropology had been unable to fix the racial characteristics of Indians, in part because "we cannot yet determine which features are purely Indian, nor determine the proportion of Indian blood in those who appear to be mestizos." More significantly, he argued that the anthropometric and physiological characteristics that had been traditionally used as racial indicators were incorrect because "some of these vary if the local conditions change, and others rest purely in the individual, and are not hereditary."[82] He repeated this claim regularly in later years, using his status as director of the III to claim that the social sciences (anthropology in particular) had "deauthorized in a definitive manner the supposed scientific value previously attributed to the concept of 'Race.'"[83]

This was the most prominent Indigenista in the nation denying race as a discrete category, and suggests a definitive end to the race question. Yet Gamio, like others, never had such a simple understanding of race as he professed at the III. Always interested in creating precise classifications of the national population, in the summer of 1936 Gamio responded excitedly to the discovery of a series of pre-Columbian skeletons in the Federal District. He hoped to compare the data gathered from those skeletons with living indigenous peoples in order to determine the extent of racial mixing that current-day indigenous groups had undergone. This would in turn reveal whether or not there were any "pure" Indians in Mexico.[84] If he no longer subscribed to racist theories, why would Gamio be interested in this issue?

The answer to this question reveals one of the deeper contradictions in the Indigenista effort to deauthorize race as a discrete category. To be sure, Gamio and other Indigenistas believed that cultural differences were the key barriers to national integration, but they never lost interest in uncovering essential differences rooted in blood.[85] His enthusiasm for the skeletons was due to his belief that science could not determine which contemporary Indians were racially pure without some source of comparative data. Although he claimed his interest was purely scientific—an effort to produce precise racial data and show the extent of mestizaje in the national population—he implicitly suggested that this racial data would be useful to national development. He never lost interest in this project, later expressing hope that the modern scientific methods then being developed in the United States could actually determine an individual's race to a biological certainty. His only reservation about these practices was that the costs of testing all Mexicans for their race would be prohibitive.[86]

In his defense, Gamio would have claimed that his real interest lay in biotype, not race. Gamio used biotype to account for minor variations from one ethnic population to another, and denied that this implied essential differences in mental and physical capacity. He defined biotypology as consisting "primarily in understanding, through investigation, if the biological development of individuals or groups is normal or abnormal, and if they are the latter, to formulate and apply methods that correct that abnormality." He drew concepts from somatology, physiology, and psychology to discover the "normal" state of any group, and described inherited diseases, mental illness, sexual deviance, physiological deficiencies, and tendencies towards certain illnesses as factors that created abnormalities. In this, he remained committed to understanding the Indian's cultural deficiencies, but argued that "certain hereditary afflictions caused by physiological or mental abnormalities of the parents correspond exclusively to biotypological investigations, and generally could be combated without developing an understanding of cultural factors."[87]

Biotype gained popularity throughout Latin America during the 1930s, and was promoted most aggressively in Mexico by Carlos Basauri. He was first introduced to biotype by a group of Italian anthropologists who used these measures to demonstrate the racial deficiencies of the Mexican, but Basauri's own use of biotype was more complex. While impressed by the suggestion that abnormalities resulted from endocrinological problems and stunted development, he suggested that many of these imbalances could be corrected through environmental improvements and a less toxin-laden diet. Observing that children displayed few of the degenerated qualities of older residents in the Otomí communities he studied, Basauri concluded that with early intervention, future abnormalities could be resolved. Likewise, his superiors in the SEP found some of the promises of biotypology attractive, but they were careful to note that degeneration did not seem to be a problem that all indigenous populations suffered from, and was therefore more likely the result of environmental factors than essential differences.[88]

Gamio too adopted biotype in a selective fashion. He never wavered in asserting that most of the abnormalities he identified were entirely a product of poverty and poor nutrition. Even if the biological development of Indians was generally deficient, he always asserted that this was the result of illnesses and cultural factors, not a fixed heredity. Though he acknowledged somatological, psychological, and physiological deficiencies, he remained optimistic that most of the problems identified by biotypological studies could be remedied. Neo-Lamarckians to the end, he and Basauri never wavered in arguing that degeneration could be relatively easily reversed. Nevertheless, at a time when other Indigenistas were describing the Indian as a member of an oppressed nation or part of the proletariat, the turn to biotype suggested that Gamio was increasingly willing to describe the Indian as an infirm, or abnormal being.[89]

In this, Basauri and Gamio remained interested in blood in ways that other Indigenistas would have found appalling. Moreover, as they moved from one type of hierarchy to another, the Indian remained for them an object of study, a passive being with limited capacities. Based in part on this, Elías Trabulse argues that the move from race to biotype was of little significance. Both race and biotype gave the scientist the power to diagnose, made the Indian a simple object of study without human agency, and rationalized the paternalistic power of the state. Furthermore, the notions of normal and abnormal inherent to biotypology, defining criminals, alcoholics, and the infirm according to characteristics of the blood, could serve the same ends as theories of racial inferiority.[90]

These criticisms remind us that whether done with reference to biotype, psychology, culture, or race, all those practices that made Indian alterity immutable had similar effects. More seriously, exclusionary strategies based in social, cultural, economic, or psychological distinctions would be able to withstand the test of time more effectively than racial ones. Totalizing systems of racial exclusion have proved to be the cause of their own downfall during the past century, while more subtle systems, which offer rights to some and rely on informal economic, social, educational, and cultural mechanisms of discrimination, make more elusive targets.[91] Elite Mexicans could congratulate themselves for the absence of racism in their community, and maintain expectations that indigenous Mexicans could and should modernize their communities and become factors in the nationality. Those who did not were simply lazy, uneducated, abnormal, or psychologically deficient, and did not deserve the rights and privileges that others enjoyed.

For his part, during the 1940s Gamio increasingly argued that an inferiority complex, rooted in the "ancestral and inexplicable pessimism of the autochthonous soul" was the most important problem that indigenous Mexicans faced. Gamio suggested that this psychological state led to racial prejudice, which could only be combated through economic elevation and education.[92] He brought this point home in a 1945 essay in which he went so far as to argue that in contrast to the United States, there was no racial prejudice in Mexico; those incorporated into occidental culture faced no barriers. "The inferiority complex that one has before ascending to superior strata, is transformed, due to explicable psychological phenomena, into a superiority complex. But it is social, not racial; an attempt to separate oneself from or ignore groups to which one once belonged."[93]

As these words would suggest, Gamio repeatedly proclaimed the "advantages of mestizaje" while he served as president of the III. In this, Gamio did not speak for all Indigenistas. He would have faced severe criticism from any number of the social scientists who occupied positions of power during the 1930s, but for various reasons after the demise of Cardenismo most of these individuals lost access to the public prominence that Gamio enjoyed. Having maintained a low profile during the Cárdenas sexenio, Gamio was one of the few individuals who emerged relatively untainted by a leftist past, and was ultimately able to parlay this into a profile as the most prominent Indigenista in Mexico. As president of the III, and self-appointed spokesman for the regime, he offered a welcome alternative to the pluralistic concerns of the late 1930s. Gone was the focus on empowerment of the Cárdenas sexenio. In its place Gamio reasserted the power of the modernizing state over the Indian, who was this time crippled not by race, but by biotype and psychological complexes.[94]

Conclusion

The Indígena Capacitado

Struggling to remake their society in the aftermath of a bloody civil war, Indigenistas believed that a more inclusive national community was the key to a prosperous and stable future. It was with this goal in mind that they studied, educated, and aided indigenous peoples, bringing the national state into local communities and providing an understanding of the Indian problem to those at the highest levels of power. Through their efforts Indigenismo acted both as a set of values used by elite intellectuals to theorize about the nation, and as an everyday set of practices with which pedagogues, social scientists, and bureaucrats sought to build connections between the revolutionary state and diverse indigenous communities. Indigenous actors themselves also played important roles in this process, transforming Indian-state relations in significant and often unforeseen ways.

Hoping that Mexico would become a democratic society through education, land reform, cultural revival, and social scientific knowledge, most early Indigenistas believed indigenous peoples should be assimilated into the nation. This was the underlying desire embodied in their initial attempts to solve the Indian problem, including Manuel Gamio's ethnographic study of the Valley of Teotihuacán, and the creation of the Casa del Estudiante Indígena in Mexico City. In the end, these efforts proved that Indians were as capable as any other Mexican, but also revealed the superficial assumptions of their benefactors. The indigenous Mexicans who benefited from these programs proved less compliant than Indigenistas had imagined, and the wholesale incorporation of the Mexican Indian remained an elusive goal.

By the early 1930s the failures of assimilation converged with a shift to the left under President Lázaro Cárdenas to produce a series of projects that pushed Indigenismo in innovative directions. Under the influence of a newly professional corps of social scientists, indigenous empowerment and pluralism became important concerns, as was reflected in the programs undertaken in the internados indígenas, the Departamento de Asuntos Indígenas, and regional indígena congresses.

At various points during these decades, assimilationism, pluralism, and socialism each had turns as the reigning perspective on the Indian question. Yet the ideological gyrations that accompanied political shifts tell only part of the story. Struggles over Indigenista initiatives also contributed to the creation of new political subjects: Indians empowered to demand rights as citizens and act as agents in their own redemption. In communities throughout the country the ideas and programs advocated by Indigenistas wrought subtle yet important transformations, allowing a generation of young indigenous males to use the tools of Indigenismo to challenge the limits and form of the state. Although their power was limited by a national context in which the word *Indian* would remain for the most part a racial slur, the indígenas capacitados (as these young men were known) ultimately played a central role in ensuring seventy years of PRI hegemony. Their ascendance, and the new forms of caciquismo they created, represents perhaps the most important but least understood outcome of revolutionary Indigenismo.

In early 1940, Mónico Chín and four others from the ejido of Chunhuas, Quintana Roo, wrote to President Cárdenas with a series of demands. They requested that certain federal authorities be removed, that others be affirmed, and that a new representative of the DAI be assigned to the region. Added to this was another request, "that the government delegate from the zone be a *nativo maya capacitado*."[1] On the surface, this request was not unlike thousands of others during the Cárdenas sexenio. Community leaders all over the country regularly tried to exercise control over which officials could be present in their community, and demanded self-representation in all levels of government. It was different from others, however, in that it used language which to that point had been reserved mostly for federal officials. In requesting a nativo maya capacitado, Chín adopted the state's own idiom to demand local representation in government, using a term that was directly rooted in the Mexican state's project of producing a uniform citizenry. Most Indians might have needed close federal supervision because of their primitive state, but a capacitado was just the kind of person federal officials had long believed was the key to the redemption of the Indian. According to Chín, if there was a capacitado in a community, that capacitado had a right to represent the community.[2]

Bicultural and bilingual Indians have played an important intermediary role in Mexico as far back as the colonial period, but their role in revolutionary Mexico was unique in many respects. The revolutionary state had abandoned the principles of separateness that underpinned the colonial *república de indios,* along with the nineteenth-century racism that had denied the Indian any possibility of claiming to be a rational political actor. The capacitado thus occupied a place of privilege that had been traditionally reserved for people of European ancestry, or at least for those who aspired to a European identity, for most of the century since Independence. Their newfound symbolic capital invested them with the right to represent their communities and address the state, but they did so in a very different way than those indigenous elites who had acted as interlocutors between the colonial state and the Indian. The capacitado was not simply a mediator, but meant to be the agent who would bring Indian and nation together in one community.

Chín asserted the role of the capacitado as the legitimate representative of the community by using this Indigenista term, implicitly disqualifying both non-capacitados and non-Indians. Likely he had someone in mind for the position, since the small number of capacitados in the region meant there were very few people who could fulfill his demand. More importantly though, Chín was taking part in a process whereby indígenas capacitados throughout the country positioned themselves as the only legitimate representatives of the Indian before the revolutionary state. Using a strategy that Bourdieu identifies as cultural distinction, they ensured their right to act as both agents of the state and representatives of their communities (Bourdieu 1984).

In the forums examined in this study, the Casa del Estudiante Indígena, the internados, the DAI, and the congresos regionales indígenas, Indigenistas consciously endeavored to produce men who would be social leaders, not caciques. The distinction may seem academic, but to Indigenistas it represented the difference between an agent of emancipation and an oppressor. Their hope was that, in the absence of a state that could enforce democratic practices, the content of their pedagogy (the socializing school of the 1920s, and the Socialist School of the Cárdenas sexenio) and practice would produce a more democratic community. To be sure, they always recognized the danger that some would fail as teachers or become repressive caciques, but they believed that theirs was the best way to bring modern values to the countryside. The indígena capacitado, as they envisioned him, would be part agent of modernity, part representative of the Indian community before the state—the perfect interlocutor with an understanding of both the Indian community (from whence he came) and the modern world (in which he believed). As such, the indígena capacitado was essential in the elimination of one form of hierarchy (race) and implantation of another (education).[3]

Capacitados could dissent, but only as long as they accepted the overarching goals of "modernization," national integration, and an expanding corporatist nation-state. In accepting these projects they distinguished themselves as "political" citizens from "nonpolitical" primitives. The concept of the capacitado was thus as important in silencing certain members of indigenous communities as it was in empowering others to speak. Other members of their communities, illiterate, monolingual, and sometimes openly hostile to revolutionary programs that promised to undermine community institutions and local cultures, were relegated to the vast community that Claudio Lomnitz identifies as "silent Mexico." As such, the capacitados were integral to the creation of a postrevolutionary order that was based more on the reproduction of hierarchy than on a notion of citizenship rights. They drew from a long tradition of Mexican nationalism, in which those Mexicans who have been unable to claim the identity "modern" have been silenced, and where a public sphere, based on the principle of equal access for all citizens, has never existed. After 1940, when the state turned its focus to governmentalism instead of democracy, the capacitados became "the metonymic signs of an imaginary democracy" (Lomnitz, 2001: 206). Emerging in the absence of deeper transformations and penetrations, the capacitados were uniquely powerful.

Capacitados did not simply rely on efforts by federal officials to silence dissent, they were active participants in the process. We see a powerful example of this in a poem that the Zapotec teacher Adolfo Velasco wrote about his work in 1936. The chief of the Misión Cultural in Tezoatlán, Oaxaca, Velasco characterized his charges in his composition "Panorama Indígena."

Strange being in this socialist century
Thin of flesh
Muscles, but no fat, like a beast of burden
Threadbare clothing
Gathered from wherever it could be found
Their copper flesh
Their calloused feet, covered by dirty huaraches
Filthy scabs on their hands, legs, and torso

The woman is
As repugnant as the man
Indian eyes reveal
Incipient culture
A sullen misanthrope
Long-suffering and submissive
Resistant, caught in alcohol's vice

These poor Indians, living tragic lives
A simple and monotonous life
Sleeping, working, eating, and dressing poorly
Never improving, never changing
Routine is everything
In the way they sow, harvest, and in their life

Working like beasts
But their produce is worth little
We must go to the Indian
Wake them from their spiritual slumber
From their mental incapacity
From their ignorance of their rights
So that they know
They too deserve a better life[4]

Undoubtedly seeking advantage within the revolutionary state, Velasco was careful to show his affinity for Educación Socialista and incorporation in his poems. In this, he was not unlike Nicolás Flores and Esteban García, Indian agraristas who took part in the Congreso Económico y Asuntos Educativos e Indígenas in Atlacomulco, México, during July 1937. Though the congress was almost entirely vanguardist, a forum where teachers and agraristas complained about the "chronic ignorance" of the Indians and called for a strongly didactic approach to "incorporating them to modern life,"[5] Flores and García were able to escape being objects of these laments because they came to the congress as representatives of the local agrarian league.[6] Claiming the hybrid identity of Indian/agrarista, Flores and García were among the many young activists who promoted their identity as Indians, but as Indians who, through their political or educational affiliations, were modern subjects. As such, they were entitled to speak on behalf of the community and act as agents of modernity.

Some of the delegates to the regional congresses tried to use these forums to press for greater local autonomy, but Flores and García represented a different strategy. They endeavored to ingratiate themselves to the revolutionary state as much as possible, likely in an effort to escape rural poverty through employment in the federal bureaucracy. This was a common practice in revolutionary Mexico, and had in fact been one of the problems that undermined the Casa del Estudiante Indígena, where class after class of students tried to pursue an education that would allow them to remain in well-paid urban jobs after graduation rather than return to the countryside. Likewise, the Asociación Mexicana de Profesionales Indígenas e Intelectuales (AMPII), created in 1948 by a group of young Indian professionals who were mostly graduates of internados and beneficiaries of Cardenista social reform, would promote a straightforward incorporationist ethos as a key element of their professional and organizational strategies. Rejecting any trace of the pluralistic ethos that had once animated the DAI, they chose as their slogan "Let us Mexicanize Indians, not Indianize Mexico."[7]

These public proclamations could be dismissed as false consciousness or cynical manipulations designed to promote personal interests, but another explanation is also possible. Graduates of the Casa, teachers like Flores and García, and members of the AMPII had all succeeded in the assimilationist programs of the state, and many likely believed that these programs represented the best hope for their indigenous brethren. A successful capacitado could believe that their path to success was the best way for all to follow, especially given the harsh response of many federal officials to the pluralistic efforts of the 1930s.

Their story is also very much told by the radical shifts in the Mexican state after 1940, when social science and education were reduced from important forums for imagining the nation to simple mechanisms for modernization. After 1940 Indigenismo was similarly divested of its mandate to undertake revolutionary and egalitarian social reforms, and instead became a tool for promoting capitalist accumulation and social control. Stability was no longer pursued through major social reforms and mass organizations. Instead, the federal state would rely on strategically located individuals to act as its agents on the ground, supporting them as local authorities in return for their role in ensuring order. As part of this process the indígenas capacitados often became the chief agents of the modernizing state in indigenous communities.

Thus was the indígena capacitado transformed into what Luz Olivia Pineda calls the *cacique cultural,* as young, bilingual males ascended to positions of power in indigenous communities throughout the country during the 1940s and 1950s (Pineda 1993). In Mexico's highly segmented cultural landscape, the capacitados were uniquely qualified to act as the cultural brokers between the state and the Indian. They mobilized a diverse set of strategies to both protect local cultures and allow the gradual (though highly uneven) intrusion of federal authority and capitalist development. In a practice Paul Friedrich identifies as "double agenting," these men could assume a variety of identities to reinforce their power (Friedrich 1986). In their home communities indigenous leaders often distinguished themselves from their fellows with dress and habits that marked them as "modern" and mestizo. Simultaneously, the indígena capacitado portrayed himself to the outside world as a simple Indian from a community undifferentiated by class in order to sell merchandise, build patronage networks, and reinforce his right to speak on behalf of the community.[8]

Centrally important to maintaining PRI hegemony after 1940, in many regions indigenous leaders acted as the lynchpins in a system described by Guillermo de la Peña as a "hierarchical patronage network" (de le Peña 1986). Far from being a truly centralized state, the political system that emerged in the aftermath of the Revolution was more a series of political arrangements that allowed local elites to monopolize power with the consent of federal officials, as long as they supported federal officials on certain key issues. At best, they used their position as interlocutors to defend local interests, demand concessions and resources from the state, and preserve limited autonomy for their communities. In the worst cases, caciques used this authority to expel opposition families from the community, funnel money for material improvements into their own pockets, and murder adversaries.[9]

It would be possible to interpret the ascendance of the capacitados as simply an extension of the long tradition of political bossism in Mexico, and to view the democratic promises of Cardenismo and Indigenismo as an aberration. Yet they were very much a product of revolutionary Indigenismo. As much as they were agents of control, they relied on popular support to rule, and rose to power through the institutions of revolutionary Indigenismo.[10] Moreover, even as they limited federal power by protecting local cultures and practices from outside authorities, they oversaw the expansion of roads, capital investments in the form of dams, trucks for the transportation of goods, and agricultural aid (credit, seed, fertilizers, tractors). The modernizing projects they oversaw in their communities may have been a far cry from Indigenismo's emancipatory utopia, but they did ultimately transform the lifestyles of the communities they ruled.[11]

When asked about these developments in the Valle de Mezquital, locals invariably recall a man named Maurilio Muñoz Basilio. His legend begins with the story of a chance encounter with President Lázaro Cárdenas at the age of thirteen, when Cárdenas came to the region to inaugurate a bridge on the Rio Tula in 1935. Muñoz Basilio was a poor Otomí youth from Tasquillo, Hidalgo, the oldest of seven brothers, who pastured sheep and sold newspapers to help the family make ends meet (most of those who tell his story omit the information that his father was a rural teacher). He sold Cárdenas a newspaper, and the president, impressed by the enterprising youth, promised him a scholarship to study for a career as a rural teacher. Over the next decade Maurilio received an education, took a position teaching at the internado in Los Remedios, moved on to study anthropology at the University of New Mexico (where he received his doctorate), and began a long and distinguished career working for the INI in Ixmiquilpan.[12]

As both student and teacher, Muñoz Basilio was one of the successes of Cardenista education, and never forgot the promises he made to work for Otomí redemption. Even though he left the valley for a time, Muñoz Basilio maintained close relationships with former students and colleagues, and participated actively in the Patrimonio Indígena del Valle de Mezquital, founded during the 1950s. Though the Patrimonio provided employment opportunities for members of the local elites, many of whom were not Otomí, it also represented a forum for the growing cohort of educated Otomí to hold political office, publicize indigenous issues, and pursue their own careers.[13] In Ixmiquilpan a small group of mestizo merchants still monopolized municipal and federal political offices, but during these years a growing number of graduates from Los Remedios, El Nith, and El Domo successfully promoted their own professional and political interests. Some found work as teachers in the internados or in rural schools in the area, where their skills as bilingual Indians and relationships with local political bosses gave them opportunities to influence local political arrangements. Others, ambitious for rewards that went beyond their home villages, migrated out of the valley to pursue professional careers.

Clearly talented at using the language of modernity to work within the federal state while maintaining his local ties, Muñoz Basilio became a central figure in local power arrangements when he founded the Consejo Supremo Ñhañhu (CSN) in 1970.[14] The timing of his decision was propitious. Native teachers had worked in both Otomí and Spanish in local schools for almost three decades, and successful schools had long blended a respect for Otomí traditions with a modernizing message.[15] Prior to the early 1970s these had been informal arrangements, frowned upon by a state that distrusted any expression of Indianness that it had not officially sanctioned. However, once Luis Echeverría came to power in 1972 the climate was right for organizations that departed from a strictly incorporationist ethos. Muñoz Basilio's strategic choice for the organization, taking the ancient name of his people and discarding the Hispanic, was a clear statement in this regard. He would affiliate both with the PRI and the CNC, but the CSN was to be run by and for the Ñhañhu alone. Ranging ever further from academia into politics, Muñoz Basilio ran successfully for deputy to the state congress, where he represented Ixmiquilpan from 1975 to 1978.[16]

Built on many of the ideals of revolutionary Indigenismo, the CSN was envisioned as an intermediary between federal, state, and local authorities and local indigenous peoples. Today it numbers twenty-two members, and is made up of rural teachers, social scientists, and the director of the local Museo de la Cultura Ñhañhu. Support from federal sources ensures that its offices, though meager, have a computer, working telephones, and necessary facilities. It coordinates the distribution of federal aid funds into villages, petitions for irrigation, potable water, electricity, and paved roads, and no doubt receives credit when those benefits arrive. In return for this, the CSN has played a role in keeping the peace, bringing out demonstrators for PRI rallies, and getting out the vote in elections.[17] Through the CSN, Muñoz Basilio and his cohort could play the roles of both "mediators and enforcers" in their communities, preserving a space for Ñhañhu language and culture, but doing so within the parameters dictated by their patrons in the PRI, INI, and CNC.[18]

As Muñoz Basilio's career suggests, political mobilization in postrevolutionary Mexico has often relied on state patronage, particularly for those movements that used a language and articulated agendas that synchronized with national initiatives. Agrarismo, Educación Socialista, and the indígena congresses were among the phenomena that relied on state patronage, and thus never reflected unmitigated expressions of the popular will. This does not mean, however, that they were simply instruments of control, or that agrarismo and other phenomena of this type lacked any popular support. Rather, they were forums in which members of popular groups gave conditional support to federal authorities in return for certain concessions. By and large these undertakings produced thin performances. Nationalist efforts resonated on a local level only as much as they met local needs, and participation in national movements was strategic, reflecting a decision to take part in a practice that offered benefits which, while limited, were better than the alternatives.[19] For its part, the long shadow cast by Muñoz Basilio and the CSN's historic ability to deliver limited results has meant that it has survived for decades where other organizations did not; supported, if conditionally, by the campesinos who come to its functions and the individuals who seek its patronage.

The CSN is also important as one of the means through which educated Ñhañhu can gain a little prestige and some political power in their community. That most of the members are teachers reflects one of the most common trends in social mobility in postrevolutionary Mexico. Young, impoverished males have for decades opted for careers as educators, which provide a regular (if limited) salary, membership in a union, and some professional prestige, all with a minimum of education (in the 1930s sometimes as little as three years).[20] Throughout Mexico, this was one of the most important impacts of the internados, and one of the reasons that so many members of the CSN and older members of the community still remember them fondly as "great successes." These schools provided the means for a generation of young men to first become teachers, and then power brokers in their home communities. Some, like Juan Ramírez Pedraza, ultimately used the opportunities provided in Los Remedios to enjoy a relatively comfortable middle class life. Others entered an active life in politics, as did the current members of the CSN.[21]

As for Muñoz Basilio, central to his legend is the story that he took advantage of his education, founded the CSN, became an important power broker in the region, and still never lost touch with his roots. The earnestness with which people relate this aspect of his life history—that he died poor because he never wanted wealth, that he gave everything to his beloved brothers—is indicative of how rare a story like this is in postrevolutionary Mexico.[22] Most of those empowered to speak on behalf of the Indian and act as intermediaries between the Indian and the state in recent decades have clearly endeavored to take care of their own interests first and foremost. The stories from Chiapas, Michoacán, Oaxaca, and other places are legion. Indigenous caciques appropriated tractors, trucks, and fertilizers provided by the INI and CNC, monopolized land and political offices, and used murder and intimidation to remain in power.[23]

Indigenismo and Revolutionary Hegemony

When the few tourists who find their way to Ixmiquilpan today ask locals for things to see, they are generally pointed in the direction of the Museo de la Cultura Ñhañhu, built along Highway 85 in the center of town. Run by a current member of the CSN, the museum is like dozens of other museums that can be found in similar sized cities throughout Mexico, the oldest dating to the late 1930s. These museums have always had multiple purposes, providing employment for local intellectuals and artisans through a combination of tourism and government subsidies, as well as celebrating the local and national cultures through archeological, historical, and contemporary artistic exhibits.[24] Never having had a need to generate revenue from admissions, museums like the Museo de la Cultura Ñhañhu are generally little more than pedagogical tools for schoolchildren and relatively sterile institutionalized spaces. They provide employment opportunities for a few lucky individuals, but beyond this their role as cultural centers is ambiguous at best, and negligible at worst.

The museum's place in Ixmiquilpan reflects some of the complex roles that Indigenismo has played since the Revolution. In its earliest manifestation as a nationalist discourse, Indigenismo failed to resonate amongst all but a very few indigenous activists, who used the opportunities opened up by Indigenistas to their own ends. If Indigenismo was to have the power to mobilize and unify the citizenry, it needed to resonate in indigenous communities, but these were often the places where these revolutionary nationalists faced their greatest challenges. Indian cultures may have been a national patrimony in the eyes of Indigenistas, but to the community members who refused to lead them to ancient ruins, hid archeological artifacts, and murdered the occasional federal official, their cultures were local—not national—patrimonies, worth defending against outsiders.[25]

When Indigenistas later designed projects that sought to respect local cultures and customs, their initiatives resonated more broadly. However, even as they found allies on the ground, pluralistic Indigenismo found few allies within the state. Efforts at bilingual education and community control of schools were canceled abruptly once high-level officials decided that they were not in keeping with their agenda, only to emerge decades later as the preferred method of indigenous education. The youths educated in these programs fulfilled one part of the Indigenista agenda, but by and large failed to act as the agents of emancipation that their benefactors hoped they would become. Nonetheless, through these youths Indigenismo played an important role in the complex series of political arrangements after 1940 that scholars have described as the hegemony of the revolutionary state.

That hegemony was in part a product of institutions like the rural school, the DAI, and agrarian league, in part produced through rituals that articulated local cultures to the nation, and in part the product of actual political arrangements whereby federal officials assumed more authority in indigenous communities. Though these practices subordinated Indian communities to the state, Mary Kay Vaughan notes that they also produced a mutual language for consent and dissent, and legitimized the claim to a multiethnic nation. She shows that the federal and local authorities usually had to accommodate one another, and that locals only adopted selected elements of the national project, making federal programs conform to local traditions and power configurations.[26]

The role of the capacitados, however, suggests we should add another layer to this conception of hegemony. As the key interlocutors between many indigenous communities and the state, the capacitados were in a uniquely powerful position to control access to the "language of contention." The role of the capacitados suggests that we should consider the power blocs and networks that framed and often limited that language, especially in regions where the revolutionary state was weak. Some, like Muñoz Basilio, defended their communities and promoted local interests, but others used their power to stifle dissent and monopolize power.

The long history of caciquismo to which Indigenismo ultimately contributed, whereby political bosses ruled without clear or effective implementation of national laws or policies, suggests that hegemony was as much a function of personalistic rule as the result of discursive practices. In the place of a civil society based on a collection of rights, we instead find communities where the right to have rights was limited by a hierarchy that was justified through reference to the modernizing ethos of Indigenismo. And in the absence of a federal state that could effectively protect civil rights, it would be strategically located intermediaries, often the capacitados, who would act as the state. In this sense, the capacitados were not so much agents of a hegemonic state as hegemony themselves, essential mediators between a highly segmented population and the Mexican state. Like the museums that some of them oversaw, the hegemony they created was very thin, rested mostly on the personal qualities of particular capacitados, and thus, was always at risk of collapse.[27]

Appendix A

Distribution of Centros de Educación Indígena as of August 1937

Location	Municipio	Ethnicity
Amatenango del Valle	Las Casas (Chiapas)	Tzotziles
Chijtón	Ixtapa (Chiapas)	Tzotziles
Rincón Chamula	Nuevo Solistahuacán (Chiapas)	Tzotziles
S. Pedro Chenalhó	C. Las Casas (Chiapas)	Tzotziles
Bachajón	Chilón (Chiapas)	Tzendales
Cieneguita	Urique (Chihuahua)	Tarahumaras
Norogáchic	Batopilas (Chihuahua)	Tarahumaras
Sisoguíchic	Bocoyna (Chihuahua)	Tarahumaras
Tónachic	Batopilas (Chihuahua)	Tarahumaras
Misión Chichimecas	San Luis de la Paz (Guanajuato)	Pames
Amapilca	Alcozauca (Guerrero)	Mixtecos and Tlapanecos
Ejido de Carmen	San Luis Acatlán (Guerrero)	Mixtecos, Tlapanecos, Amuzgos, and Aztecas
San Gabriolito	Tepecoacuilco (Guerrero)	Aztecas and Tlapanecos
La Estancia	Actopan (Hidalgo)	Otomíes
Techímal	Teanguistengo (Hidalgo)	Mexicano
Bolaños	Colotlán (Jalisco)	Huicholes
Caró	Jocotitlán (México)	Masahuas and Otomíes
Paracho	Uruapan (Michoacán)	Tarascos
Jesús María	Ruiz (Nayarit)	Coras
Ayutla	Villa Alta (Oaxaca)	Mixes
Chalcatongo	Tlaxiaco (Oaxaca)	Mixtecos and Zapotecos
Guelatao	Ixtlán (Oaxaca)	Zapotecos
San Fdo. Matamoros	Zimatlán (Oaxaca)	Mixtecos and Zapotecos
Comaltepec	Zacapoaxtla (Puebla)	Mexicano
Zongozotla	Zacapoaxtla (Puebla)	Totonacas
Jacal de San Felipe	Amealco (Querétaro)	Otomíes
Quitiyé	Cadereyta (Querétaro)	Otomíes

Location	Municipio	Ethnicity
Matlapa	Tamazunchale (San Luis Potosí)	Mexicano
Pequetzén	Tancanhuitz (San Luis Potosí)	Huastecos
Vícam	Guaymas (Sonora)	Yaqui
Tlanepaquila	Zongolica (Veracruz)	Mexicano
Chichimilá	Valladolid (Yucatán)	Maya

Source: SEP, 1937b, vol. 1, 406–407.

Appendix B

Work of the Comisión Intersecretarial de Estudio y Planeación en el Valle de Mezquital as of September 1939

Secretaría de Hacienda y Crédito Público

The Secretaría de Hacienda y Crédito Público had conducted a study of consumption and production of pulque and taxes on intoxicants, studied regional cooperatives, studied production of ixtle, and studied local taxes to determine which to abolish and which new ones should be created.

Secretaría de la Defensa Nacional

The Secretaría de la Defensa Nacional had constructed four barracks in order to protect the Mexico–Laredo highway and guarantee the safety of the inhabitants of the region, and was in the process of organizing Indians of the valley militarily to prepare them for armed service and train them in discipline.

The Secretaría de Economía Nacional

The Secretaría de Economía Nacional had examined social and economic conditions in Arbolado and Tetzú with the aim of establishing a cooperative wool-spinning and weaving workshop, organized cooperative societies in both communities, constructed workshops and a regional gallery, and undertaken a project to perfect certain articles and introduce others of greater utility. The Secretaría de Economía Nacional had promoted the fabrication of sombreros and furniture, created a Centro de Reunión for cultural improvement in Tetzú, and was examining means to develop the deposits of kaolin in Orizabita.

Secretaría de Agricultura y Fomento

The Secretaría de Agricultura y Fomento had undertaken a disinfection and seed selection campaign, formed a collective orchard in the Escuela Vocacional para Indígenas in Los Remedios, and was planting three thousand fruit trees, along with twenty-five hundred eucalyptus trees. The agency was also studying the best means of agriculture in the region, and endeavoring to provide the best animals for the region, along with a local veterinary service.

Comisión Nacional de Irrigación

The Comisión Nacional de Irrigación had introduced potable water in several schools and villages, constructed water and gasoline pumps close to the highway, dug several wells, conducted studies for the construction of several canals, and initiated work on a water tunnel in El Tecolote.

Secretaría de Comunicaciones y Obras Públicas

The Secretaría de Comunicaciones y Obras Públicas had completed 6.162 km of road building, constructed a building for an Indian Agricultural Vocational School in Los Remedios, and was directing the construction of the hospital in Ixmiquilpan.

Secretaría de Educación Pública

In 1937 Secretaría de Educación Pública had provided 2,500 daily breakfasts for 90,250 pesos (serving 25 percent of the local children). It had also spent 2,500 pesos on soap, provided sewing machines to 101 schools, haircutting tools to 180 schools, and generally supplied clothes, sombreros, sandals, and medical attention for children. A reduced budget in 1938 and 1939 meant that only two thousand children benefited from the program during that period. Secretaría de Educación Pública had also undertaken an intercultural exchange with Mexico City where one thousand Otomí children visited the capital and an equal number of children from the capital visited the valley. To this date children from 40 schools in the capital had participated.

Secretaría de la Asistencia Pública

Secretaría de la Asistencia Pública had undertaken studies of infant mortality, established a maternity service in Ixmiquilpan and Actopan, established an infant social assistance service in the Ejido de Estancia, Hidalgo, and contributed 8,000 pesos to the construction of a hospital in Ixmiquilpan.

Departamento Agrario

In 1937 the Departamento Agrario oversaw eight provisional possessions and six definitive possessions (while twenty-two more were pending), conducted thirty-seven inspection visits, conducted nineteen ethnic censuses, and formed fourteen ligas feminiles. In 1938 Departamento Agrario oversaw nine provisional possessions and nine definitive possessions, with nine more pending. In 1939 Departamento Agrario oversaw two definite possessions.

Departamento de Salubridad Pública

The Departamento de Salubridad Pública had undertaken 25,664 consultations; 9,439 cures; 203 operations; 9,433 injections; 20,631 formulas dispatched; 1,091 external visits; 548 house calls; 23,737 immunizations for smallpox (the vast majority), typhoid, whooping cough, rabies, and others; 1,288 conferences; 84 births; 112 pregnancy exams; distributed 1,056 pamphlets of hygienic propaganda; conducted 6 prenuptial exams; 84 sanitary inspections; 663 blood analyses; and numerous other unspecified examinations.

Departamento Forestal y de Caza y Pesca

The Departamento Forestal y de Caza y Pesca had conducted a study of resources, was undertaking reforestation efforts, and had created the nursery in El Mexe, which by December 1937 had 129,362 plants. Other nurseries were also being built.

Departamento de Asuntos Indígenas

The Departamento de Asuntos Indígenas had created a Procuraduria de Comunidades Indígenas in Ixmiquilpan in January 1936, and was continuing to work for defense of the interests of Indians in the zone. The agency had organized four cooperatives, provided motorized corn mills, haircutting tools, baths, and medical assistance, built several workshops, provided potable water to several communities, and was helping in the installation of telephone lines and other public works.

Departamento de Educación Física

The Departamento de Educación Física had built thirty-three courts for basketball and volleyball with the help of teachers. It had put on thirty-two sporting events, and donated sports equipment to various communities.

Banco Nacional de Crédito Ejidal

The Banco Nacional de Crédito Ejidal reported loans of over 52,000 pesos for cultivation and acquisition of machines and work animals to several ejidos in 1937, benefiting 2,739 ejidatarios working a total of 3,168 hectares. In 1938 the agency had continued to help the same ejidatarios, who were cultivating 2,365 hectares (803 fewer) because they did not have sufficient irrigation to work the rest. In 1939 they were only cultivating 1,216 hectares, due to massive failures and a lack of irrigation. Declining loans were provided each year in accordance with reduced levels of cultivation, but an additional 47,000 pesos for attention to the crops was provided in 1939. The agency also reported ongoing efforts to give ejidatarios more control over their credit and better systems of cultivation. Two experimental fields were dedicated to new varieties of grain and alfalfa in Actopan to determine which resists rot better, and which provides more protein. The agency was bringing varieties from other parts of the country and foreign sources.

Gobierno del Estado de Hidalgo

The state government reported construction and repair of schools, potable water, irrigation systems, roads, telephone lines, sports equipment.

Universidad Nacional Autónima de México

The UNAM reported various social, educational, biological investigations.

Source: Chávez Orozco, Informe of the Comisión Intersecretarial de Estudio y Planeación en el Valle de Mezquital, 26 September 1939.

Notes

Note: Abbreviations used in the notes are listed under Archival Sources in the Bibliography.

Introduction

1. For reporting on the congress, see "Gran Congreso de Otomies habra en Ixmiquilpan," *El Nacional,* 6 September 1936; "Iran al Congreso Regional Indígena en Ixmiquilpan," *La Prensa,* 24 September 1936; "Quince mil campesinos se reunieron en Ixmiquilpan en el congreso de indios," *Excelsior,* 26 September 1936; "Que la raza Otomí salga de su sopor," *El Nacional,* 30 September 1936; "Con las razas indígenas estan las obligaciones del Gobierno," *El Nacional,* 26 September 1936; "El Congreso Indígena de Ixmiquilpan," *El Universal,* 26 September 1936; "Un Congreso pro razas indígenas," *Excelsior,* 20 September 1936. On the populist dimensions, see Knight, 1998, 223–236.

2. "Fue de interes el Congreso de Ixmiquilpan, Hgo.," *Excelsior,* October 4 1936; "Frutos del Congreso Indígena de Ixmiquilpan," *El Nacional,* 28 September 1936.

3. L. Martínez Cosío, "Proyecto para reorganizar el Museo Regional Queretaño," April 1939, AH—INAH vol. 17, 1939, exp. 21.

4. See, for example, Bantjes, 1998, 144–149.

5. See Hobsbawm, 1983, 6–12; Morris, 1999, 364–367; Scott, 1998.

6. See Sayer, 1994, 367–398; Butler, 1990, 24–25, 140–149; Mallon, 1995, 6–7; Vaughan, 1997, 189–201.

7. On the Zapatistas, see Womack, 1968; Brunk, 1995. On Villa, see Katz, 1998. See also Knight, 1986; Joseph, 1988; Purnell, 1999.

8. On the emergence of the social sciences see Dalhgren Jordán, 1988, 86–87; Comas, 1964, 101–103; Kemper, 1984, 139–156. See also Bourdieu, 1990, 123–149.

9. See, for example "Primer Congreso de Misioneros de Educación Pública," Mexico City, 18 September to 8 October 1922, AHSEP—ER 1327/25.

10. See for example, Knight, 1986, 518–519; Joseph, 1988, 105–107.

11. Lomnitz, 2001, 125–144, esp. 140.

12. Delpar, 1992, 96–99; de la Peña, 1996, 41–81.

13. Other critics of Indigenismo include Bartra, 1986, 324–351; Brading, 1988, 75–89; Knight, 1990, 71–114; Lomnitz-Adler, 1992; Hewitt de Alcántara, 1984, 9–13; Pérez Montfort, 1994, 345–352; Tenorio-Trillo, 1996, 65–80; Morales Garza, 1998, 141–172; Lomnitz, 2001, 228–262. A less critical tradition, including Comas (1964), dominated scholarship on Indigenismo from the 1940s until the 1970s, but has largely fallen out of favor. Nonetheless, one can still find relatively sympathetic readings of Indigenismo in Marzal, 1989; Favre, 1998; González Gamio; 1987.

14. de la Peña, 1996, 41–81. Lomnitz, 2001, xvi–xviii.

15. More broadly, see Stocking, 1976, 1–15; Aguirre Beltrán, 1992, 189–206; Fabian, 1985, 7–23.

16. Laclau and Mouffe, 1985: 114–121.

17. Laclau and Zac, 1994, 31–37.

18. On the difficulty of state building, see Benjamin, 1985, 195–217; Gledhill, 1991, 28–30, 114–115; Nugent, 1993; Joseph and Nugent 1994, 3–23; Knight, 1994b, 73–107; Becker, 1995, 4–9, 151–162; Alonso, 1995; Purnell, 1999. On education specifically, see Vaughan, 1994, 213–247; Rockwell, 1994; Vaughan, 1997, 25–46; Loyo, 1999. On orientalism, see Said, 1978.

19. In this sense, many of the traditional aspects of hegemony as rule in the absence of coercion are not entirely relevant here. On the Gramscian concept of hegemony and its application to other societies, see Barrett, 1995, 235–240. On capacitados as metonymic signs, see Lomnitz, 2001.

20. Scholars remain divided on the deeper meaning of these efforts. Adolfo Gilly sees Cardenismo as central to a new relationship between state and society. See Gilly, 1994, 391–461, esp. 414. Others, however, render Cardenismo as fundamentally paternalistic and bourgeois. See Córdova, 1974; Becker, 1995; González y González, 1997, 105–123.

21. These were thus similar to other struggles between popular groups and federal officials over the nature of the state. See for example, Knight, 1994, 31–63; Purnell, 1999, 172–178; Friedrich, 1986; Rubin, 1997; Lomnitz-Adler, 1992, 61–247; Becker, 1995; Bantjes, 1998, 175–203; Vaughan, 1997; Knight, 1994b, 73–107; Gledhill, 1991, 33–94, 95–115; Fallaw, 2001.

Chapter 1. The Indian and the Nation

1. Carlos Samper, "La incorporación del Indio," n.d., AHSEP—ER (1210) 1835/16.

2. Tresierra, 1994, 193–194; González y González, 1996, 313–326; Tenorio–Trillo, 1996, 64–95.

3. "Primer Congreso de Misioneros de Educación Pública," Mexico City, 18 September to 8 October 1922, AHSEP—ER 1327/25.

4. See Alonso, 1995, 51–103; Aguirre Beltrán, 1992, 189–206; Mallon, 1995, 91–133, 175; Vaughan, 1982, 26–29; Lomnitz, 2001, 40–46, 50–51.

5. Schwarcz, 1993, 44–68; Hannaford, 1996, 187–276, 325–368; Trabulse, 1996, 86–95; Knight, 1990, 78–80; Buffington, 2000, 43–63.

6. Trabulse, 1996, 79–81; Stepan, 1991, 145–153; Raat, 1973, 44–45, 48–49; Raat, 1970, 426–427; Powell, 1968, 19–36; Knight, 1990, 71–113; Buffington, 2000, 145–146.

7. Lomnitz, 2001, 50–52, 240–250; Favre, 1998, 40–44; Monsiváis, 1996, 55–57. González y González, 1997, 313–326; Stocking, 1982, 13–132.

8. On the congress, see Serrano and Villanueva, 1988, 15–16; Comas, 1964, 9–13; Tenorio–Trillo, 1996, 88–95. On Sierra, see Olivé Negrete, 1988, 57–70; Comas, 1964, 14–19. On Molina Enríquez, see Trabulse, 1996, 92. See also Aguirre Beltrán, 1992, 189–206; Stabb, 1959, 405–423; Monsiváis, 1996, 55–57; Favre, 1998, 40–44.

9. Strug, 1986, 161–182, 207–233; Stocking, 1976, 1–15; Stocking, 1982, 133–233; de la Peña, 1996, 45–47.

10. Gamio, 1919b, 15–18.

11. Olivé Negrete, 1981, 62–63.

12. Gamio, 1960, 7–26, 47–55, 61–70, 81–82, 103–109, 167–170, 183; Gamio, 1922, 9.

13. Alvaro Obregón (n.d.), in AIMG, box 5, exp. 9. See also González Gamio, 1987, 45–47, 124; Miller, 1999, 139–140.

14. The DA was granted a $175,000 budget. Gamio to Boas, 27 February 1918, AIMG box 1, exp. 38; Gamio to Boas, 29 June 1917, INAH—DA box 1, exp. 4; AIMG box 1, exp. 33; Gamio to Boas, 23 August 1917, AIMG box 1, exp. 35. See also Gamio, 1919b; Gamio, 1918, 3; Olivé Negrete, 1988, 57–70.

15. Butler, 1990, 98; Clifford, 1986, 99–101; Abrams, 1988, 58–89; On the program, see Gamio, 1918, 9–10, 14–15; Gamio, 1922, 12; Gamio, 1919b, 8–10.

16. Scott, 1998, 9–84.

17. Gamio, 1918, 10–14.

18. Gamio, 1918, 14–15; Gamio, 1922, 10; Gamio, 1924, 21–22; Gamio, memo, 8 September 1917, INAH—DA box 1, exp. 7.

19. This was the first of what he hoped would be ten studies of the ten distinct cultural zones into which he divided the country. Gamio, "Origin, Programa, y Tendencias de la Direccion de Antropología," AIMG box 10, exp. 6; Gamio, 1918, 16–17; Gamio, 1922, 11–12.

20. Paul Silicio Pauer to Boas, 21 January 1924, AIMG box 2, exp. 13. Gamio, 1922, 25; Gamio, 1924, 9.

21. Gamio, 1922, 22.

22. Gamio, 1924, 9.

23. His classification of the Catholic practices of residents of the valley reinforced these numbers. He claimed that many of the indigenous people of the valley practiced a modern, as opposed to "pagan" form of Catholicism. Gamio, 1922, 24–34, 40. See also Manuel Gamio to Frank Glass, 20 April 1926, AGN—Obregón/Calles 713–G-26.

24. Gamio, 1922, 33.

25. Gamio, 1922, 26.

26. Gamio, 1922, 11–30, 41–43, 52–54.

27. Gamio, 1922, 22.

28. Gamio, 1922, 67–70.

29. Gamio, 1922, 80–81.

30. Manuel Gamio, "Reforma de la dieta de indios y mestizos," n.d., AIMG box 9, exp. 7. See also Comas, 1975, 48–50.

31. Gamio, 1922, 26–28, 80–81; Gamio, 1924, 14; Gamio, 1960, 171–181; Gamio, 1926, 121–126.

32. *Ethnos* was published intermittently from April 1920 to May 1925. See "Estatutos de la asociación editora Ethnos," 1 February 1920, INAH—DA box 1, exp. 11; Paul Siliceo Pauer to Ignacio B. Castillo, 21 February 1920, INAH—DA box 1, exp. 11. On the nationalist ethos in these journals, see, among others, José G. Montes de Oca., "The Festival of St. John," *Mexican folk-ways* (hereafter *MF*) 2:7 (June–July 1926) 35; Delfin Ramirez Tovar," El Carnival en Huixquilcan," *MF* 5:1 (January–March, 1929) 35; Diego Rivera, "Mexican Painting: Pulquerias," *MF* 2:7 (June–July 1926) 6–10; Manuel Gamio, "The New Conquest," *Survey Graphic,* 1 May 1924, 145–146. See also Delpar, 1992, 37; Loyo, 1992, 263–265; López, 2001, 157–209.

33. Gamio, 1922, 71. See also Rene D'Harnoncourt, "Las Artes populares de México," *MF* 6:2 (1930) 56–64; Jose M. Puig Casauranc, in *Forma: Revista de Artes Plasticas* 1:1 (October 1926) 1; Sáenz, 1929, 15–16; Mendizabal, 1922, 3–21; Pablo González Casanova, "The Origin of the Stories of Indian Mexico," *MF,* 2:8 (August–September

1926) 12–17; *Ethnos* 1:1 (1920) 25–26; Campos, 1929, 21; Miguel O. de Mendizabal, "Los cantares y la música indígena, las canciones y bailables populares de México," *MF,* 3:2 (1927) 109–121.

34. "La revolución artistica mexicana — una lección," *Forma: Revista de Artes Plasticas* 1:4 (1927) 8–16; Salvador Novo, "Aims of the Open Air Schools of Painting," *MF* 4:1 (January–March 1928) 24; "Las industrias indígenas y la cerámica teotihuacana," *Ethnos* 2 ep. 1:1, 52–54; Manuel Gamio, "El reurgimiento de Arte Plumero," *Ethnos* 1:5 (August 1920) 117–120; Manuel Gamio, "Possibilities of Indigenous Art of Mexico," n.d., AIMG box 8, exp. 1; Murillo, 1922, vol. 1, 11; Best Maugard, 1923, 11–14; Frances Toor, "The Old and New Jarabe," *MF,* 6:1 (1930) 26–36. See also de la Peña, 1998, 53.

35. Gamio, 1922, 80. See also Stocking, 1982, 195–233.

36. Gamio, "Consideraciones sobre la Politica Indigenista," n.d., AIMG box 6, exp. 57.

37. See, for example, Fellipe Carillo Puerto, "The New Yucatan," in *Survey Graphic,* 1 May 1924, 139; Catherine Vesta Sturges, "Along the way with Rural Institutes (Misiones Rurales)," *MF* 3:3 (1927) 165–166; Sáenz, 1929, 8.

38. SEP, 1927b, xxv.

39. He worked with Gamio at Teotihuacán. Basauri, 1928, 18.

40. Gutiérrez y Oliveros, 1929, 11–13.

41. Gamio, "El Indio Mexicano en la Olimpiada Mundial," n.d., AIMG box 8, exp. 36.

42. Knight, 1990, 76–77, 82–83, 87–95.

43. Vasconcelos, 1997, 16.

44. Vasconcelos, 1926, 77–79, 90; Stepan, 1991, 147–153.

45. Buffington, 2000, 155.

46. Lomnitz-Adler, 1992, 261, 306–307.

47. Basauri, 1928, 5–6, 13; Vasconcelos, 1926, 77–79; Francisco Ramírez, "El Indio," *El Maestro Rural* (hereafter *MR*) 1:3 (1 April 1933) 7.

48. "La condición de las razas indígenas en México es la misma que tenian in 1811," *Excelsior,* 18 July 1931. See also "El problema del indio," *Excelsior,* 20 July 1931; Luis L. Leon, "Al Margen de la campaña cardenista. La incorporación de los núcleos indígenas," *El Nacional,* 28 June 1934.

49. "Sección Editorial. El problema del indio," *El Universal,* 5 January 1938.

50. Manuel Gamio, "El racismo y la población Indígena" (1942) in Gamio, 1948, 36–37; Manuel Gamio, "Consideraciones sobre el problema Indígena," (1942) in Gamio 1948, 1–9; Manuel Gamio, "Editorial: ventajas del mestizaje," July 1954, AIMG box 7, exp. 5.

51. Enrique Corona, "Pensamos así . . . desenvolvimiento mental y limitado," *El Nacional,* 13 August 1931. See also Carlos Basauri to Rafael Ramírez, 15 May 1931, AHSEP — ER 1327/2.

52. Adolfo Velasco, "Algunos consideraciones de orden antropológico aplicadas a la educación," 14 October 1933, 1–6, AHSEP — ER (1052) 1677/4.

53. Stepan, 1990, 117–119, 134–145; Stern, 1999, 41–81; Buffington, 2000, 160–161.

54. Stepan, 1990, 110–152.

55. "Nueva Orientación a Internados Indígenas," *El Nacional,* 14 July 1936.

56. See, among others, Insp. Abel Ortega, in San Francisco de la Tables, in Municipio

de Chapa de Moto, 6 October 1930; Roberto L. Razo, in San Francisco de la Tables, in Municipio de Chapa de Moto, 26 June 1933; AHSEP—DEPM (6288) 6/11.

57. "La rendción del indio es una necesidad panamericana," *El Nacional,* 25 March 1935; Gamio, 1987, 32–33; Ing. Norberto Aguirre, "Apuntes sobre el problema indígena de México," *Agricultura,* February 1939.

58. Pierre M. Morpeau, "El problema racial de México y la cultura indígena," *El Nacional Revolucionario,* 18 May 1931.

59. "Sección Editorial. El problema del indio," *El Universal,* 5 January 1938.

60. de la Cadena, 2000, 4–20, 306–330.

61. See, among others, J. B. Durand, "Diferencias entre las mentes citidana y rural," *MR* 3:5 (1 March 1934) 7–8; Genaro Vázquez, "Plan de Acción en favor de los indios, dirigido a los maestros rurales," October 1926, CONDUMEX 082.172.72 OAX.

62. Sáenz, 1929, 15–16. See also "Primer Congreso de Misioneros de Educación Pública," México, 18 September to 8 October 1922, AHSEP—ER 1327/25; Antonio Vela "La civilización de la raza de bronce. "Dedicado a los mexicanos patriotas," (Puebla, 1922), 2–3, AHSEP—ER 1327/808/26; "Dos Criterios acerca del Problema Indígena," *Excelsior,* 17 August 1931. See also Vaughan, 1997, 25–46; Joseph, 1988, 101–128.

63. Aguirre Beltrán, 1992, 68–69.

64. Manuel Puig Casauranc, "Programa Para la Escuela Rural—Actividades para el año preparatorio," 1926, AHSEP—ER 1463/15.

65. Puig Casauranc, "Programa Para la Escuela Rural—Actividades para el año preparatorio."

66. Stepan, 1991, 56–57, 77–81.

67. See, for example, Moisés Sáenz, "Our Rural Schools," *MF* 3:1 (Feb–Mar 1927), 46.

68. Circular by Director, EDFED in Puebla, 21 June 1927, AHSEP—ER 1796, unclassified. See also Rockwell, 1994, 199–204.

69. See "Discurso pronunciado por the Srta. Profa. Luz Vera en la sesión de clausura del Congreso de Misioneros . . ." 6 October 1922, AHSEP—ER 1327/308/26; Sáenz, "Our Rural Schools," 45–46.

70. Loyo, 1999, 168–173.

71. Loyo, 1999, 180–185, Aguirre Beltrán, 1992, 69–74; Loyo, 1996b, 102–103; Lewis, 1999, 12.

72. SEP, 1927, 15–17, 31, 37, 51. See also Dawson, 2001, 329–361.

73. SEP, 1927, 35; Memorandum by Enrique Corona, 3 January 1927, AHSEP—ER box 1628, exp. 2.

74. SEP, 1927, 59–60.

75. Director, Educación Federal in Tepic, Nay, to Corona, 1 March 1926, 12 July 1926, AHSEP—ER, box 1628, exp. 1. See also Corona to chief, Escuelas Rurales, 18 November 1927, AHSEP—ER, box 1628, exp. 2.

76. Dr. Santiago Ramírez to Corona, 16 March 1931, AHSEP—ER box (849) 1474, exp. 7.

77. Corona to Ignacio Ramírez, 16 August 1926; Ramírez to Corona, 27 August 1926; Corona to Ramírez, 14 September 1926, AHSEP—ER box (859) 1658, exp. 1.

78. Dr. Alejandro Cerisola to Corona, 1 October 1931, AHSEP- ER box (849) 1474, exp. 4.

79. Corona, *Informe,* 5 November 1930, AHSEP—ER box 6214, exp. 34; Corona to

Ramírez, 14 May 1926, AHSEP—ER box (859)1658, exp. 1; SEP, 1927, 59–60, 72, 76, 110–116. See also Aguirre Beltrán, 1992, 100–101; Loyo, 1996b, 109–111.

80. Corona to Ramírez, 15 December 1926, AHSEP—ER box (859) 1658, exp. 1.

81. Corona, *Informe,* December 1930, AHSEP—ER box (1327) 1400, exp. 10.

82. Corona to Director of Misiones Culturales, 18 January 1929, AHSEP—ER box 6214, exp. 24.

83. See, for example, Corona, *Informe* for 1930, AHSEP—ER box (1327)1400, exp. 7; Prof. Braulio Rodríguez, *Informe,* 4 May 1931, AHSEP—ER box (849)1474, exp. 17.

84. Samuel Ramos to Oficial Mayor, Sec. de Relaciones Exteriores, 21 November 1931, AHSEP—ER box (849) 1474, exp. 3. See also R. Ramírez to Sub-Secretary of the SEP, 27 October 1930, AHSEP—ER box 1624, exp. 36; "Internados Regionales para Indios," *El Nacional* 15 December 1931; "Nuevo Centro de Indígenas," *El Nacional,* October 1931.

85. Braulio Rodríguez, *Informe,* 4 May 1931, 3–10; Corona, *Informe* for January 31 1932 to May 1932, 7 June 1932, AHSEP—ER box (849) 1474, exp. 41; Corona, *Informe,* 30 April 1929, AHSEP—ER box 6214, exp. 13. See also R. Ramírez, "Finalidades que persiguen el Departamento de Enseñanza Rural y Primaria Foránea," 15 July 1931, AHSEP—ER box (1099) 1724, exp. 16.

86. SEP, 1927, 132, 140–142. See also Corona, *Informe,* 5 November 1930, AHSEP—ER box 6214, exp. 4.

87. Corona, *Informe,* 30 April 1929, AHSEP—ER, box 6214, exp. 13. See also R. Ramírez, "Finalidades que persiguen . . . ," 15 July 1931.

88. Corona, *Informe* for 1930; Braulio Rodríguez, 4 May 1931; Agustín Rocha Saavedra to R. Ramírez, 30 June 1930, AHSEP—ER box 6214, exp. 6.

89. SEP, 1927, 38, 82, 86–87.

90. Corona, *Informe,* 17 October 1929, 3, AHSEP—ER, box 6214, exp. 13. Pamphlets for events are found in AHSEP—ER box 6214, exp. 4.

91. SEP, 1927, 67, 88.

92. Corona, *Informe,* December 1930, AHSEP—ER 1327/1400/10; Corona, *Informe,* 31 May 1932, AHSEP—ER (849) 1474/41.

93. This term appeared in several Informes for 1930 and 1931. See AHSEP—ER box (1327) 1400/7.

94. Rafael Ramírez to Sub-Secretary of the SEP, 27 October 1930, AHSEP—ER box 1624, exp. 36. See also Rafael Ramírez, *Informe* for Escuelas Rurales, 1 September 1932–31 July 1933, 8 August 1933, AHSEP—ER box (1099) 1724, exp. 2.

95. SEP, 1932, vol. 1, 70.

96. SEP, 1932, vol. 1, 30, 63–72. See also Loyo, 1996, 107–108; Lewis, 1999,13.

97. Reunion de los Directores de Educación Federal, que integran la 3/a zona Escolar de la República, Celaya, Gto., 3 May 1932, AHSEP—ER (870) 1495/1.

98. Jesus Valejo C. to Manuel Mesa, chief of EANR, 14 September 1934, 30 December 1934, AHSEP—EANR (3253) 365/8; Report of Roberto Peréz Basulto, Enfermero Especialista on mission, 30 December 1934, EANR (3253) 365/8; Gustavo Jarquín, chief of the Misión Cultural at Dzitbalché, Camp. to Manuel Mesa, chief of EANR, 25 January 1934, AHSEP—EANR (1359) 370/1; Report by A. Pereyra, Jefe de Misión Cultural in Dzitbalché, Camp, 30 April 1934, AHSEP—EANR (1359) 370/1.

99. "Dos Criterios acerca del Problema Indígena," *Excelsior,* 17 August 1931; ER Informe for 1928, AHSEP—ER 1795/16.

100. Rafael Ramírez to Basauri, 11 May 1931, AHSEP—ER 1327/2.

101. Basauri to SEP, 6 February 1931, AHSEP—ER 1327/2; Basauri, "Proyecto . . . Comisión de Investigaciones Indias para 1932," 2 December 1931, AHSEP—ER 1327/3; Rafael Ramírez to Basauri, 11 May 1931; Ignacio Ramírez, and Basauri to chief, ER, 8 April 1931, AHSEP—ER 1327/2.

102. Sáenz, 1936, 13–16, 28–38, 259–260; SEP, 1932, vol. 2, 11–13.

103. Sáenz, Report of 6 August 1932, AHSEP—ER 1327/3. See also Sáenz, 1936, 39, 259–260; ER *Informe* for 1931–1932, AHSEP—ER (1099) 1724/15.

104. Sáenz, 1936, 2–3, 10–11, 20–28, 43–55, 62–66, 87–103. Rafael Ramírez, ER *Informe* for 1933, 8 August 1933, AHSEP—ER (1099) 1724/2. See also Becker, 1995, 104–110; Purnell, 1999, 68–69.

105. Becker, 1995, 54–55.

106. Sáenz, 1936, xiii; 29–38, 60, 130–203, 227–276, 295–309; Rafael Ramírez, ER *Informe* for 1933, 8 August 1933, AHSEP—ER (1099) 1724/2; Rafael Ramírez, ER *Informe* General for 1933–1934, 31 July 1934, 9, 38–40, AHSEP—ER (1260) 1746-1723/8. See also Hewitt de Alcántara, 1984, 14–16.

107. Sáenz, 1936, 189; Manuel Velázquez Andrade, "¿Conocemos al Indio?" *El Nacional,* 13 August 1935.

108. Sáenz, 1936, 304–309.

Chapter 2. The Problems and Promise of the Internados Indígenas

1. Luis Monzón to Rafael Ramírez, chief of ER, 10 November 1933, 9, AHSEP—ER box (859) 1582, exp. 59.

2. Rufino Tamayo, "Opinion sobre la labor de las Misiones Culturales," 1 December 1932, AHSEP—ER (869) 1494/23.

3. Rafael Ramírez, ER *Informe General de la Labores de 1933,* 8 August 1933, AHSEP—ER (1099) 1724/2; "Centros de Educación Indígena," 1932, AHSEP—ER (1099) 1724/2. See also Ignacio García Tellez, Acuerdo no. 2409, 23 April 1935, AHSEP—ER (1328) 186/2.

4. "Centros de Educación Indígena," 1932; ER *Informe General de las labores de 1933;* Luis Monzón to R. Ramírez, 20 December 1933, AHSEP—ER 859 1683/8; ER *Informe* for 1933/34, AHSEP—ER (1260) 1746 1723/8.

5. SEP, 1937, 6–7.

6. "Centros de Educación Indígena," 1932; AHSEP—ER, *Informe General de las labores de 1933.*

7. Centros de Educación Indígena, 1932. See also "Juntas de los Directores de Educación Federal de los Estados de Yucatán, Campeche, Tabasco, y territorios de Quintana Roo, en la Ciudad de Merida, Yuc.," 21 October 1935, AHSEP—ER (189) 1331/11.

8. See Vaughan, 1997, 155–156.

9. The number of students enrolled in the internados represented only a small percentage of the Indian students enrolled in SEP schools; only about 3,000 of the 140,000 Indian students ever enrolled in SEP schools were students in the internados. They did, however, represent a significant endeavor for their pedagogy and efforts at teacher training. Rafael Ramírez, ER *Informe,* 1 September 1932 to 31 July 1933, 8 August 1933, AHSEP—ER (1099) 1724/2; Isidro Candia, *Informe* of the DAI, August 1941, AGN—MAC 606.3/44; SEP, 1937, 6–10; "Término de la situación miserable de nuestros Indígenas," *El Nacional,* 4 February 1938. See also critique of Lucio Mendieta y Núñez, *Los Tarascos,* 1940, AH—INAH vol. 21, exp 19.

10. ER, *Informe General de las Labores de 1933,* 8 August 1933, 14; Rafael Ramírez, *Informe General de la acción desarollada por el Departamento de Enseñanza Rural y Primaria Foránea durante el ejercicio de 1933–1934,* 31 July 1934, AHSEP—ER (1260) 1746–1723/8. See also Manuel Torres, Amuzgos, Oax., to Lázaro Cárdenas, 13 March 1936, AGN—LCR 533.4/12; Jenaro Domínguez, Florencia de Jesús and others, Ayutla, Oax., to Cárdenas, 14 June 1936, AGN—LCR 545.3/147. See also Loyo, 1996, 156–157.

11. Flores Zamora to Elena Torres, 10 May 1935, AHSEP—ER (1328) 186, exp. 8.

12. See Rubén Rodriguez Lozano, "Estudio General de la Huasteca Potosina para fundar la necesidad de crear una Direccion de Educacion Federal," March 1938, AGN—LCR 433/30329. See also Friedrich, 1986, 27–41.

13. Monzón to Rafael Ramírez, 27 September 1933, AHSEP—ER (859) 1582/59; Monzón to Ramírez, 10 November 1933, AHSEP—ER (859) 1582/59; Monzón to Ramírez, 24 August 1933, AHSEP—ER (859) 1582/59; Ramírez to Monzón, 22 June 1933, AHSEP—ER (859) 1582/59; Rafael Ramírez, ER *Informe* for May 1933, 8 June 1933, AHSEP—ER (1099) 1724/2.

14. Rafael Ramírez, ER *Informe* for April 1934, 30 April 1934, AHSEP—ER (1260) 1746–1723/8.

15. Rafael Ramírez, ER *Informe* for April 1934; Rafael Ramírez, ER *Informe* for June 1934, 30 June 1934, AHSEP—ER (1260) 1746–1723/8; ER *Informe* for 1934, AHSEP—ER (1260) 1746–1723/8.

16. Rafael Ramírez, ER *Informe* for June 1933, 30 June 1933, AHSEP—ER (1099) 1724/2.

17. Monzón to R. Ramírez, 10 November 1933, AHSEP—ER (859) 1582/59.

18. Monzón to R. Ramírez, 10 November 1933.

19. Monzón to R. Ramírez, 20 December 1933, AHSEP—ER 859 1683/8; ER *Informe* for 1933/34, AHSEP—ER (1260) 1746–1723/8; R. Ramírez to Monzón, 28 September 1933, AHSEP—ER 859 1583/55; Monzón, "Que puede hacer la escuela por los Indios mexicanos durante seis años," AHSEP—ER 859 1583/55; Monzón to R. Ramirez, 20 July 1933, AHSEP—ER 859 1683/8; Monzón to Ramírez 10 November 1933, AHSEP—ER (859) 1582/59.

20. Monzón to R. Ramírez, 12 October 1934, AHSEP—ER 859 1683/8.

21. Monzón to R. Ramírez, 12 October 1934.

22. Luis Monzón, "La elevación del indio mexicano mediante el funcionamiento de un DEPARTAMENTO AUTOCTONO. Motivos y puntos fundamentales," AHSEP—ER (859) 1683/8.

23. Luis Monzón, "La elevación del indio mexicano . . ."

24. See, for example, Díaz Polanco, 1997; Tresierra, 1994.

25. R. Ramírez, ER *Informe* for 1933–1934, 31 July 1934, AHSEP—ER (1260) 1746–1723/8.

26. R. Ramírez, ER *Informe* for April 1934; R. Ramírez, ER *Informe* for May 1934, 31 May 1934, AHSEP—ER (1260) 1746–1723/8; R. Ramírez, ER *Informe* for July 1934, 31 July 1934, AHSEP—ER (1260) 1746–1723/8; R. Celso Flores Zamora, ER *Informe* for November 1935, 30 November 1935, AHSEP—ER (1331) 189/5; Prof. Jacinto A. Téllez, report on SLP, 18 May 1935, AHSEP—ER (1328) 186.3/2.

27. SEP, 1937b, vol. 1, 406–410.

28. "Nueva orientación a internados indígenas," *El Nacional,* 14 July 1936.

29. "Nueva orientación a internados indígenas," *El Nacional,* 14 July 1936.

30. "El problema indígena. Puntos de vista de los comisionados de la Secretaría de

Educación, en el congreso de Ixmiquilpan, Hgo.," *El Nacional,* 30 Sept 1936; SEP, 1935, 100–110, SEP, 1937, 7–8.

31. SEP, 1937b, vol. 1, 401.

32. SEP, 1937b, vol. 1, 401.

33. SEP, 1937b, vol. 1, 403; "Activa campaña en favor de la cultura indígena,"*El Nacional,* 16 February 1938; Celso Flores Zamora, ER *Informe* for May 1935, AHSEP—ER (1331) 189/5; Ignacio García Tellez (SEP), Acuerdo no. 2409, 23 April 1935, AHSEP—ER (1328) 186/2.

34. "Término de la situación miserable de nuestros indígenas," *El Nacional,* 4 February 1938; "Para acrecentar la economía de los campesinos indígenas," *El Nacional,* 20 April 1939.

35. SEP, 1937b, vol. 1, 408–410.

36. See, among others, José Ruiz and others, Nacajuca, Tab. to Cárdenas, December 1939, AGN—LCR 151.3/1384; Ayuntamiento de Hueyapan, Pue., to Cárdenas, 31 May 1940, AGN—LCR 151.3/1704; 13 signatories from Atliaca, Gro., to Cárdenas, 22 February 1940, AGN—LCR 404.1/7395; "Pliego de Peticiones que presenten las Autoridades, vecinos y Director de la Escuela Primaria Federal del Pueblo de Huauclilla, Nochix, Oax. Ante el C. Presidente de la Republica Gral. Lázaro Cárdenas," 7 November 1936, AGN—LCR 545.3/147; "Un Internado Indígena en Paracho, Mich.," *El Nacional,* 30 October 1935; "Solicitudes Para Centros de Indígenas," *Excelsior,* 3 July 1937; Loyo, 1996, 153–155.

37. See, among others, Autoridades y Vecinos (23 signatories) of San Fernando de Matamoros, Zimatlán, Oax., to SEP, 26 July 1938, AGN—LCR 533.4/31; Gustavo de la Cruz, "Comité Regional Agrario "Primo Tapia," Naranja, Mich., to Cárdenas, 28 October 1939, AGN—LCR 533.4/32; Estéban Espinosa to Cárdenas, 10 August 1937, AGN—LCR 533.4/32; Rockwell, 1994, 171.

38. Presidente Municipal, Presidente Comité Agrario, the Comité de Educación, and the Comité del PNR, along with 38 actual signatures, and 14 more who signed on behalf of over 100 others, from the Pueblo of Coapilla, Chiapas, to Cárdenas, 8 November 1936, AGN—LCR 533.4/20.

39. Autoridades y Vecinos, San Fernando de Matamoros, Zimatlán, Oax., to SEP, 26 July 1938.

40. See, among others, Rosendo García and others, Zongozotla, Pue., to Cárdenas, 9 December 1937; Federico López and others, Amuzgos, Oax., to Cárdenas, 21 May 1937; Jenaro Domínguez and others, Ayutla, Oax., to Cárdenas, 14 June 1936. All citations in AGN—LCR 545.3/147.

41. See, for example, Ramon Entzana Reyes y José Torres, San Juan Yautepec, Mex., to Cárdenas, 1 November 1938, AGN—LCR 534.1/847.

42. See, among others, Angel Corzo to SEP, 25 February 1930, 2 July 1930; J. Guadalupe Aguilera to SEP, 12 April 1932. All cited in AHSEP—DEPM, caja 6 6288/1. See also Rockwell, 1994, 191–199.

43. See, for example, Sociedad de Alumnos in Techímal, Hgo., to Avila Camacho, 15 December 1941, AGN—MAC 534.4/2; Autoridades y Vecinos, San Fernando de Matamoros, Zimatlán, Oax., to SEP, 26 July 1938.

44. Prof. Juan F. Campos G., Bolaños, Jal., to Cárdenas, 12 April 1937, AGN—LCR 534/126.

45. Federico Antuna H., Bolaños, Jal., to Cárdenas, 20 December 1936, AGN—LCR 534/126.

46. Federico Antuna H., Bolaños, Jal., to Cárdenas, 27 December 1936, AGN–LCR 534/126.

47. Cenovio de la Cruz, Tuxpan, Jal., to Cárdenas, 24 December 1937, AGN–LCR 534/126.

48. Ten signatories from Chenalhó, Chis., to Cárdenas, 28 March 1940, AGN–LCR 606.1/625.

49. Pedro Manuel, José Luciano, and 44 others, all illiterate, Techimal, Hgo., to Cárdenas, 4 February 1937, AGN–LCR 534.3/545.

50. See, for example, Maria Del Carmen Navarro, El Caró, Mex., to Cárdenas, 10 August 1938, AGN–LCR 704.3/190.

51. See, for example, Rosendo García y otros, Zongozotla, Pue., to Cárdenas, 9 Dec. 1937; Federico López, Amuzgos, Oax., to Cárdenas, 21 May 1937; Jenaro Domínguez, Florencia de Jesús y otros, Ayutla, Oax., to Cárdenas, 14 June 1936; Profs. Alvaro R. Mendoza, Arturo Trujillo, and others, Cacate, Ixtapa, Chis., to Cárdenas, 16 March 1936; Manuel Torres, Amuzgos, Oax., to Cárdenas, 13 March 1936. All cited from AGN–LCR 545.3/147. See also Raúl Noriega, "Dirección Revolucionaria en los Asuntos Indígenas," *El Nacional,* 18 April 1937; José Salinas, C. Santos, SLP, to Cárdenas, 16 February 1937, AGN–LCR 533.4/24.

52. Gregorio Vázquez, Trinidad González and others, Cuatepec, Pue., to Cárdenas, 3 January 1938, AGN–LCR 534.6/850.

53. Fifteen Yaqui representatives, Vicám, Son., to Cárdenas, 20 August 1937, AGN–LCR 533.11/1; Guadalupe Santiago, Chalcatongo, Oax., to Cárdenas, 3 January 1937, AGN–LCR 130/405; Avelino García, Chalcatongo, Oax., to Cárdenas, 24 January 1937, AGN–LCR 130/405.

54. R. Ramírez, ER *Informe* for July 1934, 31 July 1934.

55. See, among others, Fausto García R. and Victoria García de Quintero to Cárdenas, 20 February 1937, AGN–LCR 534.6/624; Martín Díaz, Ametanango del Valle, Chis., to Cárdenas, 19 February 1937, AGN–LCR 534.6/624; Ezequiel A. Sánchez, San Luis Acatlán, Gro., to Cárdenas, 28 January 1939, AGN–LCR 534.6/499; Francisco Reyes, Caró, Mex., to Cárdenas, 22 April 1938, AGN–LCR 534.6/664; Tobías Cardoso, San Gabriolito, Gro., to Cárdenas, 11 January 1938, AGN–LCR 533.4/25. See also, Loyo, 1996, 146–152; Sotelo Arévalo, 1996, 50–56, 95; Becker, 1995, 124–128.

56. See, for example, Luis Felipe Obregón to chief of ER, 31 October 1934, AHSEP–ER (1151) 1725/5; ER *Informe* for 1933/34; R. Ramírez, ER *Informe* for April 1934, 30 April 1934.

57. Juan Gallardo Moreno to Secretaría de Communicaciones y Obras Públicas, 15 August 1939, AGN–LCR 151.3/1251.

58. See, among others, Fidel Chávez, Tlaxiaco, Oax., to Cárdenas, 23 June 1938, AGN–LCR 533.4/39; Agustín Lanuza Jr. to Governor of Oaxaca, 30 June 1938, AGN–LCR 533.4/39; Pablo García León, Tlaxiaco, Oax., to Cárdenas, 27 June 1938, AGN–LCR 533.4/39.

59. Aguirre Beltrán, 1992, 110–111. González y González, 1997, 105–123, 274.

60. Rockwell, 1994, 186–199.

61. Gabriela López, and others, Caró, Mex., to Cárdenas, 30 May 1937 AGN–LCR 534/205; Prof. Fernando Basauri. F. Vázquez M. and others, Caró, Mex., to Cárdenas, 11 July 1937, AGN–LCR 534/205.

62. See proclamation of Sindicato de Trabajo of Asuntos Indígenas, Chenalhó, Chis., 13 August 1943, AGN–MAC 541.1/60.

63. Sindicato de Trabajo of Asuntos Indígenas, in Chenalhó, Chis., 13 August 1943.

See also student and teacher protests in August 1943, AGN—MAC 541.1/60; Governor Isidrio Fabela, Toluca, Mex., to Avila Camacho, 29 July 1943, AGN—MAC 541.1/60.

64. Francisco Estrada and others, Matlapa, SLP, to their fellow students in Comalco, 5 August 1943, AGN—MAC 541.1/60.

65. SEP, 1937b, vol. 1, 406–410.

66. Dir. Prof. Elpidio López, reporting on Chiapas, 20 May 1935, AHSEP—ER (1328) 186.3/2; Prof. Rosario C. Martínez, Tónachic, Chih., June 1944, AGN—MAC 404.1/3381.

67. Conferencia de Jóvenes Mexicanos, (DF) to Avila Camacho, 10 February 1945, AGN—MAC 485.1/1.

68. Iwanska, 1977, 19–39.

69. Interview with Jesús Pedraza and Sabin O. Roque, of the Consejo Supremo Ñhañhu del Valle de Mezquital, Ixmiquilpan, Hgo., 26 April 2000.

70. Interview with Prof. Juan Ramírez Pedraza, Ixmiquilpan, Hgo., 25 April 2000.

71. Interview with Prof. Juan Ramírez Pedraza, 25 April 2000; Loyo, 1996, 148–152.

72. Proclamation of Porfirio Hernández and others, Caró, Mex., 18 August 1938, AGN—LCR 534/205.

73. Loyo, 1996, 159.

74. Report of Prof. Rosario C. Martínez, June 1944, AGN—MAC 404.1/3381; "Estudio de la Región Tarahumara. Presentado por el Departamento de Trabajo," June 1936, AGN—LCR 533.4/12; Reyes Rocha et al., 1991, 33–35.

75. Loyo, 1996, 148–152. See also Basauri, 1940, vol. 3, 256–266.

76. Vaughan, 1997, 155–156.

77. Raúl Donde (DF), to SEP, 29 March 1935, AGN—LCR 533.11/1.

78. Luis Chávez Orozco to Cárdenas, 3 August 1939, AGN—LCR 533.11/1.

79. Fifteen Yaqui representatives, Vicám, Son., to Cárdenas, 20 August 1937, AGN—LCR 533.11/1.

80. Ingacio García Téllez to Col. J. Manuel Núñez, 14 October 1937, AGN—LCR 533.11/1; Graciano Sánchez to private secretary of Cárdenas, 26 January 1938 AGN—LCR 533.11/1; Cárdenas to Román Yocupicio (Governor of Sonora), 12 June 1939, AGN—LCR 533.11/1. See also Vaughan, 1997, 155–156; Bantjes, 1998, 144–149.

81. Mauricio Swadesh to Cárdenas, 1 August 1939, AGN—LCR 533.3/18.

82. DAI, 1940, 8–10, 81–82, 90–103.

83. "Plan del Proyecto Tarasco" AH—INAH vol. 17, 1939, exp 9.

84. Jorge A. Vivo, "México y el Indio," *El Nacional,* 14 May 1937.

85. Reyes Rocha et al., 32–33.

86. Luis I. Rodríguez (private secretary, Cárdenas) to Gonzalo Vazquez Vela (SEP), 20 July 1936; Victorio E. Góngora to Francisco Múgica (Sec. de Comunicaciones y Obras Públicas), 4 July 1936; SEP to Rodríguez, 29 July 1936. All in AGN—LCR 531.2/244.

87. Mauricio Swadesh to Cárdenas, 1 August 1939.

88. "Plan del Proyecto Tarasco."

89. DAI, 1940, 20–21, 33–34; "Plan del Proyecto Tarasco."

90. "Plan del Proyecto Tarasco"; Aguirre Beltrán, 1992, 126–131; Reyes Rocha et al., 33–35.

91. DAI, 1940b; "Plan del Proyecto Tarasco."

92. Prof. Antonio Luna, Paracho, Mich., to Cárdenas, 10 May 1940. On 12 May 1940, Cárdenas ordered that most of the requests be carried out. Both cited in AGN—LCR 534.3/1565. See also thirty-seven signatories from Paracho to Cárdenas, 11 May 1940, AGN—LCR 534.3/1565.

93. Swadesh to Cárdenas, 21 May 1940, AGN—LCR 151.3/1124.

94. Reyes Rocha et al., 33–35.

95. Vaughan, 1997, 4, 8–9; Rockwell, 1994, 199–204.

96. Cárdenas to Autoridades municipales y vecinos de los Pueblos correspondientes a la Sierra de Juárez y circunvecinos al pueblo de Guelatao, Guelatao de Juárez, Oax., 25 April 1939, AGN—LCR 533.4/22.

97. Margarito García, Agente Municipal, Ixtlán de Juárez, Oax., to Cárdenas, 17 February 1937; Margarito García to Cárdenas, 18 February 1937. Both cited in AGN—LCR 30/405. Maximiliano García Moguel to Lic. Gonzalo Vázquez Vela (SEP), 30 June 1937, AGN—LCR 533.4/22.

98. Francisco I. Ramírez, Presidente Municipal of Ixtlán de Juárez, Oax., to Maximiliano García Moguel, 14 June 1937, AGN—LCR 533.4/22.

99. Maximiliano García Moguel to Lic. Gonzalo Vázquez Vela (SEP), 30 June 1937.

100. Speech by Agustín M. García Moguel, personal secretary of Maximiliano García Moguel, 27 June 1937, AGN—LCR 533.4/22. Maximiliano García Moguel to Lic. Gonzalo Vázquez Vela, 30 June 1937.

101. Fifty signatories from the "Agrupación Indígena Regional Benito Juárez," Guelatao de Juarez, Oax., to Cárdenas, 15 March 1938, AGN—LCR 533.4/22.

102. José Ochoa Rentería to Cárdenas, 3 October 1938, 9 October 1938, 20 March 1940. All in AGN—LCR 702.2/104–20.

103. Cárdenas to Autoridades Municipales y vecinos de los Pueblos correspondientes a la Sierra de Juárez y circunvecinos al pueblo de Guelatao, Guelatao de Juárez, Oax., 25 April 1939, AGN—LCR 533.4/22.

104. J. González Gallo to Ávila Camacho, 6 November 1942; Chief of SEP to González Gallo, 16 November 1942. Both in AGN—MAC 534.3/103. Hermenegildo Luis to Avila Camacho, 4 March 1941, 27 December 1943. Both in AGN—MAC 151.3/37.

105. Manuel Torres, Ixtlán de Juárez, Oax., to Ávila Camacho, 12 November 1941, AGN—MAC 151.3/37.

106. Mónico Chín, Presidente del Comisario Ejidal de Chunhuas, QR, and four others, to Cárdenas, 12 January 1940, AGN—LCR 151.3/1407; Ignacio M. Beteta, to Cárdenas, 19 August 1938, AGN—LCR 533.11/1. Benjamín Gómez H., Procurador de Comunidades Indígenas, Zacatepec, Oax., to Cárdenas, 1 July 1939, AGN—LCR 533.4/48.

107. Basauri, 1940, vol. 1, 513–516.

108. Petition of Pedro I. Pérez, Guelatao, Oax., 18 February 1941, AGN—MAC 534.3/103; Prof. Leopoldo Carrando Carasco, Jefe Departamento Indígena, to director of the internado in Guelatao, 3 May 1941, AGN—MAC 534.3/103.

109. Leopoldo Carrando Carasco to director of the internado in Guelatao, 3 May 1941.

110. Comparatively, see Boyer, 1998, 413–454.

Chapter 3. Science and State Formation in the Departamento de Asuntos Indígenas

1. "Editorial. Nueva actitud del estado frente a la masa india," *El Nacional,* 20 April 1937.

2. "Proyecto de reforma a la Ley de Secretaros de Estado, para fundar un organismo nuevo en favor de los indios de México," 10 September 1935, AGN—LCR 545.2/45.

3. Eulogio R. Valdivieso and Andrés Molina Enríquez, of the "Organización de los

Indios de la o, República," to Cárdenas, 14 February 1936, AGN—LCR 533.4/1. See also, among others, Ricardo Ramiro Matamoros A. to Cárdenas, 1 January 1935, AGN—LCR 545.3/147.

4. Sáenz, 1936, 313–322; Sáenz, "Sobre la creación de un Departamento de Población Indígena," 6 November 1935, AGN—LCR 533.4/1.

5. Sáenz, "Sobre la creación . . ."

6. Sáenz, "Sobre la creación . . ."

7. Sáenz, "Sobre la creación . . ."; Sáenz, 1936, 335–336.

8. Sáenz, "Sobre la creación . . ."; Sáenz, 1936, 343.

9. Sáenz, "Sobre la creación . . ."

10. Sáenz, 1936, 325–335; Sáenz, "Sobre la creación . . ."

11. Sáenz, 1936, 336–337.

12. Sáenz, "Sobre la creación . . ."

13. Sáenz, 1936, 340.

14. Sáenz, 1936, 334; Sáenz to Cárdenas, 6 November 1935, AGN—LCR 533.4/1.

15. Sáenz to Cárdenas, 6 November 1935.

16. Lázaro Cárdenas, "Parrafos de la iniciativa de reformas a la ley de secretarias de estado, en lo referente a la creación del Departamento de Asuntos Indígenas," 1935, AGN—LCR 533.4/1; "Programa de Acción del Departamento de Asuntos Indígenas," 1936, AGN—LCR 545.2/45. See also Durán, 1972, 167–168.

17. DAI, 1938e, 28–34; "Los Centros de educación indígena," *MR* 10:1 (July 1937) 10.

18. See, for example, "Las miserias de los indios," *El Nacional,* 10 May 1936; "En defensa de los indígenas, casi esclavos," *Excelsior,* 5 April 1936; "Como tratan en Chiapas a los infelices indios," *El Universal,* 5 April 1936.

19. Cárdenas, "Parrafos de la iniciativa . . . Asuntos Indígenas," 1935. See also, among others; "El Despertar Socialista Indígena," *MR* 7:3 (1 August 1935) 25–26; "Los nuevos misioneros de la cultura y de la civilización," *MR* 4:8 (1 April 1934) 8–9; "Mejoría de Nuestra Población Aborigen," *El Nacional,* 6 July 1937. See also Guevara Niebla, 1985; Becker, 1995, 70–75, 111–115; González y González, 1997, 105–123.

20. Raúl Noriega, "Dirección Revolucionaria en los Asuntos Indígenas," *El Nacional,* 18 April 1937.

21. See, for example, "No ha mejorado nada la condición de los indígenas de Chiapas," *Excelsior,* 1 July 1934; Ignacio Morelos Zaragoza, "El Eterno crimen de los hombres blancos," *Excelsior,* 7 July 1934; Rafael López Ocampo, "La Campaña Pro-Indio en el Estado de Chiapas," *El Nacional,* 12 August 1934; F. Rodríguez Cabo, Insp. Federal de Trabajo, Study of Labor Problems in Chiapas, 30 Sept 1935, 3–5, AGN—LCR533.4/12. See also Cortés Zavala, 1995.

22. Sánchez to SHCP, 9 June 1936, AGN—LCR 568.1/5.

23. Cárdenas, "Parrafos de la iniciativa . . . Asuntos Indígenas," 1935; "Programa de Acción del Departamento de Asuntos Indígenas," 1936. See also "Editorial. Nueva actitud del estado frente a la masa india," *El Nacional,* 20 April 1937.

24. "Término de la Situación Miserable de Nuestros Indígenas," *El Nacional,* 4 February 1938; "Programa de Acción del Departamento de Asuntos Indígenas," 1936.

25. "Proyecto . . . organismo nuevo en favor de los indios de México."

26. DAI, 1938f, 3–4; "Proyecto . . . organismo nuevo en favor de los indios de México"; "Explotación vergonzosa," *El Universal,* 10 May 1936.

27. Córdova, 1995, 451.

28. Basilia R., widow of Trevino Solis, Cd. Victoria, Tamaulipas, to Cárdenas, 10 March 1935, AGN—LCR 444.1/81.

29. See among others, Federico Fernández V. and J. Carmen Carreto A., Tlaxcala Tlax., to Cárdenas, 18 June 1935, AGN—LCR 403/143; Manuel Luque, and others, Higuera de Zaragoza, Sin., to Cárdenas, 3 December 1934, AGN—LCR 702.12/3.

30. "Programa de acción del Departamento de Asuntos Indígenas," 1936.

31. Sánchez to Hacienda y Crédito Público, 9 June 1936; Sánchez to Cárdenas, 10 June 1936; Cárdenas to Sánchez, 18 September 1936. All in AGN—LCR 568.1/5. See also Mendieta y Núñez, 1938, 26–33; "Dept. de Asuntos Indígenas," *Excelsior,* 2 January 1937.

32. Cárdenas, "Parrafos de la iniciativa . . . Asuntos Indígenas," 1935; "Programa de Acción del Departamento de Asuntos Indígenas," 1936; "Proyecto . . . organismo nuevo en favor de los indios de México."

33. Proyecto . . . organismo nuevo en favor de los indios de México"; "Programa de acción del Departamento de Asuntos Indígenas"; Sánchez to SCHP, 9 June 1936, AGN—LCR 568.1/5.

34. Mendieta y Núñez, 1938, 26–33.

35. Sánchez to SCHP, 9 June 1936, AGN—LCR 568.1/5.

36. Gov. Efrain A. Gutiérrez, Chis., to Lic. Raúl Castellanos, (personal secretary of Cárdenas), 24 August 1938, AGN—LCR 533.31/9.

37. See, among others, Leopoldo Payán, Tlaxiaco, Oax., to Cárdenas, 6 January 1940, AGN—LCR 531.2/244; Federico Hernandez Lopez, DF, to Cárdenas, 3 November 1937, AGN—LCR 704.3/246; Prof. Diego Hernández Topete, Morelia, Mich., to Cárdenas, 28 January 1937, AGN—LCR 531.2/244.

38. "Dept. de Asuntos Indígenas," *Excelsior,* 2 January 1937; "Dept. de Asuntos Indígenas," *Excelsior,* 2 September 1936; DAI, 1938f, 12–14.

39. Sánchez to Cárdenas, 1 April 1937, AGN—LCR 533.11/1; DAI, 1938f, 12–14; Mendieta y Núñez, 1938, 26–33.

40. "Término de la situación miserable de nuestros indígenas," *El Nacional,* 4 February 1938; Cárdenas to DAI 13 January 1938, AGN—LCR 545.3/147; "Activa campaña en favor de la cultura indígena," *El Nacional,* 16 February 1938; DAI, 1938f, 4–5, 8–11. The budget for the INAH in 1940 was $705,000.00. Alfonso Caso to Lic. Aurelio Bueno (SHCP), 4 July 1940, AH—INAH vol. 19, 1940, exp. 4. The following is from SHCP, *Cuenta Pública,* comparing expenditures of the DAI and SEP, from 1936 to 1946:

	DAI	SEP
1936	666,684.04	51,480,593.91
1937	381,162.90	63,946,292.38
1938	2,171,261.83	64,037,263.23
1939	2,885,519.09	67,037,263.23
1940	2,958,801.43	74,952,145.32
1941	3,038,373.34	76,722,686.35
1942	2,889.347.34	85,662,201.90
1943	3,105,776.83	94,415,901.87
1944	3,698,392.36	129,720,006.88
1945	3,860,046.41	170,035,182.05
1946	4,031,064.77	199,065,663.23

41. Octavio Campos Salas to Cárdenas, 15 July 1939, AGN—LCR 533.4/12; DAI, 1938f, 4–5; Isauro Villareal Barte to Cárdenas, 25 April 1938, AGN—LCR 545.3/147; Prof. José Aguero García, Ing. Efraín Castro, El Mexe, Hgo., to Cárdenas, 8 April 1938, AGN—LCR 545.3/147; Guillermo Durán to Cárdenas, 23 March 1939, AGN—LCR 432/1035; Antonio González V. to Cárdenas, 1 February 1939, AGN—LCR 432/1035; Manuel Espinosa and others, Cd. Obregón, Son., to Cárdenas, 8 August 1938, AGN—LCR 703/26.

42. Francisco Huizar R., Maestro Rural Federal, Colotlán, Jal., to Cárdenas, 11 August 1938, AGN—LCR 53.4/41. See also Salomón Córdoba, Ayotzinapa, Gro., to Cárdenas, 29 August 1938, AGN—LCR 704.3/246; sixty signatories from the Sindicato Unico de Trabajadores de la Enseñanza Superior Campesina (Huamantla, Tlax.), to Cárdenas, 25 August 1938, AGN—LCR 704.3/246.

43. Five internado directors to Cárdenas, 21 June 1938, AGN—LCR 545.3/147.

44. Sixty signatories from the Sindicato Unico de Trabajadores de la Enseñanza Superior Campesina (Huamantla, Tlax.), to Cárdenas, 25 August 1938.

45. See Comisario Ejidal, Ramón Chávez, San Jorge de Bellavista, Canatlán, Dgo., to Cárdenas, 6 August 1938, AGN—LCR 703/26; Pedro Gallegos G., Presidente Muncipal, Cd. Valles, SLP, to Cárdenas, 6 February 1937, AGN—LCR 703.4/205. See also Sánchez to Roberto Espinoza Pérez and Ingnacio Olivas, Fed. Uniones y Sindicatos Obreros, 21 September 1938, AGN—LCR 703/26.

46. Gilberto Loyo to Cárdenas, 27 December 1938, AGN—LCR 703/26. See also Prof. Antonia García M. and Manuel Rubio Jaime to Cárdenas, September 1938, AGN—LCR 703/26.

47. Enedino Torres and Pantaleón Torres, Ixmiquilpan, Hgo., to Cárdenas, 12 June 1938, AGN—LCR 545.3/147.

48. Fidencio Zavala, Ixmiquilpan, to Cárdenas, 7 June 1938; Manuel Rubio Jaime to Cárdenas, 24 May 1938. Both in AGN—LCR 534/276.

49. See, among others, Fidencio Zavala to Cárdenas, 17 June 1938, AGN—LCR 534/276. Sindicato Unico de Trabajadores de la Enseñanza Superior Campesina (Huamantla, Tlax.), to Cárdenas, 25 August 1938; Salomón Córdoba, Ayotzinapa, Gro., to Cárdenas, 29 August 1938, AGN—LCR 704.3/246.

50. Salomón Córdoba, Ayotzinapa, Gro., to Cárdenas, 29 August 1938; Gildardo Salinas, Amuzgos, Oax., to Cárdenas, 20 July 1938, AGN—LCR 704.3/246.

51. Prof. Eusebio Sánchez to C. Pataleón Torres, Ixmiquilpan, Hgo., 18 July 1938, AGN—LCR 534/276; Graciano Sánchez to Raúl Castellano (personal secretary of Cárdenas), 23 June 1938, AGN—LCR 534/276; Graciano Sánchez to C. E. Rubio V., Ozuluama, Ver., 27 August 1938, AGN—LCR 704.3/246; Eusebio Sánchez to Manuel Villarreal M. (Durango), 2 August 1938, AGN—LCR 704.3/246.

52. Pantaleón Torres to Cárdenas, 29 June 1938, AGN—LCR 534/276.

53. See Manuel Gamio, "Algunas consideraciones sobre niveles culturales de los grupos indios y mestizos," PCII, April 1940, AIMG, box 9, exp. 51; Moisés Mendoza, "Panorama de México. El mixteco, idioma vivo," *El Nacional,* 30 March 1939; J. de la Fuente, "El Congreso Indígena Huasteco," *El Nacional,* 10 December 1939; DAI, 1940, 57–62; "La Población Indígena de México," Información del DAI para el Primer Congreso Demográfico Interamericano, (section de Etnología y Eugenesia) Mexico, 12 October 1943, AGN—MAC 433/164. See also de la Peña, 1998, 71.

54. See Lombardo Toledano, 1936, 97–120. See also Sáenz, 1933; Sáenz, 1933b; Chávez Orozco, 1933; Marzal, 1989, 432–433.

55. Elena Torres to chief, EARN, 18 February 1935, AHSEP—EANR box 3307/418, exp. 418.8. See also Prof. Alfredo Granguillhome O., "Opiniones de Maestros. La Alfabetización Indígena," *El Nacional,* 8 December 1937.

56. "La dignificación de las lenguas indígenas," *MR* (15 March 1934) 9; Jorge A. Vivo, "México y el indio," *El Nacional,* 14 May 1937; Basauri, 1940, vol. 1, 113–131; "Término de la situación miserable de nuestros indígenas," *El Nacional,* 4 February 1938.

57. DAI, 1940, 8–10.

58. In all, there were fifty-seven delegates. DAI, 1940, xiv.

59. DAI, 1940, 43–44, 81–82. See also Díaz Polanco, 1997.

60. DAI, 1940, x, 18.

61. DAI, 1940, vi–x, 33–34.

62. Their efforts were aimed at developing literacy in indigenous languages in Mexico. Townsend met hostility because he was both American and Protestant, but in 1935 used his connections to Sáenz to establish an experimental station in Tetelcingo, Morelos, for Nahuatl. de la Peña, 1996, 64–68; Comas, 1964, 37–39.

63. See, for example, Sáenz to Cárdenas, 5 January 1939, AGN—LCR 533.4/1.

64. Sáenz, 1939, x–xii.

65. Sáenz, 1939, 13–19, 20–23, 39–52, 72, 94–110.

66. Sáenz, 1939, 114–115.

67. Sáenz, 1939, 116–128, 203–208, 212–219.

68. Sáenz, 1939, 223–233.

69. Luis Chávez Orozco to Cárdenas, 18 December 1939, AGN—LCR 533.4/1.

70. Comas, 1964, 41–49; Kemper, 1984, 143.

71. Delegates voted to create the Instituto Indigenista Interamericano (III), to be based in Mexico City, with an executive committee headed by Luis Chávez Orozco and Moisés Sáenz. For pluralist views expressed at the PCII, see Profa. Dolores Medina Guzmán, presentation of the Instituto Nacional de Psicopedagogia, BNAH—PCII; Javier Piña y Palacios et al., "Las razas indígenas y la defensa social," BNAH—PCII; Ramon G. Bonfil, "La integración de la comunidad indígena como base para promover el desenvolvimiento de los grupos autóctonos," BNAH—PCII; Conclusions from "Seccion Juridica," BNAH—PCII; "Educación Indígena," Acta Final of the PCII, AGN—LCR 533.4/1.

72. Mari. De los Angeles Azcarate de Chávez Orozco, "Ponencia del Comite Nacional de Ayuda al Niño Indígena ante el PCII," BNAH—PCII; Jorge A. Vivo, "Rasgos tribales y nacionales del problema indígena," BNAH—PCII.

73. See, among others, Prof. Luis Alvarez Barret, "La política de educación indígena de la revolución mexicana," BNAH—PCII; Ramon G. Bonfil, "La integración de la comunidad indígena . . ."; Acta 25 and Acta 30 of the Acta Final of the PCII, AGN—LCR 533.4/1.

74. Jorge A. Vivo, "Rasgos tribales y rasgos nacionales . . ."

75. Jorge A. Vivo, "Rasgos tribales y rasgos nacionales . . ."

76. Alvarez Barret, "La política de educación indígena . . ."; Alfonso Villa Rojas, "Sobre la Organización Política de los indios Tzeltales del estado de Chiapas, Mex.," BNAH—PCII.

77. Alvarez Barret, "La política de educación indígena . . ."

78. See, among others, Alfonso Caso, "Protección de las artes populares," BNAH—PCII; Alfonso Pulido Islas, "Las artes populares indias," BNAH—PCII.

79. Cárdenas, Address to the PCII, BNAH—PCII.

80. Cárdenas, Address to the PCII.

81. Durán, 1972, 171–175.

82. Cárdenas, Address to the PCII.

83. See, for example Hamilton, 1982; Bantjes, 1998; González y González, 1997. See also Scott, 1998.

84. Edmundo Domínguez, "Ponencia Otomí," BNAH—PCII; Adrian Plácido López, (delegado de la raza mixteca del estado de Oaxaca), "Ponencia que el Delegado al Congreso Interamericano . . . ," BNAH—PCII. On the objections, see Grl. Eduardo Hay (SRE) to Cárdenas, 24 November 1939; Cárdenas to Hay, 27 November 1939. Both in AGN—LCR 533.4/1.

85. *MR* 13:3–4 (March–April, 1940) 10.

86. On this tendency see, among others, "Los nuevos misioneros de la cultura y de la civilización," *MR* 4:8 (1 April 1934) 8–9; Prof. Rafael Ramírez, "Formación y capacidad de los maestros rurales para hacer eficaz la acción de la escuela en los pueblos indígenas," *MR* 7:7 (1 October 1935) 11–12; Basauri, 1940, vol. 1, 101.

87. "Una conferencia sobre el problema indígena," *El Universal,* 25 March 1935; "Discurso del señor general Cárdenas," *El Universal,* 26 September 1936. See also Aguirre Beltrán, 1992, 120–125.

88. Luis L. León, "Al margen de la campaña cardenista. La incorporación de los núcleos indígenas," *El Nacional,* 28 June 1934.

89. José Pavia Crespo, "El indígena al margen de la ley," *El Nacional,* 30 December 1937; José Pavia Crespo, "El indígena y el mundo político," *El Nacional,* 5 November 1937. See also Gamio, 1987, 22–23. 54–70.

90. Elena Torres to chief, EARN, 18 February 1935, AHSEP—EANR box 3307/418, exp. 418.8.

91. "Sección Editorial. El mensaje de la realidad," *Grafico,* 20 May 1937.

92. de la Peña, 1996, 41–81.

93. SEP, 1937b, vol. 1, 411–412; "Investigación científica de las condiciones de que se hallan los indios de México," *Excelsior,* 16 June 1937.

94. See Blaut, 1993; Clifford, 1988; Warman, 1970; Knight, 1990; González y González, 1997, 105–123.

95. Luis Castillo Ledón (MN) to INAH, 29 June 1939, AH—INAH vol. 16, 1938–1936, exp. 6; "Investigación científica de las condiciones de que se hallan los indios de México," *Excelsior,* 16 June 1937; Angel M. Corzo, "Cuestionario para fijar la cultura de las razas indígenas de México," n.d., AGN—LCR 533.4/1; Angel Corzo to Cárdenas, 8 March 1940, 22 April 1940, AGN—LCR 533.11/5; Basauri, 1940, vol. 1, 7–11,

96. SEP, 1937b, vol. 1, 411–412; Corzo, "Cuestionario para fijar . . ."

97. Corzo, "Cuestionario para fijar . . ."

98. Corzo, "Cuestionario para fijar . . ."

99. Corzo, "Cuestionario para fijar . . ."

100. Clifford, 1986, 99–101.

101. See, for example, Basauri, 1940, vol. 3, 295–298, 300–310.

102. Basauri, 1940, vol. 3, 522–523, 536, 567–576.

103. Basauri, 1940, vol. 1, 42–105; Basauri, 1940, vol. 3, 574–576.

104. Basauri, 1940, vol. 3, 115, 287–289, 539.

105. Basauri, 1940, vol. 1, 40. See also chapter 5.

106. Basauri, 1940, vol. 1, 38–39.

107. Basauri, 1940, vol. 1, 39, 46. See also Carlos Basauri, "La supuesta degeneración de la raza indígena," *El Nacional,* 8 July 1936; Stepan, 1991, 84–95, 145–153.

108. Basauri, 1940, vol. 1, 39–40.

109. Basauri, 1940, vol. 1, 40–42.

110. See Stocking, 1976, 16–17.

111. Basauri, 1940, vol. 3, 333–342.

112. Carlos Basauri, "Importancia de la economía doméstica en la población indígena," *El Nacional,* 14 July 1936.

113. Basauri, 1940, vol. 3, 342–344.

114. Alfonso Caso (INAH) to Alfonso Reyes, 5 June 1940, AH—INAH vol. 21, 1940, exp. 19.

115. On this, see Clifford, 1988.

116. Gamio, 1987, 22–23.

Chapter 4. Empowering the Masses at the Congresos Regionales Indígenas

1. "Decidida Ayuda para el Indio," *El Nacional,* 25 December 1939.

2. González y González, 1997, 105–123; Gilly, 1994, 391–461, esp. 414.

3. See, for example, Becker, 1987, 458–459; Guerrero, 1989, 192–194. On the congress that included Indians, see Alfonso Unda Ruiz and Ismael Velasco, from the "Primer Congreso Obrero Campesina Indígena," Oaxaca, Oax., to Cárdenas, 26 December 1934, AGN—LCR 404.4/8. See also "Federación Indigenista Revolucionaria Oaxaqueña, estatutos, circulares, declaraciones," 1 January 1939, CONDUMEX 082.172.72 OAX.

4. DAI, 1938, 10; DAI, 1938c, 19; DAI, 1938b, 29; Cárdenas to C. Eliseo Rosas, 12 November 1938, AGN—LCR 151.3/1124.

5. "El Congreso Tarasco dio ya comienzo," *El Nacional,* 15 December 1937; "Inauguración de magno congreso," *Excelsior,* 17 March 1938; "Clausura del Congreso de Tamazunchale," *El Nacional,* 19 March 1938; "Preparación del congreso de indígenas," *El Nacional,* 25 April 1938; "Un congreso de indígenas," *Excelsior,* 27 August 1938; *El Universal,* 3 September 1938; "Primer Congreso de la Raza Huasteca," *El Nacional,* 23 September 1939; J. de la Fuente, "El Congreso Indígena Huasteco," *El Nacional,* 10 December 1939.

6. DAI, 1938c, 38–39.

7. "Congreso de aborigenes," *El Universal,* 15 June 1936; "El segundo congreso de indígenas," *El Universal,* 21 October 1936.

8. "El congreso de indígenas," *El Nacional,* 21 September 1936.

9. "El congreso de indígenas," *El Nacional,* 21 September 1936; "Los congresos de indígenas," *El Nacional,* 29 August 1936; DAI, 1939, 9.

10. de la Peña, 1998, 72.

11. Jorge A. Vivo, "Tamazunchale" *El Nacional,* 15 May 1938; DAI, 1939, 10, 26; DAI, 1938c, 38–39; DAI, 1940c, 10–11; "Con las razas indígenas estan las obligaciones del gobierno," *El Nacional,* 26 September 1936.

12. Ignacio García Tellez (from the Tercer Congreso Regional Indígena in Tamazunchale) to Cárdenas, 17 March 1938, AGN—LCR 433/303.

13. Tancanhuitz saw 8 percent under 20, 32 percent 21–30, 50 percent 31–40, 6

percent 41–50, 4 percent 51–70. J. de la Fuente, "El Congreso Indígena Huasteco," *El Nacional,* 10 December 1939.

14. Julio de la Fuente, "Conflictos en la organización social y política de los zapotecos," BNAH—PCII.

15. Rubén Novelo Gil, "Nuevas apuntes que dan a conocer cosas muy propias . . . de la zona maya del ex-Territorio de Quintana Roo," June 1934, AHSEP—EANR (3243) 354.9. See also Mallon, 1995; Purnell, 1999; Friedrich, 1986.

16. "Congresos de los indígenas," *El Nacional,* 5 August 1938; DAI, 1939, 34; DAI, 1938b, 30, 48; DAI, 1938c, 37–39; DAI, 1938, 15–17. See also Marcos Bernal to Cárdenas, 25 September 1936, AGN—LCR 505.1/39; "El Congreso Indígena de Ixmiquilpan," *El Universal,* 26 September 1936. Rubén Rodríguez Lozano to Cárdenas, 18 March 1938, AGN—LCR 433/303; "Se inauguró el congreso indígena de Tamazunchale," *El Nacional,* 18 March 1938.

17. DAI, 1938, 13, 15; DAI, 1938c, 25; "Clausura del congreso de Tamazunchale," *El Nacional,* 19 March 1938.

18. "Gran Congreso de Otomies habra en Ixmiquilpan," *El Nacional,* 6 September 1936; DAI, 1940c, 5.

19. DAI, 1939, 16–17; DAI, 1938b, 6; DAI, 1938c, 5–11, 21.

20. DAI, 1938b, 33.

21. "El segundo congreso de indígenas," *El Nacional,* 23 October 1936.

22. DAI, 1938, 6–7. More generally, see DAI, 1938b, 9; Los congresos de indígenas," *El Nacional,* 29 August 1936.

23. "Solicitudes y quejas de los otomies," *El Nacional,* 4 October 1936.

24. "Clausura del congreso de Tamazunchale," *El Nacional,* 19 March 1938. See also "Importantes resoluciones en la sesión de clausura del congreso de Uruapan," *El Nacional,* 17 December 1937; Jorge A. Vivo, "Tamazunchale," *El Nacional,* 15 May 1938.

25. Jorge A. Vivo, "Tamazunchale," *El Nacional,* 15 May 1938.

26. DAI, 1938c, 18; Jorge A. Vivo, "Tamazunchale," *El Nacional,* 15 May 1938.

27. DAI, 1938b, 9, 19, 25–29.

28. DAI, 1939, 5, 19; DAI, 1938, 6; DAI, 1938c, 31–32.

29. "Clausura del Congreso de Tamazunchale," *El Nacional,* 19 March 1938. See also Lomnitz-Adler, 1992, pp. 8–13; Bourdieu, 1990.

30. Butler, 1990, 24–25, 132–149. See also Roseberry, 1994; Sayer, 1994. For the primitive moniker, see, for example, "Protesta por los asesinatos de maestros rurales" *MR* 6:4 (15 February 1935) 8.

31. "Que la raza otomí salga de su sopor," *El Nacional,* 30 September 1936. See also "Declaración de principios de los indios de Ixmiquilpan, Hidalgo, *El Universal,* 30 September 1936.

32. DAI, 1939, 37. See also meeting of Indigenistas in the DF, 29 August 1939, AGN—LCR 533.4/1.

33. J. de la Fuente, "El Congreso Indígena Huasteco," *El Nacional,* 10 December 1939; DAI, 1939, 45.

34. DAI, 1939, 19.

35. DAI, 1939, 18–19.

36. DAI, 1939, 7, 17–20. See also Ignacio León to Cárdenas, April 1940, AGN—LCR 433/294.

37. DAI, 1939, 20–21, 27, 35. See also Stephen, 1996, 20.

38. See, for example, Roberto M. Crespo to Cárdenas, 29 August 1938, AGN—LCR 433/303; Marcos Bernal to Cárdenas, 25 September 1936, AGN—LCR 505.1/39; Ignacio Morelos Zaragoza, "El eterno crimen de los hombres blancos," *Excelsior,* 7 July 1934; Rafael López Ocampo, "La campaña pro-indio en el estado de Chiapas," *El Nacional,* 12 August 1934. See also Schryer, 1990, 250–251, 322–323.

39. Antonio Bautista, Yolomecatl, Oax., to Cárdenas, 18 March 1938, AGN—LCR 433/304; DAI, 1939, 10, 24.

40. "El segundo congreso de indígenas," *El Universal,* 21 October 1936.

41. See, for example, Prof. Manuel Ruíz Mercado and Prof. José Ventura Gonzalez to Cárdenas, 24 July 1937, AGN—LCR 433/212.

42. Key organizers of the Ixmiquilpan Congress, Vincente Ordoñez and Marcos Galindo, were local businessmen. Interview with Jorge Trejo Cadena and María Concepción Galindo Barrera, 24 April 2000. See also "Gran Feria Regional y Exposition Industrial, Agricola y Ganadaria en la ciudad de Ixmiquilpan, Hgo.," 13–23 August 1936, AGN—LCR 505.1/39.

43. Interview with Jorge Trejo Cadena and María Concepción Galindo Barrera, 24 April 2000.

44. Vicente Pérez and others to Cárdenas, 24 March 1940, AGN—LCR 542.1/987; Domingo Flores and others to Cárdenas, 7 April 1936, AGN—LCR 542.1/987.

45. Victoriano Rosales, Estanislao Aguilar, and others, Santo Domingo Agua Zarca, Hgo., to Cárdenas, 12 August 1935; Vicente Pérez and others to Cárdenas, 24 March 1940; Domingo Flores and Reyes Rojas to Cárdenas, 7 April 1936; Carmen García de Hernández to Cárdenas, 17 May 1935; Perfecto Hernández and others to Cárdenas, 17 May 1935; Estanislao Angeles to Cárdenas, 17 May 1937. All in AGN—LCR 542.1/987.

46. Guillermo Obregón to Cárdenas, 24 September 1936; Alberto Lechuga to Cárdenas, 24 September 1936; Marcos Bernal to Cárdenas, 25 September 1936; Guillermo Galindo and others to Cárdenas, 24 September 1936. All in AGN—LCR 505.1/39.

47. "Quince mil campesinos se reunieron en Ixmiquilpan en el congreso de indios," *Excelsior,* 26 September 1936; "El congreso indígena de Ixmiquilpan," *El Universal,* 26 September 1936.

48. Chávez Orozco to Cárdenas, 25 May 1940, AGN—LCR 433/482; Angel Corzo to Cárdenas, 6 June 1940, AGN—LCR 433/482.

49. Gilberto Tello N. to Cárdenas, 16 May 1940, AGN—LCR 433/482.

50. Erasto Urbina to Governor Gutiérrez (Chis.), 11 May 1940, AGN—LCR 433/482.

51. Chávez Orozco to Cárdenas, 27 May 1940; Corzo to Cárdenas, 6 June 1940, AGN—LCR 434/482.

52. Gutiérrez to Cárdenas, 19 July 1940, AGN—LCR 433/482.

53. Corzo to Cárdenas, 6 June 1940; Corzo to Cárdenas, 28 May 1940; Chávez Orozco to Cárdenas, 27 May 1940; Chávez Orozco to Cárdenas, 25 May 1940. All in AGN—LCR 433/482.

54. "Se Otorga Ayuda a los Indígenas de la Huasteca," *Excelsior,* 12 July 1937.

55. "Con las razas indígenas estan las obligaciones del Gobierno," *El Nacional,* 26 September 1936.

56. Roberto M. Crespo to Cárdenas, 29 August 1938, AGN—LCR 433/303.

57. "Redención de los otomís," *El Nacional,* 17 December 1936.

58. Augusto Focil Díaz, "Importante junta convocó ayer el señor presidente," *El*

Nacional, 27 September 1936; "Ayuda a los otomies de Ixmiquilpan," *El Nacional,* 3 October 1936.

59. DAI, 1940c, 13–14; DAI, 1939, 41.

60. See, for example, Cárdenas to C. Eliseo Rosas, 12 November 1938, AGN—LCR 151.3/ 1124; DAI, 1938c, 19; DAI, 1938b, 29; DAI, 1938, 10.

61. "Solicitudes y quejas de los otomies," *El Nacional,* 4 October 1936. See also Report on Primer Congreso Regional Indígena, BNAH.

62. DAI, 1938c, 21.

63. DAI, 1938c, 21.

64. See memo by Graciano Sánchez, 11 March 1936, AGN—LCR 609/280.

65. Mateo Antonio and others (four of whom cannot sign their names) to Cárdenas 30 July 1936, AHSEP—DEPH, box 1, exp. 4389. See also memo by Rafael Ramírez, 27 July 1934, AHSEP—DEPH, box 1, exp. 4389.

66. Edmundo Domínguez, "Ponencia Otomi," BNAH—PCII.

67. See, for example, "Primer Congreso Indígena," BNAH. See also Augustín M. Cano and others to Cárdenas, 31 October 1939, AGN—LCR 534.3/1217.

68. DAI, 1939, 48–69.

69. DAI, 1938c, 21; DAI, 1939, 48–69.

70. DAI, 1939, 28.

71. Adrian Plácido López, (delegado de la raza mixteca del estado de Oaxaca), "Ponencia que el delegado al Congreso Interamericano . . . ," BNAH—PCII; DAI, 1939, 61–62; DAI, 1938b, 33–35; DAI, 1938c, 22; DAI 1940c, 9–10. See also German Chable and others to Cárdenas, 22 December 1939, AGN—LCR 151.3/1383.

72. "Solicitudes y quejas de los otomies," *El Nacional,* 4 October 1936; DAI, 1938, 16.

73. DAI, 1939, 58–69; DAI, 1938b, 33–44; DAI, 1938c, 32–33; DAI, 1940c, 5–7.

74. DAI, 1939, 58–69; DAI, 1938b, 33–44; DAI, 1940c, 5–7.

75. DAI, 1938b, 33–35; DAI, 1940c, 5–7; "Primer Congreso Indígena," BNAH; Plácido López, "Ponencia que el delegado . . ."

76. DAI, 1938e, 37.

77. DAI, 1938c, 31.

78. DAI, 1939, 54–57, 63–69; DAI, 1938b, 33–44; DAI, 1940c, 8–9.

79. DAI, 1939, 54–57.

80. DAI, 1938b, 33–44.

81. DAI, 1938b, 33–44, 38–39.

82. See, for example, Purnell, 1999; Becker, 1995; and González y González, 1968.

83. On these types of requests, see DAI, 1938b, 33–44, 38–39; DAI, 1939, 54–57, 63–69; Rubén Rodríguez Lozano to Cárdenas, 18 March 1938, AGN—LCR 433/ 303; Fernando Castellanos to Cárdenas, 18 March 1938, AGN—LCR 433/303; Sotelo Arévalo, 1996, 67. More broadly, see Becker, 1995, 108; Friedrich, 1977, 78–130; Purnell, 1999, 67, 111–133; Benjamin, 1990, 74–79; Becker, 1995, 136–138.

84. See, for example, Alfonso Fabila to Cárdenas, 3 August 1938, AGN—LCR 533.11/1; Chávez Orozco to Cárdenas, 1 July 1939, AGN—LCR 533.11/1. See also Schryer, 1990, 17–26, 320; Becker, 1995, 32–38, 104–110, 136–153; Purnell, 1999, 6–7, 135–136, 180; Nugent, 1993, 88–121; Knight, 1994, 62.

85. Mateo Antonio and others to Cárdenas, 30 July 1936, AHSEP—DEPH, box 1 exp. 4389.

86. See Rockwell, 1994, 170–208.

87. A further 107 petitions requested irrigation, 12 called for livestock, and 31 for trees. "Primer Congreso Indígena," BNAH. See also German Chable and others to Cárdenas, 22 December 1939; DAI, 1939, 48–53; DAI, 1938c, 21.

88. DAI, 1938, 12; Boletín of the Segundo Congreso de la Raza Tarahumara, 1–2 June 1944, AGN—MAC 404.1/3381.

89. "Las demandas del congreso de chontales," *El Nacional,* 25 December 1939; DAI, 1940c, 8–9; German Chable and others to Cárdenas, 22 December 1939; DAI, 1938b, 33–44.

90. Alfonso Fabila to Prof. Luis Villarreal (EANR), 12 November 1935, AHSEP—EANR, box 3275/386, exp. 386.71. See also memo by Luis Chávez Orozco, 29 May 1939, AGN—LCR 533.4/12.

91. "Primer Congreso Indígena," BNAH. See also Plácido López, "Ponencia que el delegado . . ."

92. "Primer Congreso Indígena," BNAH; "Solicitudes y quejas de los otomies," *El Nacional,* 4 October 1936; DAI, 1938, 16; DAI, 1939, 48–50, 53–54, 58–61; DAI, 1938b, 4, 33–44; DAI, 1938c, 21; DAI, 1940c, 5–7.

93. "Clausura del congreso de Tamazunchale," *El Nacional,* 19 March 1938; DAI, 1938c, 22; Plácido López, "Ponencia que el delegado . . . ," "Primer Congreso Indígena," BNAH.

94. Eliseo Rosas to Cárdenas, 8 November 1938, AGN—LCR 151.3/1124.

95. José German Chable and others to Cárdenas, 22 December 1939, AGN—LCR 151.3/1383; Victor Zapata Frías to Cárdenas, 23 December 1939, AGN—LCR 704/496.

96. "Las demandas del congreso de chontales," *El Nacional,* 25 December 1939.

97. German Chable and others to Cárdenas, 22 December 1939; "Solicitudes y quejas de los otomies," *El Nacional,* 4 October 1936.

98. "Las demandas del congreso de chontales," *El Nacional,* 25 December 1939.

99. García Téllez to Cárdenas 17 March 1938, AGN—LCR 433/303; DAI, 1938c, 21–22. See also Eliseo Rosas to Cárdenas, 8 November 1938, AGN—LCR 151.3/1124.

100. Fernando Castellanos and others to Cárdenas 10 February 1938, AGN—LCR 433/303; Crescencio Mendoza and others to Cárdenas, 23 December 1939, AGN—LCR 151.3/1383.

101. Rodríguez Lozano to Cárdenas, 18 March 1938, AGN—LCR 433/303. See also Rubén Rodríguez Lozano, "Estudio General de la Huasteca Potosina para fundar la necesidad de crear una Direccion de Educacion Federal," March 1938, AGN—LCR 433/303.

102. Rodríguez Lozano to Cárdenas, 18 March 1938.

103. Castellanos to Cárdenas, Rodríguez Lozano to Cárdenas, March 1938. Both in AGN—LCR 433/303.

104. Resolutions of the Congreso Científico Americano, Sección 23—Sección de Indigenistas, September 1935, AHSEP—ER 1327 183/10/4; Rubén Rodríguez Lozano to Cárdenas, 18 March 1938.

105. See Congreso Economico y Asuntos Educativos e Indígenas, Atlacomulco, Mex., 24 July 1937, AGN—LCR 433/212.

106. Fernando Castellanos to Cárdenas, 18 March 1938, AGN—LCR 433/303. See also Corzo to Cárdenas, 6 June 1940; Corzo to Cárdenas, 28 May 1940; Chávez Orozco to Cárdenas, 27 May 1940; Chávez Orozco to Cárdenas, 25 May 1940. All in AGN—LCR 433/482.

107. See, for example, Augustín M. Cano and others to Cárdenas, 31 October 1939, AGN—LCR 534.3/1217; Colonel Ignacio M. Beteta to Cárdenas, 17 January 1939, AGN—LCR 433/212; José Ventura González to Cárdenas 7 July 1937, AGN—LCR 433/212.

108. See, for example, Bantjes, 1998, 216–226; Fallaw, 1997, 551–577.

109. Scott, 1990; Vaughan, 1997, 19; Roseberry, 1994, 360–361.

110. See, among others, Rubin, 1997; Vaughan, 1997; Purnell, 1999; Benjamin, 1990.

111. Roseberry, 1994, 360–361; Mallon, 1995, 7, 30–62.

112. Chartier, 1988, 102–104; Barthes, 1972, 109–159.

113. These included the prominent educator José María Licona, and Silvestre Pérez, later the *jefe político* of Pazuelos, Mun. de Cardonal, for many years. Manuel Basilio, another member, was likely a relative of Maurilio Basilio, later the cacique cultural of the region. Ramón G. Bonfíl, another member, was first secretary general in 1932 of the Confederación Mexicana de Maestros (predecessor of SNTE), and later a federal deputy from Hidalgo. Pérez López, 1979, 67–68, 233–234. Interview with Jesús Pedraza and Sabin O. Roque (president), of the Consejo Supremo Ñhañhu del Valle de Mezquital, 26 April 2000.

114. Rus, 1994, 265–300; Collier, 1994, 119–124; Harvey, 1998, 54–58; Pineda, 1993, 15–19, 72–90; Rubin, 1997; Schryer, 1990, 180–183, 224–226; Rockwell, 1994, 198.

115. Ignacio León Ruiz and Patricio Jaris to Avila Camacho, 31 October 1945; Lic. Roberto Amorós (Oficial Mayor of Ávila Camacho) to León et al., 6 November 1945; Avila Camacho to León, 31 May 1944; Memo by Prof. Rosario C Martínez, Tónachic, June 1944; Boletín of the Segundo Congreso de la Raza Tarahumara, 1–2 June 1944. All in AGN—MAC 404.1/3381. "Estudio de la región tarahumara. Presentado por el Departamento de Trabajo," June 1936, AGN—LCR 533.4/12; Loyo, 1996, 120–121; de la Peña, 1995, 120.

116. Pablo Baez and Cirilo Jacinto to Cárdenas, 13 December 1938, 27 January 1939, 11 April 1939; Cárdenas to Avila Camacho, 10 March 1939, 13 April 1939; Avila Camacho to Cárdenas, 4 April 1938. All in AGN—LCR 542.1/2213. On the revolutionary idiom, see Becker, 1995, 119–123.

117. Baez and Jacinto to Cárdenas, 11 April 1939.

118. Baez and Jacinto to Cárdenas, 27 January 1939, 11 April 1939.

119. Baez and Jacinto to Cárdenas, 11 April 1939.

120. Baez and Jacinto to Cárdenas, 11 April 1939.

121. See Avila Camacho to Cárdenas, 4 April 1938; Cárdenas to Avila Camacho, 10 March 1939; Baez and Jacinto to Cárdenas, 13 December 1938.

Chapter 5. Indigenismo in the Shadow

1. Matos Moctezuma, 1996, 300–301.

2. Graciano Sánchez to personal secretary of Cárdenas, 26 January 1938, AGN—LCR 533.11/1; J. B. Durand, "Estudio económico social del Valle de Mezquital," 24 January 1936, AHSEP—EANR 3623/374 exp. 999/22; Memo by Graciano Sánchez, 11 March 1936, LCR 609/280; Augusto Focil Díaz, "Importante junta convocó ayer el señor presidente," *El Nacional,* 27 September 1936; Artemisa N. Sáenz Royo, "El Valle de Mezquital," August 1939, AGN—LCR 609/280.

3. Luis Chávez Orozco, *Informe* of Comisión Intersecretarial de Estudio y Planeación en el Valle de Mezquital, 26 September 1939, Chávez Orozco, Report of the CIEPVM, 14 September 1939; Luis Chávez Orozco to Juan Gallardo Moreno, 3 October 1939. All in AGN—LCR 609/280.

4. "Redención de los otomís," *El Nacional,* 17 December 1936.

5. "La transformación de la region otomí," *El Universal,* 4 February 1937; "Dept. de Asuntos Indígenas," *Excelsior,* 2 January 1937.

6. Chávez Orozco, Informe of the CIEPVM, 26 September 1939.

7. "La política de irrigación en benficio del indio," BNAH—PCII.

8. J. B. Durand to Avila Camacho, 6 November 1942, AGN—MAC 485/1.

9. Some of the poorest communities gathered sewage water from the canal for drinking. Loose documents, AGN—MAC 485/1.

10. On the broader impact and appeal of these programs, see González y González, 1968; Purnell, 1999; Joseph 1988, 288–295; Pineda, 1993, 60; Collier, 1994, 28–29; Gledhill, 1991; Bantjes, 1998; Fallaw, 2001, 80–157.

11. Chávez Orozco, Informe CIPEVM, 26 September 1939.

12. Graciano Sánchez to SEP, 13 July 1938, AHSEP—DEPH box 10, exp. 4077; Isidro Candia to SEP, October 1941, AHSEP—DEPH, box 1, exp. 4389; Prof. Florentino Guzmán, Pachuca, Hgo., to Director General of Educación Primaria Urbana y Rural, Mex., DF, 1 October 1938, AHSEP—DEPH box 10, exp. 4075.

13. Isidro Candia, DAI *Informe,* August 1941, AGN—MAC 606.3/44. Sixty signatories from the Sindicato Unico de Trabajadores de la Enseñanza Superior Campesina (Huamantla, Tlax.), to Cárdenas, 25 August 1938, AGN—LCR 704.3/246.

14. Gamio, "Anteproyecto relativo a educación y culturización el la zona de Mezquital," n.d., AIMG, box 6, exp. 24; Avila Camacho, Acuerdo, 20 January 1943, AGN—MAC 485/1; Isidro Candia, "Memorandum al Presidente de la República," 19 January 1943, AGN—MAC 485/1; Acuerdo, between Avila Camacho, the DAI, SecAgFom, SEP, and SHCP, 3 May 1943, AGN—MAC 485/1; J. B. Durand to Avila Camacho, 6 November 1942, AGN—MAC 485/1; "Anteproyecto de reglamento para el Comite Coordinador del Valle de Mezquital," 30 March 1943, AGN—MAC 485/1; Prof. José Reyes Pimentel to Avila Camacho, 22 April 1944, AGN—MAC 485/1; SHCP, *Cuenta Pública,* 1944.

15. Of the irrigation budget, $180,000.00 [all amounts in pesos] was for repairs and $20,000.00 for studies of new systems. The following was the budget of the Comité as of 1 May 1944:

Irrigacion	200,000.00
Agricultura	912,925.00
Economia	558,500.00
Salubridad y Asistencia	585,627.00
Comunicacions	334,000.00
Educacion Publica	469,284.57
Educacion Physica	34,636.00
Asuntos Indígenas	201,800.00
Total	3,296,772.57

Prof. José Reyes Pimentel (of DAI), President of the Comité Coordinador, to Avila Camacho, 22 April 1944, AGN—MAC 485/1.

16. Manuel Santuario to SECAGFOM, 30 September 1944, AGN—MAC 485/1; Candia to Avila Camacho, 21 January 1943, AGN—MAC 508.1/267; Martiniano Marin, Ixmiquilpan, to Avila Camacho, 5 March 1945, AGN—MAC 508.1/267.

17. Gamio to Javier Desentis, Pachuca, Hgo., 12 March 1952, AIMG box 2, exp. 82. Gamio, "Nuestros Indios Monolingues," n.d., AIMG, box 7, exp. 8; Gamio to Gov. of Hgo., 1 April 1952, AIMG, box 2, exp. 85.

18. Gamio, "Consideraciones sobre problemas del Valle de Mezquital," 20 May 1952, AIMG box 7, exp. 68.

19. Gamio, "Principales Actividades . . . III," June 1950–July 1951, 29 August 1951, AIMG box 6, exp. 45; Gamio, "Consideraciones sobre problemas del Valle de Mezquital," 20 May 1952; Gamio, Report on the work of the III in Valle de Mezquital, 19 December 1951, AIMG box 6, exp. 5; Gamio, "Antecedents Sobre el Proyecto Relativo al Valle de Mezquital . . ." 31 August 1950, AIMG box 2, exp. 72; Gamio to President Miguel Alemán Valdés, 17 March 1951, AIMG box 2, exp. 74. See also Comas, 1975, 48–50.

20. J. B. Durand, "Estudio económico social del Valle de Mezquital."

21. Bartra, 1986, 326–327; Interview with Jesús Pedraza and Sabin O. Roque, of the Consejo Supremo Ñhañhu del Valle de Mezquital, 26 April 2000.

22. Harvey, 1998, 120–126; Knight, 1994b, 73–107; Bantjes, 1998, 216–226. Sotelo Arévalo, 1996, 98; de la Peña, 1998, 76–77; Medina, 1986, 173–76.

23. Loose documents, AGN—MAC 111/1595.

24. "Semblanza de Sr. Isidro Candia," AIMG box 5, exp. 11.

25. "La Población Indígena de México," Información del DAI para el Primer Congreso Demográfico Interamericano, (sección de Etnología y Eugenesia), 12 October 1943, AGN—MAC 433/164. SEP expenditures went from 76,722,686.35 to 199,065,663.23. By 1942 the budget of the DAI was $3,000,000.00. SHCP, *Cuenta Pública*, 1941–1946; Memo by Roberto Amorós G., personal secretary to Avila Camacho, 30 March 1942, AGN—MAC 545.3/115.

26. Candia, DAI *Plan General de Trabajo* for 1942, January 1942, AGN—MAC 545.2/115; Ing. Fernando F. Miramontes, "Asuntos encomendados por el C. Presidente de la República para su trámite inicial por El Departamento Agrario," 2 April 1943, AGN—MAC 522.1/1. See also Candia to chief, Oficina Administrava (DAI), 26 March 1943, AGN—MAC 404.1/338; Isidro Candia, DAI *Informe,* August 1941, AGN—MAC 606.3/44.

27. See, for example, Comisión Ejidal de Zacualpan, Gro., to Avila Camacho, 24 November 1942; Hermelindo Prudents to Avila Camacho, 27 November 1942; Municipal President of Orizaba, Ver., and others, to Avila Camacho, 20 April 1944. All in AGN—MAC 703.4/301.

28. P. López, Tetela de Ocampo, Pue., to Alemán Valdés, 2 February 1950, AGN—MAV 703.41/30.

29. Gamio, "La Politica de una institución no politica," n.d., AIMG box 6, exp. 52; Niblo, 1999, 75–147, 165, 223, 253–309; Sanderson, 1981, 137–138.

30. Angel Corzo to Avila Camacho, 14 February 1941, AGN—MAC 606.3/44.

31. Angel Corzo to Avila Camacho, 6 May 1941, AGN—MAC 704/145.

32. Medina, 1986, 173–76.

33. Comas, 1964, 23–24.

34. Gamio to Franz Boas, 9 January 1925, AIMG box 2, exp. 17; "Separación del Dr. Gamio de la Subsecretaría de Educación Pública" (n.d.), AIMG box 5 exp. 10; Gamio to

SEP, 6 October 1925, AIMG box 2, exp. 31; Gamio to Calles, 14 May 1925, AIMG box 2, exp. 23; Calles to Gamio, 16 May 1925, AIMG box 2, exp. 24; Gamio to Calles, 3 June 1925, AIMG box 2, exp. 27. See also Comas, 1975, 55.

35. See Manuel Gamio, "Acerca del problema indígena," (1947), in Gamio, 1948, 130–132.

36. Jeremías Lópes Chiñas, FIRO Circular no. 29, 2 April 1941, AGN—MAC 135.21/27. See also Jeremías Lópes Chiñas, Vicente Magdaleno, and Lic. José Pavía Crespo to Avila Camacho, 12 April 1941, AGN—MAC 135.21/27.

37. Lópes Chiñas, FIRO Circular no. 29, 2 April 1941.

38. Prof. Alberto Terán and Dr. José G. Parres to SEP, 18 November 1942, AGN—MAC 482.1/18; Aguirre Beltrán, 1992, 111–112; Doremus, 2001, 380–401.

39. Collier, 1994, 62–67.

40. Ramón Berzunza Pinto to Avila Camacho, 2 April 1941, AGN—MAC 480/5.

41. Fidel Fabián, Miguel J. Mendoza, and others, Paracho, Mich., to Avila Camacho, 4 February 1941, AGN—MAC 534.6/66; Berzunza Pinto to Avila Camacho, 2 April 1941; de la Peña, 1998, 73–74.

42. Berzunza Pinto to Avila Camacho, 2 April 1941.

43. Berzunza Pinto to Avila Camacho, 2 April 1941.

44. Prof. Ramón G. Bonfíl (DAI) to Alfonso Caso, 30 April 1941, AH—INAH vol. 24, 1942 exp. 8; Angel M Corzo to Avila Camacho, 14 August 1941, AGN—MAC 480/5. By 1941 the DAI had undertaken literacy campaigns in 10 Indian dialects, produced 5 dictionaries, and showed that adults and children could learn to read and write in Tarascan in a period of 30–45 days. Their work also influenced the *Instituto de Alfabetización en Lenguas Indígenas,* established in 1944, which published 10 million cartillas bilinguales in Tarascan, Otomí, Nahuatl, and Tarahumara. By 1951 there were 80 bilingual teachers in 63 *Centros de Alfabetización,* with 2,400 students in the country. Even this program, however, would be abruptly canceled in 1958 in spite of its successes. Memo by Lic. Roberto Amorós G. of the Oficicina Consultiva of the SECPARTIC to Avila Camacho, 30 March 1942, AGN—MAC 545.3/115. See also Reyes Rocha et al., 1991, 33–37; Comas, 1964, 41–43; Greaves, 1996, 161–194.

45. Genáro Zalpa and José Gómez B., Paracho, Mich., to Avila Camacho, 21 January 1942, AGN—MAC 534.6/225.

46. Isidro Candia to Lic. J. Jesús González Gallo, 11 April 1942, AGN—MAC 534.6/225. See also Jesús Hernández, Paracho, to Avila Camacho, 30 March 1942, AGN—MAC 534.6/225.

47. Juan Barajas, Uruapan, Mich., to Avila Camacho, 8 April 1942, AGN—MAC 534.6/225; Manuel M. Cárdenas (Oficial Mayor of Governor of Michoacán) to personal secretary of Avila Camacho, 29 April 1942, AGN—MAC 534.6/225.

48. Bernardino López, Andrés Cortés and other signatories, of the internado in Paracho, to Avila Camacho, 7 June 1943, AGN—MAC 534.6/225; Ignacio Ríos, Municipal President of Paracho, to Avila Camacho, 19 June 1943, AGN—MAC 534.6/225.

49. Isidrio Candia to Lic. Roberto Amoros G. (Oficial Mayor of Avila Camacho), 23 June 1943, AGN—MAC 534.6/225. Isidro Candia to Avila Camacho, 30 June 1943, AGN—MAC 709/4.

50. Candia, DAI *Informe,* August 1941, AGN—MAC 606.3/44; Candia, memo, 15 December 1942, AGN—MAC 482.1/18. Candia, *Plan General de Trabajo* for 1942, January 1942, AGN—MAC 545.2/115; memo by Lic. Roberto Amorós G., 30 March 1942, AGN—MAC 545.3/115. On the cuts, see, for example, Manuel Ortega, Techímal,

Hgo., to Isidro Candia, 3 December 1941, AGN—MAC 534.4/2; Sindicato de Trabajadores de la Enseñanza de la Revolución Mexicana, Ixmiquilpan, Hgo., to Avila Camacho, 4 January 1941, AGN—MAC 534.1/103.

51. Isidro Candia to Avila Camacho, 22 July 1941, AGN—MAC 433/164; Avila Camacho, "Proyecto de decreto para la creación del Patronato Indígena de Industrias Manuales," June 1944, AGN—MAC 545.3/74.

52. "La Población Indígena de México," Información del DAI para el Primer Congreso Demográfico Interamericano (section de Etnología y Eugenesia), 12 October 1943, AGN—MAC 433/164.

53. Gamio, "Anteproyecto relativo a educación y culturización el la zona de Mezquital," n.d., AIMG, box 6, exp. 24; Gamio, "Consideraciones sobre el consumo de la producción Indígena," Segundo Congreso Mexicano de Ciencies Sociales, October 1945, AIMG box 6, exp. 85; Gamio, 1987, 71–83.

54. Memo by Lic. Roberto Amorós G., 30 March 1942, AGN—MAC 545.3/115.

55. Report of the Consejo Técnico Consultivo of the DAI, 1942, AGN—MAC 545.3/115.

56. Genaro Vázquez was a former cabinet member and the man originally elected to head the Instituto Indigenista Mexicana after the PCII. Genaro Vázquez to Avila Camacho, 15 December 1942, AGN—MAC 545.3/74.

57. Miguel Alemán Valdés to the Congress, 3 December 1946, AGN—MAV 545.22/2.

58. Gamio, editorial, 1947, AIMG, box 6, exp. 48.

59. See various, dating from 1946–1947, in AGN—MAV 545.3/91; Prof. Bruno Miranda Bello to Alemán Valdés, 13 February 1947, AGN—MAV 703.2/10.

60. "Decreto por el Lic. Alemán que crea al Instituto Indigenista Nacional . . ." (1947), AIMG box 8, exp. 47.

61. Gamio, "Consideraciones sobre el Instituto Indigenista Nacional," 3 January 1947, AIMG box 2 exp. 62.

62. It also failed to promote links between indigenous and other campesino organizations. Herrasti and Ramírez, 1988, 240–265; Olivé Negrete, 1981, 133–145; Collier, 1994, 36, 62–69, 143; Pineda, 1993, 75–76; Pozas, 1986, 417–448.

63. "Plan tarasco de investigaciones antropologicas," 1941, AH—INAH vol. 24, 1942, exp. 8; Manuel Gamio, "Algunas informaciones sobre el III," n.d., AIMG box 6, exp. 53; Gamio, "Indigenismo," presentation to the Congreso Científico Mexicano, 8 March 1951, AIMG box 6, exp. 78. See also Dalhgren Jordán, 1988, 92–93, 99–107; Lomnitz, 2001, 254–259; Comas, 1964, 37–39.

64. Memorandum no. 118, Dr. Jesús Díaz Barriga to Cárdenas, 6 April 1940, AGN—LCR 544.3/1.

65. Loyo, 1999, 208–212.

66. Barthes, 1972, 109–159. On common sense, see Gramsci, 1976, 326–327. On this critique of Indigenismo, see, for example, "La condición de las razas indígenas en México es la misma que tenian in 1811," *Excelsior,* 18 July 1931; "El problema del indio," *Excelsior,* 20 July 1931; Luis L. Leon, "Al margen de la campaña cardenista. La incorporación de los núcleos indígenas," *El Nacional,* 28 June 1934; "Dos criterios acerca del problema indígena," *Excelsior,* 17 August 1931; "El problema indígena en el país," *Excelsior,* 28 September 1936. See also González y González, 1997, 105–123; Pérez Montfort, 1994, 352–363.

67. Paz, 1993; González y González, 1997, 105–123; Miller, 1999, 146–148.

68. "El problema indígena en el país," *Excelsior,* 28 September 1936. See also "El problema del indio," *Excelsior,* 20 July 1931; Gilberto Bosques, "La psicología del indio," *El Nacional,* 16 January 1932; Baqueiro Foster, "Entre los Coras y Huicholes del Nayarit," *Excelsior,* 12 January 1934; "Fatal atraso en una zona de Guerrero," *Excelsior,* 2 August 1934; Jorge Labra, "La ignorancia del indio," *Excelsior,* 9 February 1935; "Alcohol para embrutecer y explotar mejor al indio," *El Universal,* 17 May 1936; Mauricio Magdaleno, "Elogio apolítico del indio mexicano," *El Universal,* 15 June 1937. See also Vaughan, 1982, 217–238; Loyo, 1992, 245–251.

69. José Palacios, "El torno del mito del indígena," *El Nacional,* 6 August 1938; P. González "El indio y nosotros," *El Universal,* 16 November 1936; Luis L. León, "Al margen de la campaña Cardenista. La incorporación de los núcleos indígenas," *El Nacional,* 28 June 1934. León cited "recent scientific investigations by anthropologists and sociologists" for his claims.

70. "Rechazaron a los indios los vecinos blancos de cancuc," *El Universal,* 24 February 1935; Román Badillo, "El indio y los ignorantes del campo," *El Universal,* 4 July 1936.

71. Eduardo Pallares, "El mito del indígena," *El Universal,* 30 June 1938.

72. More broadly, see Monsiváis, 1996, 71–74; Morris, 1999, 376.

73. Attacking Pallares specifically, José Palacios claimed that Indian behavior was a product of slavery, abandonment, oppression, exploitation, and empty stomachs. José Palacios, "El Torno del Mito del Indígena," *El Nacional,* 6 August 1938.

74. "Término de la situación miserable de nuestros indígenas," *El Nacional,* 4 February 1938; Ing. Federico Cervantes, "La alimentación del indio," *Grafico,* 12 May 1939. See also Stepan, 1991, 84–95, 145–153.

75. "Alcohol para embrutecer y explotar mejor al indio," *El Universal,* 17 May 1936; "El problema indígena en el país," *Excelsior,* 28 September 1936.

76. Enrique Corona, "Pensamos así . . . desenvolvimiento mental y limitado," *El Nacional,* 13 August 1931.

77. Matto de Turner, 1996, 58. See also Pilcher, 1998, 77–98.

78. Stepan, 1991, 57.

79. "El problema indígena en el país," *Excelsior,* 28 September 1936.

80. Gamio, "Algunas consideraciones sobre niveles culturales de los grupos indios y mestizos," April 1940, AIMG box 9, exp. 51; Gamio, "Cuáles y cómo es el indio de raza pura," *El Nacional,* 25 July 1936; Gamio, "Algunos orientaciones del III," 19 January 1954, AIMG box 6 exp. 77.

81. Gamio, "Algunas consideraciones . . ."

82. Gamio, "Algunas consideraciones . . ."; Gamio, "Cuáles y cómo es el indio de raza pura."

83. Manuel Gamio, "¿Dia de la Raza?" (1945), in Gamio, 1948, 94–96; Gamio, "Consideraciones sobre el Instituto Indigenista Nacional," 3 January 1947, AIMG box 2 exp. 62.

84. Manuel Gamio, "Cuáles y cómo es el indio de raza pura."

85. "La rendción del indio es una necesidad panamericana," *El Nacional,* 25 March 1935. See also Luis Castillo Ledón to INAH, 29 June 1939, AH—INAH vol. 16, exp. 6.

86. Gamio, "Considerations of Indianist Policy," Published in *Science of Man,* 1943, AIMG box 9, exp. 3.

87. Gamio, "El indice cultural y el biotipo," Proceedings of the Eighth American Scientific Congress, n.d., AIMG box 10, exp. 3; Gamio, 1987, 33–35.

88. Basauri, "Proyecto complementario de labores para la Comisión de Investigaciones Indias, Durante el año de 1931"; Basauri to R. Ramírez, 6 May 1931; Basauri to R. Ramírez, 14 September 1931; Basauri to R. Ramírez, 15 May 1931; R. Ramírez to Basauri, 14 October 1931. All in AHSEP—ER 1327/2. See also Buffington, 2000, 158–160; Stepan, 1991, 59–60, 114–116.

89. Manuel Gamio, "Consideraciones sobre el problema indígena,"(1942) in Gamio, 1948, 1–9; Gamio, "Editorial: Ventajas del mestizaje," July 1954, AIMG box 7, exp. 5; Gamio, "El Racismo y la población Indígena,"(1942) in Gamio, 1948, 36–37; Gamio, 1987, 33–35.

90. Trabulse, 1996, 95–101.

91. Marx, 1998, 158–190; de la Cadena, 2000, 1–44, 306–330.

92. Gamio, "Prejucios raciales y complejos de inferioridad," (1945) in Gamio, 1948, 88–90.

93. Manuel Gamio, "Prejucios raciales y complejos de inferioridad"; Gamio, "Algunas consideraciones . . ."

94. Gamio, "Editorial: Ventajas del mestizaje," July 1954, AIMG box 7, exp. 5.

Conclusion

1. Mónico Chín, Presidente del Comisión Ejidal de Chunhuas, QR, and four others, to Cárdenas, 12 January 1940, AGN—LCR 151.3/1407.

2. See Celso V. Ordaz Vargas, in Torreón, to Avila Camacho, 17 December 1944, 28 February 1945, 3 November 1945, AGN—MAC 485/2. See also Rubén Rodríguez Lozano, "Estudio general de la huasteca potosina para fundar la necesidad de crear una Dirección de Educación Federal," March 1938, AGN—LCR 433/30329; Jesús Martínez R., Esteban Cruz, and others to Avila Camacho, 1 June 1946, AGN—MAC 534.6/728; Confederación Nacional de Jóvenes Indígenas (DF) to Avila Camacho, 20 August 1946, AGN—MAC 568.2/6. See also Butler, 1990, 132, 143–149.

3. On this trend more generally, see de la Cadena, 2000, 1–43. On the gendered quality of the process, see, for example, Ortner, 1996, 21–42.

4. Adolfo Velasco, Tezoatlán, Oax., to Cárdenas, 17 May 1936, AGN—LCR 404.4/8. See also Enriqueta de Parodi, "Mujer indígena," *El Nacional,* 3 April 1935; Gilberto Bosques, "La psicologia del indio," *El Nacional,* 16 January 1932; Jorge Labra, "La ignorancia del indio," *Excelsior,* 9 February 1935; Antonio Díaz Soto y Gama, "El indio y sus virtudes," *El Universal,* 26 April 1939; Natalia Juárez Meza, "Revindicación de la mujer indígena," *El Nacional,* 2 March 1939; Profra Celia Casas, "Mujer Mexicana," *Iris. Organo de los Alumnos del Instituto Social. Misión Cultural no. 2.* Escuela Central Agricola, Durango. 1:2 (19 August 1934) 4.

5. Prof. Manuel Ruíz Mercado and Prof. José Ventura Gonzalez, Atlacomulco, Mex., to Cárdenas, 24 July 1937, AGN—LCR 433/212; José Ventura González to Cárdenas, 7 July 1937, AGN—LCR 433/212.

6. Esteban García and Nicolas Flores, Atlacomulco, Mex., to Cárdenas, 24 July 1937, AGN—LCR 433/212.

7. Iwanska, 1977, 40–53.

8. See also Schryer, 1990, 58–60, 253–256; Lomnitz, 2001, 285; Rubin, 1997, 42–44, 260; Purnell, 1999, 30–32; Rus, 1994; Stephen, 1996, 22; García Canclini, 1993, 37–47.

9. See *Memoria* of the Audiencia Publica, Las Casas, 1992, ACM; Lipp, 1991, 8–10;

Collier, 1994; Gossen, 1999, 83–85; Joseph, 1994, 137–138, 164–169; Becker, 1995, 32–38; Rubin, 1996, 85–88, 99–121; Rubin, 1997, 42–44; Lomnitz, 2001, 266–282.

10. Rus, 1994, 265–280; Harvey, 1998, 15–23; Rubin, 1996, 103–121; Rubin, 1997, 266–274; Schryer, 1990, 62–63, 180–183; Nugent, 1993, 150–165.

11. As Rus notes, the caciques culturales in the Altos de Chiapas became key labor contractors for coffee fincas in the region during the 1940s and 1950s. Rus, 1994, 265–300; Rubin, 1996, 103–121; Mallon, 1995, 6–13, 64–88; Purnell, 1999, 10–14, 191–196; Rubin, 1997, 253. Harvey, 1998, 20–21; Pineda, 1993, 93–188.

12. His employment at the INI included a stint as subdirector from 1968–1971. He was born 1922 and died 1981. Interview with Jesús Pedraza and Sabin O. Roque (president), of the Consejo Supremo Ñhañhu del Valle de Mezquital, 26 April 2000.

13. Interview with Jorge Trejo Cadena and María Concepción Galindo Barrera, 24 April 2000. See also Villa Rojas, 1986, 153–163.

14. Interview with Jorge Trejo Cadena and María Concepción Galindo Barrera, 24 April 2000. Interview with Jesús Pedraza and Sabin O. Roque (president), of the Consejo Supremo Ñhañhu del Valle de Mezquital, 26 April 2000.

15. Interview with Jesús Pedraza and Sabin O. Roque (president), of the Consejo Supremo Ñhañhu del Valle de Mezquital, 26 April 2000. Villa Rojas, 1986, 160.

16. Pérez López, 1979, 217.

17. Interview with Jesús Pedraza and Sabin O. Roque (president), of the Consejo Supremo Ñhañu del Valle de Mezquital, 26 April 2000.

18. Mallon, 1995, 71–72, 84–85, 276–309; Schryer, 1990, 252–253.

19. Vaughan, 1994, 214–245; Mallon, 1995, 281–285, 306–307, 311–312; García Canclini, 1993, 1–16, 58–68, 81–83, 88–104; Favre, 1998, 126–147; Gutiérrez, 1999; Warren, 1992, 189–219; Cook and Joo, 1995, 33–59.

20. Interview with Prof. Juan Ramírez Pedraza, 25 April 2000.

21. Interview with Prof. Juan Ramírez Pedraza, 25 April 2000. Interview with Jesús Pedraza and Sabin O. Roque (president), of the Consejo Supremo Ñhañhu del Valle de Mezquital, 26 April 2000.

22. Interview with Prof. Juan Ramírez Pedraza, 25 April 2000.

23. Collier, 1994, 89–107, 114–119. Rubin, 1996, 103–121.

24. Medina, 1986, 173–76.

25. See, for example, Alfonso Caso, Informe Preliminar de la Exploraciones realizadas en Michoacán, 17 October 1930, 9, AHI—MNAHE—DA box 2, exp. 252.

26. Vaughan, 1997, 189–201.

27. Stavenhagen, 1986, 405–407; Lomnitz-Adler, 1992; García Canclini, 1993, 58–104; Garía Canclini, 1995, 107–205; Schryer, 1990, 245–255; Mallon, 1995, 71–85, 283–285. Recent decades have seen the collapse of hegemony in the emergence of a few ethnic movements that challenge this model, notably the COCEI in Juchitán, Oaxaca, and the EZLN in Chiapas. See Tresierra, 1994, 187–190; Rubin, 1997, 266–275; Campbell, 1993, 83–97; Stephen 1996, 19–37.

Bibliography

Archival Sources

ACM	Archivo del Congreso de Michoacán (Morelia)
AGN	Archivo General de la Nación
AGN – LCR	Acervos Presidentes, Fondo Lázaro Cárdenas del Río
AGN – MAC	Acervos Presidentes, Fondo Manuel Avila Camacho
AGN – MAV	Acervos Presidentes, Fondo Miguel Alemán Valdés
AGN – Obregón/Calles	Acervos Presidentes, Fondo Obregón/Calles
AH – INAH	Archivo Historico del INAH
AHI – MNAHE – DA	Archivo Historico Institucional, Sección Museo Nacional de Arqueología, Historia y Etnografía, Departamento de Arqueología
AHSEP	Archivo Historico de la Secretaría de Educación Pública
AHSEP – DEPH	Dirección General de Enseñanza Primaria Urbana y Rural en los Estados y Territorios (Hidalgo)
AHSEP – DEPM	Dirección General de Enseñanza Primaria Urbana y Rural en los Estados y Territorios (México)
AHSEP – EANR	Departamento de Enseñanza Agrícolas y Normal Rural
AHSEP – ER	Departamento de Enseñanza Rural y Primaria Foránea
AHSEP – MC	Misiones Culturales
AIMG	Archivo Incorporado "Manuel Gamio," Museo Nacional de Antropología e Historia – Archivo Historico
BNAH	Biblioteca Nacional de Antropología e Historia
BNAH – PCII	Primer Congreso Indigenista Interamericano. Trabajos
CONDUMEX	Centro de Estudios de la Historia Mexicana
INAH	Instituto Nacional de Antropología e Historia
INAH – DA	INAH: Sección: Secretaría de Fomento. Seríe: Dirección de Antropología

Magazines and Newspapers

Ethnos
Excelsior
Forma: Revista de Artes Plasticas
Instituto Nacional de Antropología y Historia. *Anales*
El Maestro Rural (*MR*)
Mexican Art and Life
Mexican Folk-ways (*MF*)
Museo Nacional de Arqueología, Historia y Etnología. *Anales*
El Nacional Revolucionario
La Prensa

Survey Graphic
El Universal

Books and Articles

Abrams, Philip. 1988. "Notes on the difficulty of studying the State." *Journal of Historical Sociology* 1(1): 58–89.

Aguirre Beltrán, Gonzalo. 1986. "Comentario de algunas posiciones sobre la situación del indio." In *La quiebra política de la antropología social en México,* vol. 2. See García Mora and Medina, 1986.

——. 1986b. "Sobre 'la antropología y la burocracia indigenista,'" In *La quiebra política de la antropología social en México,* vol. 2. See García Mora and Medina, 1986.

——. 1986c. "Panorama de la antropología social y aplicada." In Manuel Gamio, *Arqueología e indigenismo.* Mexico City: INI.

——. 1992 (1973). *Teoría y práctica del la educación indígena.* Mexico City: Fondo de Cultura Económico.

Alfonso Ramírez, Luis. 1986. *Chilchota: un pueblo al pie de la sierra.* Zamora: El Colegio de Michoacán.

Alonso, Ana Maria. 1988. " 'Progress' as Disorder and Dishonor." *Critique of Anthropology* 8 (1):13–33.

——. 1995. *Thread of Blood: Colonialism, Revolution, and Gender on Mexico's Northern Frontier.* Tucson, University of Arizona Press.

Anderson, Benedict. 1983. *Imagined Communities: Reflections on the Origin and Spread of Nationalism.* London: Verso.

Arizpe, Lourdes. 1986. "Primer Congreso Nacional de Indígenas." In *La quiebra política de la antropología social en México,* vol. 2. See García Mora and Medina, 1986.

Bantjes, Adrian. 1994. "Burning Saints, Molding Minds: Iconoclasm, Civic Ritual, and the Failed Cultural Revolution," In *Rituals of Rule, Rituals of Resistance: Public Celebrations and Popular Culture in Mexico.* See Beezley et al., 1994.

——. 1998. *As if Jesus Walked on Earth: Cardenismo, Sonora, and the Mexican Revolution.* Wilmington: Scholarly Resources.

Barrett, Michele. 1995. "Ideology, Politics, Hegemony: From Gramsci to Lacalau and Mouffe." In *Mapping Ideology.* Slavoj Zizek, ed. London: Verso.

Barthes, Roland. 1972. *Mythologies.* New York: Hill and Wang.

Bartra, Roger. 1986. "El problema indígena y la ideología indigenista." In *La quiebra política de la antropología social en México,* vol. 2. See García Mora and Medina, 1986.

Basauri, Carlos. 1928. *La situacion social actual de la población indígena de México y breves apuntes sinteticos sobre antropología y etnografía de la misma.* Mexico City: Talleres Gráficos de la Nación.

——. 1940. *La población indígena de México.* 3 vols. Mexico City: SEP.

Becker, Marjorie. 1987. "Black and White and Color: *Cardenismo* and the Search for a *Campesino* Ideology." *Comparative Studies of Society and History* 29 (3) 453–465.

——. 1995. *Setting the Virgin on Fire: Lázaro Cárdenas, Michoacán Peasants, and the Redemption of the Mexican Revolution.* Berkeley: University of California Press, 1995.

Beezley, William H., Cheryl English Martin, and William E. French, eds. 1994. *Rituals of*

Rule, Rituals of Resistance: Public Celebration and Popular Culture in Mexico. Wilmington: Scholarly Resources.

Behar, Ruth. 1993. *Translated Woman: Crossing the Border with Esperanza's Story.* Boston: Beacon.

Benjamin, Thomas. 1985. "The Leviathan on the Zócalo: Recent Historiography of the Postrevolutionary Mexican State." *LARR* 20(3): 195–217.

——. 1990. "Laboratories of the New State, 1920–1929: Regional Social Reform and Experiments in Mass Politics." In *Provinces of the Revolution.* See Benjamin and Wasserman, 1990.

Benjamin, Thomas, and Mark Wasserman, eds. 1990. *Provinces of the Revolution: Essays on Regional Mexican History, 1910–1929.* Albuquerque: University of New Mexico Press.

Best Maugard, Adolfo. 1923. *Método de Dibujo: tradición resurgimiento y evolución del arte mexicano.* Mexico City: SEP.

Bigas Torres, Sylvia. 1990. *La narrativa indigenista mexicana del siglo XX.* Guadalajara: Ed. Universidad de Guadalajara.

Blaut, J. M. 1993. *The Colonizers Model of the World: Geographical Diffusionism and Eurocentric History.* New York: Guilford.

Bonfil Batalla, Guillermo. 1970. "Del indigenismo de la revolución a la antropología crítica." In *De eso que llaman antropología mexicana.* See Warman et al., 1970.

Bourdieu, Pierre. 1984. *Distinction: A Social Critique of the Judgment of Taste.* Cambridge, Mass.: Harvard University Press.

——. 1990. *In Other Words: Essays Towards a Reflexive Sociology.* Cambridge: Polity Press.

——. 1991. *Language and Symbolic Power.* Cambridge, Mass.: Harvard University Press.

Boyer, Christopher R. 1998. "Old Loves, New Loyalties: Agrarismo in Michoacán, 1920–1928." *Hispanic American Historical Review* 78(3): 413–454.

Brading, David. 1985. *The Origins of Mexican Nationalism.* Cambridge: Centre of Latin American Studies.

——. 1988. "Manuel Gamio and Official Indigenismo in Mexico." *Bulletin of Latin American Research* 7(1): 75–89.

Brunk, Samuel. 1995. *Emiliano Zapata: Revolution and Betrayal in Mexico.* Albuquerque: University of New Mexico Press.

Buffington, Robert. 2000. *Criminal and Citizen in Modern Mexico.* Lincoln: University of Nebraska Press.

Butler, Judith. 1990. *Gender Trouble: Feminism and the Subversion of Identity.* New York: Routledge.

Camp, Roderic A. 1985. *Intellectuals and the State in Twentieth-Century Mexico.* Austin: University of Texas Press.

Campbell, Howard. 1993. "Tradition and the New Social Movements: The Politics of Isthmus Zapotec Culture." *Latin American Perspectives,* 78, 20:3 (Summer 1993) 83–97.

Campos, Ruben M. 1928. *El folklore y la música mexicana: investigación acerca de la cultura musical en México (1525–1925).* México: Talleres Gráficos de la Nación.

——. 1929. *El folklore literario de México: investigación acerca de la producción literaria popular (1525–1925).* Mexico City: Talleres Gráficos de la Nación.

Carr, Barry. 1992. *Marxism and Communism in Twentieth-Century Mexico.* Lincoln: University of Nebraska Press.

Charlot, Jean. 1963. *The Mexican Mural Renaissance.* New Haven: Yale University Press.

Chartier, Roger. 1988. *Cultural History: Between Practices and Representations.* Ithaca: Cornell University Press.

Chávez Orozco, Luis. 1932. *La Civilización maya-quiche.* Mexico City: Talleres Gráficos de la Nación.

———. 1933. *La civilización nahoa.* Mexico City: SEP.

———. 1934. *Historia de México.* México City: Editorial Patria.

———. 1943. *Las instituciones democráticas de los indígenas mexicanas en la época colonial.* Mexico City: INI.

Clifford, James. 1986. "On Ethnographic Allegory." In *Writing Culture: The Poetics and Politics of Ethnography.* James Clifford and George Marcus, eds. Berkeley: University of California Press.

———. 1988. *The Predicament of Culture: Twentieth-Century Ethnography, Literature, and Art.* Cambridge, Mass.: Harvard University Press.

Collier, George A., with Elizabeth Lowery Quaratiello. 1994. *Basta: Land and the Zapatista Rebellion in Chiapas.* Oakland: Institute for Food and Development Policy.

Comaroff, John, and Jean Comaroff. 1992. *Ethnography and the Historical Imagination.* Boulder, Colo.: Westview.

Comas, Juan. 1950. "Bosquejo historico de la antropología en México," *Revista Mexicana de estudios antropologicos* 11: 97–191.

———. 1964. *La antropología social aplicada en México.* Mexico City: III.

———. 1964b. *La antropología social aplicada en México. Trayectoria y antología.* Mexico City: INI.

———. 1975. "Manuel Gamio en la antropología mexicana." *Anales de Antropología* 7: 47–65.

Cook, Stephen Scott, and Jong–Taick Joo. 1995. "Ethnicity and Economy in Rural Mexico: A Critique of the Indigenista Approach." *LARR* 30: 33–59.

Córdova, Arnoldo. 1973. *La ideología de la revolución mexicana. La formación del nuevo régemin.* Mexico City: Ediciones Era.

———. 1974. *La política de masas del cardenismo.* Mexico City: Ediciones Era.

———. 1995. *La Revolución en crises. La aventura del maximato.* Mexico City: Cal y Arena.

Cortés Zavala, María Teresa. 1995. *Lázaro Cárdenas y su proyecto cultural en Michoacán, 1930–1950.* Morelia: Universidad Michoacana de San Nicolás de Hidalgo.

Craig, Ann L. 1983. *The First Agraristas: An Oral History of a Mexican Reform Movement.* Berkeley: University of California Press.

Dahlgren Jordán, Barbro. 1988. "La etnología." In *La antropología en México. Panorama histórico,* vol. 5. See García Mora et al., 1988.

Darnton, Robert. 1984. *The Great Cat Massacre.* New York: Basic Books.

Dawson, Alexander. 1998. "From Models for the Nation to Model Citizens: *Indigenismo* and the 'Revindication' of the Mexican Indian, 1920–1940." *JLAS* 30 (2): 279–308.

———. 2001. "'Wild Indians,' 'Mexican Gentlemen,' and the Lessons Learned in the Casa del Estudiante Indígena, 1926–1932." *The Americas* 57(3): 329–361.

de la Cadena, Marisol. 1998. "From Race to Class: Insurgent Intellectuals *de provincia* in

Peru." In *Shining and Other Paths: War and Society in Peru, 1980–1995*. Steve J. Stern, ed. Durham: Duke University Press.

——. 2000. *Indigenous Mestizos: The Politics of Race and Culture in Cuzco, Peru, 1919–1991*. Durham: Duke University Press.

de la Luz del Valle Berrocal, María. 1998. "Julio de la Fuente." In *La antropología en México. Panorama histórico*, vol. 10. See García Mora et al., 1988.

de la Peña, Guillermo. 1986. "Poder local, poder regional." In *Poder regional en México*. Jorge Zepeda Patterson, ed. Mexico City: El Colegio de México.

——. 1987. "Orden social y educación indígena en México: la pervivencia de un legado colonial." In *La heterodoxia recuperada*. Susana Glantz, ed. Mexico City: Fondo de Cultura Económica.

——. 1993. "Individuo, etnia, nación: Paradojas y antinomias de la identidad collectiva." In *Epistemología y cultura*. Ernesto Garzón Valdés and Fernando Salmerón, eds. Mexico City: UNAM.

——. 1995. "La ciudadanía étnica y la construcción de los indios en el México contemporáneo," *Revista Internacional de Filosofía Política* 6: 116–140.

——. 1996. "Nacionales y extranjeros en la historia de la antropología mexicana." In *La historia de la antropología en México. Fuentes y transmisión*. Mechthild Rutsch, ed. Mexico City: INI.

——. 1998. "Educación y cultura en México del siglo xx." In *Un siglo de educación en México*, vol. 1. See Latapí Sarre, 1998.

Delpar, Helen. 1992. *The Enormous Vogue of Things Mexican: Cultural Relations between the United States and Mexico, 1920–1935*. Tuscaloosa: University of Alabama Press.

Departamento de Asuntos Indígenas (DAI). 1938. *Memoria del Primer Congreso Regional Indígena celebrado en Ixmiquilpan, Hgo., 26–27 Sept. 1936*. Mexico City: DAPP.

——. 1938b. *Segundo Congreso Regional Indígena: Memoria*. Mexico City: DAPP.

——. 1938c. *Memoria del Tercer Congreso Regional Indígena (Azteca)*. Mexico City: DAPP.

——. 1938d. *Memoria del Departamento de Asuntos Indígenas. Enero—31 agosto 1936*. Mexico City: DAPP.

——. 1938e. *Memoria del Departamento de Asuntos Indígenas. 1 septiembre de 1936–31 agosto de 1937*. Mexico City: DAPP.

——. 1938f. *Memoria del Departamento de Asuntos Indígenas. Septiembre de 1937–agosto de 1938*. Mexico City: DAPP.

——. 1939. *Memoria del Primer Congreso Indígena de la Raza Huaxteca del 26 al 30 de octubre de 1939*. Mexico City: DAPP.

——. 1940. *Memoria de la Primera Asemblea de Filologos y Linguistas*. Mexico City: DAPP.

——. 1940b. *Publicaciones de la prensa tarasca. Folletos de divulgación popular publicados de agosto de 1939 a enero de 1940*. Mexico City: DAPP.

——. 1940c. *Plan de Trabajo Aprobado en el Primer Congreso Indígena de la Raza Chontal celebrado en la Ciudad Villahermosa, Tab., del 20 al 22 de diciembre de 1939*. Mexico City: DAPP.

Díaz Polanco, Héctor. 1997. *Indigenous Peoples in Latin America: The Quest for Self-Determination*. Boulder, Colo.: Westview.

Doremus, Anne. 2001. "Indigenism, Mestizaje, and National Identity in Mexico during the 1940s and the 1950s." *Mexican Studies/Estudios Mexicanos* 17(2): 375–402.

Durán, Leonel, ed. 1972. *Lázaro Cárdenas. Ideario político*. Mexico City: Ediciones Era.

Errington, Shelly. 1998. *The Death of Authentic Primitive Art and Other Tales of Progress*. Berkeley: University of California Press.

Esteva Fabregat, C. 1988. *El mestizaje en Iberoamericana*. Madrid: Editorial Alhambra.

Fabian, Johannes. 1983. *Time and the Other: How Anthropology Makes Its Object*. New York: Columbia University Press.

——. 1985. "Culture, Time, and the Object of Anthropology." *Berkshire Review* 20: 7–23.

Fallaw, Ben W. 1997. "Cárdenas and the Caste War That Wasn't: State Power and Indigenismo in Post-Revolutionary Yucatán." *The Americas* 53(4) 551–577.

——. 2001. *Cárdenas Compromised: The Failure of Reform in Postrevolutionary Yucatán*. Durham: Duke University Press.

Favre, Henri. 1998. *El Indigenismo*. Mexico City: Fondo de Cultura Económica.

Florescano, Enrique. 1994. *Memory, Myth, and Time in Mexico: From the Aztecs to Independence*. Austin: University of Texas Press.

Foucault, Michel. 1978. *The History of Sexuality: An Introduction*, vol. 1. New York: Random House.

Fowler-Salamini, Heather. 1980. "Revolutionary Caudillos in the 1920s: Francisco Múgica and Adalberto Tejada." In *Peasant and Caudillo in the Mexican Revolution*. D. A. Brading, ed. Cambridge: Cambridge University Press.

——. 1990. "Tamaulipas: Land Reform and the State." In *Provinces of the Revolution*. See Benjamin and Wasserman, 1990.

Friedlander, Judith. 1975. *Being Indian in Hueyapan: A Study of Forced Identity in Contemporary Mexico*. New York: St. Martins Press.

——. 1981. "The Secularization of the Cargo System: An Example of Post-Revolutionary Mexico," *LARR* 16: 132–144.

Friedrich, Paul. 1977 (1970). *Agrarian Revolt in a Mexican Village*. Chicago: University of Chicago Press.

——. 1986. *The Princes of Naranja: An Essay in Anthrohistorical Method*. Austin: University of Texas Press.

Frischmann, Donald H. 1994. "Misiones Culturales, Teatro Conasupo, and Teatro Comunidad: The Evolution of Rural Theater." In *Rituals of Rule, Rituals of Resistance*. See Beezley et al., 1994.

Gamio, Manuel. 1917. *El Gobierno, la Poblacion, y el Territorio*. Mexico City: Talleres Gráficos de la Nación.

——. 1918. *Programa de la Direccion de Estudios Arqueológicos y Etnográficos*, Mexico City: Secretaría de Agricultura y Fomento.

——. 1919. *Empiricism of Latin American Governments and the Empiricism of Their Relations with the United States*, Mexico City: Imprenta Nacional.

——. 1919b. *Programa de la Direccion de Antropología para el Estudio y mejoramiento de las Poblaciones Regionales de la Republica*. Mexico City: Secretaría de Agricultura y Fomento.

——. 1920. *Organizacion y Tendencias de la Secretaria de Agricultura y Fomento*. Mexico City: Secretaría de Agricultura y Fomento.

——. 1922. *La Población del Valle de Teotihuacán*. 3 vols. Mexico City: Talleres Gráficos de la Nación.

——. 1924. "The Present State of Anthropological Research in Mexico." Lecture to the Carnegie Institution, Washington, D.C., 16 April 1924.

——. 1925. *The Present State of Anthropological Research in Mexico.* Washington, D.C.: Government Printing Office.

——. 1926. "Incorporating the Indian in the Mexican Population." In *Aspects of Mexican Civilization: Lectures of the Harris Foundation.* Chicago: University of Chicago Press.

——. 1948. *Consideraciones sobre el problema Indígena.* Mexico City: INI.

——. 1960 (1916). *Forjando Patria.* Mexico City: Editorial Porrua.

——. 1966. *Consideraciones sobre el problema indígena.* 2nd ed. Mexico City: III.

——. 1973. *Antologia.* Mexico City: UNAM.

——. 1987 (1935). *Hacia una México nuevo.* Mexico City: INI.

García Canclini, Néstor. 1993. *Transforming Modernity: Popular Culture in Mexico.* Austin: University of Texas Press.

——. 1995. *Hybrid Cultures: Strategies for Entering and Leaving Modernity.* Minneapolis: University of Minnesota Press.

García Mora, Carlos, and Andrés Medina, eds. 1986. *La Quiebra Política de la Antropología Social en México.* Mexico City: UNAM.

García Mora, Carlos, et al., eds. 1988. *La antropología en México. Panorámico histórico.* 15 vols. Mexico City: INAH.

Geertz, Clifford. 1973. *The Interpretation of Cultures.* New York: Basic Books.

Gilly, Adolfo. 1971. *La Revolución interrumpida.* Mexico City: Ediciones El Caballito.

——. 1994. *El cardenismo. Una utopía mexicana.* Mexico City: Cal y Arena.

Gledhill, John. 1991. *Casi Nada: A Study of Agrarian Reform in the Homeland of Cardenismo.* Albany: SUNY Press.

Gonzalbo Aizpuru, Pilar, ed. 1996. *Educación rural e indígena en Iberoamérica.* Mexico City: El Colegio de México.

González Gamio, Ángeles. 1987. *Manuel Gamio: un lucha sin final.* Mexico City: UNAM.

González y González, Luis. 1968. *Pueblo en Vilo.* Mexico City: El Colegio de México.

——. 1996. *El indio el la era liberal.* Mexico City: Clío.

——. 1997 *Los días del presidente Cárdenas.* Mexico City: Clío.

Gossen, Gary H. 1999. *Telling Maya Tales: Tzotzil Identities in Modern Mexico.* New York: Routledge.

Gould, Stephen Jay. 1978. "Morton's Ranking of Races by Cranial Capacity: Unconscious Manipulation of Data May Be a Scientific Norm." *Science* 200: 503–509.

Gramsci, Antonio. 1976. *Selections from the Prison Notebooks.* Quintin Hoare and Geoffrey Nowell Smith, eds. London: Lawrence and Wishart.

Greaves L., Cecilia. 1996. "Entre la teoría educativa y la práctica indigenista. La experiencia en Chiapas y la Tarahumara (1940–1970)." In *Educación rural e indígena en Iberoamérica.* See Pilar Gonzalbo Aizpuru, 1996.

Guerrero, Francisco Javier. 1989. "Lázaro Cárdenas: el gran viaje." In *México: un pueblo en la historia.* Enrique Semo, ed. Mexico City: Alianza Editorial.

Guevara Niebla, Gilberto. 1985. *La Educación Socialista en México (1934–1945).* Mexico City: Ediciones El Caballito.

Gutiérrez, Natividad. 1999. *Nationalist Myths and Ethnic Identities: Indigenous Intellectuals and the Mexican State.* Lincoln: University of Nebraska Press.

Gutiérrez y Oliveros, Antonio. 1929. *Valores espirituales de la raza indígena; su educación desde los tiempos presortesianos hasta nuestros dias*. Mexico City: Talleres Gráficos de la Nación.

Gutmann, Matthew C. 1996. *The Meanings of Macho: Being a Man in Mexico City*. Berkeley: University of California Press.

Hamilton, Nora. 1982. *The Limits of State Autonomy: Post Revolutionary Mexico*. Princeton: Princeton University Press.

Hannaford, Ivan. 1996. *Race: The History of an Idea in the West*. Washington: The Woodrow Wilson Center Press.

Harvey, Neil. 1998. *The Chiapas Rebellion: The Struggle for Land and Democracy*. Durham: Duke University Press.

Herrasti, Lourdes, and Axel Ramírez. 1988. "Instituto Nacional Indigenista." *La antropología en México. Panorama histórico*, vol. 7. See García Mora et al., 1988.

Hewitt de Alcántara, Cynthia. 1984. *Anthropological Perspectives on Rural Mexico*. London: Routledge and Kegan Paul.

Hobsbawm, Eric. 1983. "Introduction: Inventing Traditions." In *The Invention of Tradition*. See Hobsbawm and Ranger, 1983.

Hobsbawm, Eric, and Terence Ranger, eds. 1983. *The Invention of Tradition*. Cambridge: Cambridge University Press.

Holt, Thomas C. 1995. "Marking: Race, Race-making, and the Writing of History." *AHR* 100: 1–20.

Iwanska, Alicja. 1977. *The Truths of Others: An Essay on Nativistic Intellectuals in Mexico*. Cambridge, Mass.: Schenkman Publishing.

Joseph, Gilbert. 1988 (1982). *Revolution from Without: Yucatán, Mexico, and the United States, 1880–1924*. Durham: Duke University Press.

——. 1994. "Rethinking Mexican Revolutionary Mobilization: Yucatán's Seasons of Upheaval, 1909–1915." In *Everyday Forms of State Formation*. See Joseph and Nugent, 1994.

Joseph, Gilbert, and Daniel Nugent, eds. 1994. *Everyday Forms of State Formation: Revolution and the Negotiation of Rule in Modern Mexico*. Durham: Duke University Press.

——. 1994b. "Popular Culture and State Formation in Revolutionary Mexico." In *Everyday Forms of State Formation*. See Joseph and Nugent, 1994.

Katz, Friedrich. 1998. *The Life and Times of Pancho Villa*. Stanford: Stanford University Press.

Kemper, Robert V. 1984. "From Nationalism to Internationalism: The Development of Mexican Anthropology." In *The Social Contexts of American Ethnology, 1840–1984*. June Helm, ed. Washington: American Ethnological Society.

Knight, Alan. 1986. *The Mexican Revolution*. 2 vols. Cambridge: Cambridge University Press.

——. 1990. "Racism, Revolution, and *Indigenismo:* Mexico, 1910–1940." In *The Idea of Race in Latin America, 1870–1940*. Richard Graham, ed. Austin: University of Texas Press.

——. 1990b. "Revolutionary Project, Recalcitrant People: Mexico, 1910–1940." In *The Revolutionary Process in Mexico: Essays on Political and Social Change, 1880–1940*. Jaime E. Rodríguez O., ed. Los Angeles: Latin American Center, UCLA.

——. 1994. "Weapons and Arches in the Mexican Revolutionary Landscape," in *Everyday Forms of State Formation*. See Joseph and Nugent, 1994.

——. 1994b. "Cardenismo: Juggernaut or Jalopy?" *JLAS* 26: 73–107.

——. 1998. "Populism and Neo-populism in Latin America, especially Mexico." *JLAS* 30(2): 223–248.

Krause, Enrique. 1985. *Caudillos culturales en la revolución mexicana.* Mexico City: Siglo 21.

Laclau, Ernesto. 1977. *Politics and Ideology in Marxist Theory.* London: Humanities Press.

Laclau, Ernesto, and Chantal Mouffe. 1985. *Hegemony and Socialist Strategy: Towards a Radical Democratic Politics.* London: Verso.

Laclau, Ernesto, and Lilian Zac. 1994. "Minding the Gap: The Subject of Politics." In *The Making of Political Identities.* Ernesto Laclau, ed. London: Verso

Latapí Sarre, Pablo, ed. 1998. *Un siglo de educación en México.* 2 vols. Mexico City: Fondo de Cultura Económica.

Lewis, Stephen. 1997. *Revolution and the Rural Schoolhouse: Forging State and Nation in Chiapas, Mexico, 1913–1948.* Ph.D. diss., University of California–San Diego.

——. 1999. "A 'Collective Psychological Experiment' for the Mexican Nation: The Success and Failure of the Casa del estudiante Indígena, 1926–1932." Presented at the *Rocky Mountain Council on Latin American Studies.*

Lipp, Frank J. 1991. *The Mixe of Oaxaca: Religion, Ritual, and Healing.* Austin: University of Texas Press.

Lombardo Toledano, Vincente. 1936. "Como resolvio el régimen sovietico el problema de las nacionalidades oprimidas." In *Un viaje al mundo del porvenir.* Vincente Lombardo Toledano and Victor Manuel Villaseñor, eds. Mexico City: Publicaciones de la Universidad obrera de México.

Lomnitz, Claudio. 2001. *Deep Mexico, Silent Mexico: An Anthropology of Nationalism.* Minneapolis: University of Minnesota Press.

Lomnitz-Adler, Claudio. 1992. *Exits from the Labyrinth: Culture and Ideology in the Mexican National Space.* Berkeley: University of California Press.

López, Rick Anthony. 2001. *Lo más mexicano de México: Popular Arts, Indians, and Urban Intellectuals in the Ethnicization of Postrevolutionary National Culture, 1920–1972.* Ph.D. diss., Yale University.

Loyo, Engracia. 1992. "Lectura Para el Pueblo, 1921–1940." In *La educación en la historia de México.* Mexico City: El Colegio de México.

——. 1994. "Popular Reactions to the Educational Reforms of Cardenismo." In *Rituals of Rule, Rituals of Resistance: Public Celebrations and Popular Culture in Mexico.* See Beezley et al., 1994.

——. 1996. "Los centros de educación indígena y su papel en el medio rural (1930–1940)." In *Educación rural e indígena en Iberoamérica.* See Gonzalbo Aizpuru, 1996.

——. 1996b. "La empresa redentora. La Casa del Estudiante Indígena." *Historia Mexicana.* 46 (1): 99–131.

——. 1999. *Gobiernos revolucionarios y educación popular en México, 1911–1928.* Mexico City: El Colegio de México.

Maldonado Gallardo, Alejo. 1995. *La Educación Socialista en Michoacán. Historia de una experiencia pedagógica.* Morelia: Universidad Michoacana de San Nicolás de Hidalgo.

Mallon, Florencia. 1995. *Peasant and Nation: The Making of Postcolonial Mexico and Peru.* Berkeley: University of California Press.

Marx, Anthony W. 1998. *Making Race and Nation: A Comparison of South Africa, the United States, and Brazil.* Cambridge: Cambridge University Press.

Marzal, Manuel M. 1989. *Historia de la antropología indigenista: México y Peru,* Lima: Pontifica Universidad Catolica del Peru, Fondo Editorial.

Matos Moctezuma, Eduardo. 1996. "El indigenismo: pasado y presente." In *Cultura y derechos de los pueblos indígenas de México.* Mexico City: AGN.

Matto de Turner, Clorinda. 1996. *Birds Without a Nest.* Austin: University of Texas Press.

Medina, Andrés. 1986. "Tres puntos de referencia en el indigenismo mexicano contemporáneo." In *La quiebra política de la antropología social en México,* vol. 2. See García Mora and Medina, 1986.

———. 1986b. "Antropología e indigenismo. Los compromisos contradictorios de la ciencia en México." In *La quiebra política de la antropología social en México,* vol. 2. See García Mora and Medina, 1986.

Mendieta y Núñez, Lucio. 1938. *Valor economic y social de las razas indígenas de México.* Mexico City: DAPP.

Mendizabal, Miguel Othon de. 1922. *Las artes aborigenes mexicanas.* Mexico City: Museo Nacional de Arqueologia, Historia y Etnografía.

———. 1924. *Ensayos sobre las civilizaciones aborigenes americanas.* Mexico City: Museo Nacional.

———. 1936. *Historia economica y social de México.* Mexico City: SEP.

Meyer, Jean. 1976. *The Cristero Rebellion: The Mexican People between Church and State, 1926–1929.* Cambridge: Cambridge University Press.

Miller, Nicola. 1999. *In the Shadow of the State: Intellectuals and the Quest for National Identity in Twentieth-Century Spanish America.* London: Verso.

Monsiváis, Carlos. 1996. "Versiones nacionales de lo indígena." In *Cultura y derechos de los pueblos indígenas de México.* Mexico City: AGN.

Morales Garza, Sofialeticia. 1998. "La educacion indígena, especial e inicial: de 'modelos complementarios' a estrategias claves para reivindicar la igualidad en la diferencia." In *Un siglo de educación en México,* vol. 2. See Latapí Sarre, 1998.

Morris, Stephen D. 1999. "Reforming the Nation: Mexican Nationalism in Context." *JLAS* 31: 363–397

Murillo, Gerardo [Dr. Atl, pseud.]. 1922. *Las artes populares en México.* 2 vols. Mexico City: Editorial Cultura.

Nájera-Ramírez, Olga. 1997. *La Fiesta de los Tastoanes: Critical Encounters in Mexican Festival Performance.* Albuquerque: University of New Mexico Press.

Nolasco Armas, Margarita. 1970. "La Antropologia aplicada en México y su destino final: El Indigenismo." In *De eso que llaman antropología mexicana.* Mexico City: Editorial Nuestro Tiempo.

Nugent, Daniel. 1989. " 'Are we not (Civilized) Men?': The Formation and Devolution of Community in Northern Mexico." *Journal of Historical Sociology* (2/3): 206–239.

———. 1993. *Spent Cartridges of Revolution: An Anthropological History of Namiquipa, Chihuahua.* Chicago: University of Chicago Press.

Olivé Negrete, Julio César. 1981. *La antropología mexicana.* Mexico City: Colegio Mexicano de Antropologos.

———. 1988. "Dirección de Estudios Arqueológicos y Etnográficos de la Secretaría de Fomento (Dirección de Antropología)." In *La antropología en México. Panorama histórico,* vol. 7. See Garcia Mora et al., 1988.

Ortner, Sherry. 1996. *Making Gender: The Politics and Erotics of Culture.* Boston: Beacon.

Pagden, Anthony. 1990. *Spanish Imperialism and the Political Imagination: Studies in European and Spanish-American Social and Political Theory, 1513–1830*. New Haven: Yale University Press.

Paz, Octavio. 1980. "Social Realism in Mexico: The Murals of Rivera, Orozco, and Siqueiros." *ArtsCanada* 36: 57–60.

——. 1981 (1950). *El laberinto de la soledad*. Mexico City: Fondo de Cultura Económica.

——. 1993. *Essays in Mexican Art*. New York: Harcourt Brace.

Pérez López, Abraham. 1979. *Diccionario Biográfico Hidalguense*. San Salvador, Hgo.: Editorial Cuathémoc.

Pérez Montfort, Ricardo. 1994. "Indigenismo, Hispanismo, y panamericanismo en la cultura popular mexicana de 1920 a 1940." In *Cultura e identidad nacional*. Roberto Blancarte, ed. Mexico City: Fondo de Cultura Económica.

Pilcher, Jeffrey M. 1998. *¡Que vivan los Tamales! Food and the Making of Mexican Identity*. Albuquerque: University of New Mexico Press.

Pineda, Luz Olivia. 1993. *Caciques Culturales (El caso de los maestros bilingues en los altos de Chiapas)*. Puebla: Altres Costa–Amic.

Powell, T. G. 1968. "Mexican Intellectuals and the Indian Problem in Porfirian Mexico." *HAHR* 68: 19–36.

Pozas, Ricardo. 1986. "La antropología y la burocracia indigenista." In *La quiebra política de la antropología social en México*, vol. 2. See García Mora and Medina, 1986.

Pratt, Mary Louise. 1992. *Imperial Eyes: Travel Writing and Transculturation*. New York: Routledge.

Purnell, Jennie. 1999. *Popular Movements and State Formation in Revolutionary Mexico: The Agraristas and Cristeros of Michoacán*. Durham: Duke University Press.

Rappaport, Joanne. 1990. *The Politics of Memory: Native Historical Interpretation in the Colombian Andes*. New York: Cambridge University Press.

Raat, William D. 1970. "Los intelectuales, el positivismo y la cuestión indígena." *Historia Mexicana* 20: 412–427.

——. 1973. "Ideas and Society in Don Porfirio's Mexico," *The Americas* 30: 32–53.

Ramos, Samuel. 1951 (1934). *El Perfil del hombre y la cultura en México*. Mexico City: Colección Austral.

Reyes Rocha, José, María Luisa Miaja Isaac, and Abelardo Torres Cortés. 1991. *La educación indígena en Michoacán*. Morelia: Universidad Michoacana de San Nicolás de Hidalgo.

Rockwell, Elsie. 1994. "Schools of the Revolution: Enacting and Contesting State Forms in Tlaxcala, 1910–1930." In *Everyday Forms of State Formation*. See Joseph and Nugent, 1994.

Roseberry, William. 1989. *Anthropologies and Histories: Essays in Culture, History, and Political Economy*. New Brunswick: Rutgers University Press.

——. 1994. "Hegemony and the Language of Contention." In *Everyday Forms of State Formation*. See Joseph and Nugent, 1994.

Rubin, Jeffrey W. 1996. "Decentering the Regime: Culture and Regional Politics in Mexico." *LARR* 31(3): 85–126.

——. 1997. *Decentering the Regime: Ethnicity, Radicalism, and Democracy in Juchitán, Mexico*. Durham: Duke University Press.

Rus, Jan. 1994. "The 'Comunidad Revolucionaria Institucional': The Subversion of

Native Government in Chiapas, 1936–1968." In *Everyday Forms of State Formation.* See Joseph and Nugent, 1994.
Sáenz, Moisés. 1926. *Some Mexican Problems. Lectures on the Harris Foundation.* Chicago: University of Chicago.
——. 1928. *La educacion rural en México.* Mexico City: Talleres Gráficos de la Nación.
——. 1929. *Mexico: An Appraisal and a Forecast.* New York: Committee on Cultural Relations with Latin America.
——. 1933. *Sobre el indio ecuatoriaño.* Mexico City: SEP.
——. 1933b. *Sobre el indio peruaño.* Mexico City: SEP.
——. 1936. *Carapan. Bosquejo de una experiencia.* Lima: Librería e Imprenta Gil.
——. 1939. *México Integro.* Lima: Imprenta Torres Aguirre.
——. 1970. *Antologia de Moisés Saenz.* Mexico City: Ediciones Oasis.
Said, Edward. 1978. *Orientalism.* New York: Vintage.
Sanderson, Steven E. 1981. *Agrarian Populism and the Mexican State: The Struggle for Land in Sonora.* Berkeley: University of California Press.
Sayer, Derek. 1994. "Everyday Forms of State Formation: Some Dissident Remarks on 'Hegemony.'" In *Everyday Forms of State Formation.* See Joseph and Nugent, 1994.
Schneider, William H. 1990. *Quality and Quantity: The Quest for Biological Regeneration in Twentieth-Century France.* Cambridge: Cambridge University Press.
Schryer, Frans. 1990. *Ethnicity and Class Conflict in Rural Mexico.* Princeton: Princeton University Press.
Schwarcz, Lilia Moritz. 1993. *The Spectacle of the Races: Scientists, Institutions, and the Race Question in Brazil, 1870–1930.* New York: Hill and Wang.
Scott, James C. 1976. *The Moral Economy of the Peasant: Rebellion and Subsistence in Southeast Asia.* New Haven: Yale University Press.
——. 1985. *Weapons of the Weak: Everyday Forms of Peasant Resistance.* New Haven: Yale University Press.
——. 1990. *Domination and the Arts of Resistance: Hidden Transcripts.* New Haven: Yale University Press.
——. 1998. *Seeing Like a State: How Certain Schemes to Improve the Human Condition Have Failed.* New Haven: Yale University Press.
Secretaria de Agricultura y Fomento (SECAGFOM). 1918. *Programa de la Direccion de Arqueología y Etnografía.* Mexico City: Secretaria de Agricultura y Fomento.
Secretaría de Educación Pública (SEP). 1926. *Monografia de las escuelas de pintura al aire libre.* Mexico City: Talleres Gráficos de la Nación.
——. 1927. *La Casa del Estudiante Indígena; 16 meses de labor en un experimento psicologico colectivo con indios, febrero de 1926–junio de 1927.* Mexico City: Talleres Gráficos de la Nación.
——. 1927b. *El sistema de escuelas rurales en México.* Mexico City: Talleres Gráficos de la Nación.
——. 1932. *Memoria relativa al estado que guarda el Ramo de Educación Pública, el 31 de agosto de 1932.* 2 vols. Mexico City: Talleres Gráficos de la Nación.
——. 1933. *Misiones Culturales 1932–1933.* Mexico City: Talleres Gráficos de la Nación.
——. 1935. *Memoria relativa al estado que guarda el Ramo de Educación Pública, el 31 de augusto de 1935.* 2 vols. Mexico City: Talleres Gráficos de la Nación.
——. 1935b. *La Revolucion en una etapa de madurez social.* Mexico City: Talleres Gráficos de la Nación.

———. 1936–1937. *Biblioteca del obrero y campesino.* 23 vols. Mexico City: DAPP.

———. 1937. *Centros de Educacion Indígena. Plan general de trabajo para el año de 1937.* Mexico City: DAPP.

———. 1937b. *Memoria relativa al estado que guarda el Ramo de Educación Pública, septiembre de 1936–agosto de 1937.* 2 vols. Mexico City: DAPP.

Semo, Enrique, ed. 1989. *México, un Pueblo en la historia.* 8 vols. Mexico City: Editorial Nueva Imagen.

Serrano, Carlos, and María Villanueva. 1988. "La antropología física." In *La antropología en México. Panorama histórico,* vol. 5. See García Mora et al. 1988.

Shulgovski, Anatoli. 1968. *México en la encrucijada de su historia.* Mexico City: Ediciones de Cultura Popular.

Sotelo Arévalo, Salvador. 1996. *Historia de mi vida. Autobiografía y memorias de un maestro rural en México, 1904–1965.* Mexico City: INEHRM.

Spivak, Gayatri Chakravorty. 1988. "Can the Subaltern Speak?" In *Marxism and the Interpretation of Culture.* Cary Nelos and Lawrence Grossberg, eds. Urbana: University of Illinois Press.

Stabb, Martin. 1959. "Indigenism and Racism in Mexican Thought, 1857–1911." *Journal of Inter-American Studies* 1: 405–423.

Stavenhagen, Rodolfo. 1986. "Congreso de Pueblos, El indigenismo cuestionado." In *La quiebra política de la antropología social en México,* vol. 2. See García Mora and Medina, 1986.

———. 1986b. "Veinticinco años de indigenismo, tareas para el futuro." In *La quiebra política de la antropología social en México,* vol. 2. See García Mora and Medina, eds., 1986.

Stepan, Nancy Leys. 1990. "Eugenics in Brazil, 1917–1940." In *The Wellborn Science: Eugenics in Germany, France, Brazil, and Russia.* Mark B. Adams, ed. Oxford: Oxford University Press.

———. 1991. *"The Hour of Eugenics": Race, Gender, and Nation in Latin America.* Ithaca: Cornell University Press.

Stephen, Lynn. 1996. "The Creation and Re-creation of Ethnicity: Lessons from the Zapotec and Mixtec of Oaxaca." *LAP* 23(3): 17–37.

Stern, Alexandra Minna. 1999. "Buildings, Boundaries, and Blood: Medicalization and Nation-Building on the U.S.–Mexico Border, 1910–1930." *HAHR* 71(1): 41–81.

Stocking, George W. Jr. 1976. "Ideas and Institutions in American Anthropology: Thoughts Toward a History of the Interwar Years." In *Selected Papers from the American Anthropological Association.* Washington, D.C.: American Anthropological Association.

———. 1982 (1968). *Race, Culture, and Evolution: Essays in the History of Anthropology.* Chicago: University of Chicago Press.

Strug, David. 1986. "Manuel Gamio, la Escuela internacional y el origen de las excavaciones estratigraficas en la Américas," In *Arqueología e indigenismo.* Mexico City: INI.

Taylor, Diana. 1997. *Disappearing Acts: Spectacles of Gender and Nationalism in Argentina's Dirty War.* Durham: Duke University Press.

Tenorio–Trillo, Mauricio. 1996. *Mexico at the World's Fairs: Crafting a Modern Nation.* Berkeley: University of California Press.

Trabulse, Elías. 1996. "Los orígenes científicos del indigenismo actual." In *Cultura y derechos de los pueblos indígenas de México.* Mexico City: AGN.

Tresierra, Julio C. 1994. "Mexico: Indigenous Peoples and the Nation-State." In *Indigenous Peoples and Democracy in Latin America.* Donna Van Lee Cott, ed. New York: St. Martins Press.

Tutino, John. 1986. *From Insurrection to Revolution in Mexico: Social Bases of Agrarian Violence, 1750–1940.* Princeton: Princeton University Press.

Vasconcelos, Jose. 1926. "The Race Problem in Latin America." In *Aspects of Mexican Civilization: Lectures of the Harris Foundation.* Chicago: University of Chicago Press.

——. 1997 (1924). *La raza cosmica. Misión de la raza Iberoamericana.* Baltimore: Johns Hopkins.

Vaughan, Mary Kay. 1982. *The State, Education, and Social Class in Mexico, 1889–1928.* Dekalb: Northern Illinois University Press.

——. 1994. "The Construction of the Patriotic Festival in Tecamachalco." In *Rituals of Rule, Rituals of Resistance.* See Beezley et al., 1994.

——. 1997. *Cultural Politics in Revolution: Teachers, Peasants, and Schools in Mexico, 1930–1940.* Tucson: University of Arizona Press.

Vento, Arnoldo Carlos. 1998. *Mestizo: The History, Culture and Politics of the Mexican and the Chicano.* Lanham, Md.: University Press of America.

Villa Rojas, Alfonso. 1986. "El resugimiento del indigenismo mexicano." In *La quiebra política de la antropología social en México,* vol. 2. See García Mora and Medina, 1986.

Villoro, Luis. 1992. "La Cultura Mexicana de 1910 a 1960." In *Cultura, Ideas, y Mentalidades: Lecturas de Historia Mexicana* 6. Mexico City: El Colegio de México.

Warman, Arturo. 1969. "Cultura popular y cultura nacional." In *Caracteristicas de la cultura nacional.* Leopoldo Zea, ed. Mexico City: Instituto de Investigaciones Sociales.

——. 1970. "Todos santos y todos difuntos: Crítica histórica de la antropología mexicana." In *De eso que llaman antropología mexicana.* See Warman et al., 1970.

Warman, Arturo, et al., eds. 1970. *De eso que llaman antropología mexicana.* Mexico City: Editorial Nuestro Tiempo.

Warren, Kay B. 1992. "Transforming Memories and Histories: The Meanings of Ethnic Resurgence for Maya Indians." In *Americas: New Interpretive Essays.* Alfred Stepan, ed. Oxford: Oxford University Press.

Williams, Raymond. 1973. *The Country and the City.* Oxford: Oxford University Press.

Womack, John Jr. 1968. *Zapata and the Mexican Revolution.* New York: Vintage.

Zolov, Eric. 1999. *Refried Elvis: The Rise of the Mexican Counterculture.* Berkeley: University of California Press.

Index

About the Author

Alexander Dawson received his Ph.D. in Latin American History from the State University of New York at Stony Brook, and taught at Montana State University–Bozeman and the University of Florida while completing this book. Articles related to this project were published in the *Journal of Latin American Studies* in 1998 and *The Americas* in 2001. He is an assistant professor at Simon Fraser University in Vancouver, Canada.